The Bifurcation of the Self

Library of the History of
Psychological Theories
Series Editor: Robert W. Rieber, *Fordham University, New York, NY*

THE BIFURCATION OF THE SELF
The History and Theory of Dissociation and Its Disorders
Robert W. Rieber

CRITIQUE OF PSYCHOLOGY
From Kant to Postcolonial Theory
Thomas Teo

PERCEPTION AND ILLUSION
Historical Perspective
Nicholas J. Wade

A continuation Order Plan is available for this series. A continuation order will bring delivery of each new volume immediately upon publication. Volumes are billed only upon actual shipment. For further information please contact the publisher.

THE BIFURCATION OF THE SELF
The History and Theory of Dissociation and Its Disorders

ROBERT W. RIEBER
Fordham University
New York, New York

 Springer

Library of Congress Control Number: 2005928493

ISBN-10: 0-387-27413-8   e-ISBN 0-387-27414-6
ISBN-13: 978-0387-27413-3

Printed on acid-free paper.

© 2006 Springer Science+Business Media, Inc.
All rights reserved. This work may not be translated or copied in whole or in part without the written permission of the publisher (Springer Science+Business Media, Inc., 233 Spring Street, New York, NY 10013, USA), except for brief excerpts in connection with reviews or scholarly analysis. Use in connection with any form of information storage and retrieval, electronic adaptation, computer software, or by similar or dissimilar methodology now known or hereafter developed is forbidden.
The use in this publication of trade names, trademarks, service marks and similar terms, even if they are not identified as such, is not to be taken as an expression of opinion as to whether or not they are subject to proprietary rights.

Printed in the United States of America.   (SPI/EB)

9 8 7 6 5 4 3 2 1

springer.com

To Herb Spiegel, my friend and colleague without whose . . . this book would never have been achieved

Foreword

There is an old saying that "it is a wise hypnotist who knows who is hypnotizing whom." One can think of hypnosis as scuba diving in the dark. What one sees in the narrowly focused beam of light may be a remarkable revelation emerging (a glowing jellyfish), it may look like something other than what it is (a shark rather than a parrot fish), or it may be misunderstood because one is in the dark about its surrounding context (a small gray fin is part of a huge manta ray). The related phenomena of hypnosis and dissociation are central components of this book.

Dissociation has been around for millennia—trance dancing in Bali, possession trance states in India, whirling Dervishes in Turkey, and demonic possession in the West. For the past two centuries, prominent psychologists and psychiatrists including Pierre Janet, Sigmund Freud, and William James have made detailed observations about dissociative symptoms—a failure to integrate various aspects of identity, memory, and consciousness. Such cases and descriptions are well documented in *The Bifurcation of the Self*. One might call such a bifurcation "being of two minds" about oneself. We have all had moments of conscious ambivalence like that—feeling unsure about whether or not to accept an invitation, being undecided about the value of an argument or a potential investment. But dissociation implies a more profound inconsistency, being in some way not only divided but unaware of the division or at least some of its components. And this lack of awareness and control makes rational assessment difficult, because all of the influences on one's current state may not be evident.

For some reason, rational evaluation of the dissociative disorders has always been problematic. Despite centuries of clinical observation, the drama and intensity that sometimes accompanies these disorders has rendered them a hot topic over a very long period of time. Neither the bizarreness of schizophrenic delusions, the chaotic hyperactivity associated with mania in bipolar disorder, the irrational fears of phobics, nor the morbid self-denigration of those with depression evoke the claims of factitiousness so often hurled at those who have and treat dissociation. We don't believe the delusions of someone with schizophrenia, we observe them. In the same way, the DSM-IV-TR (American psychiatry's latest diagnostic manual), observes the "presence" of more than one identity or personality state as a diagnostic criterion for Dissociative Identity Disorder. Such individuals experience themselves as fragmented, have amnesic episodes in their current and earlier portions of their lives, and show marked fluctuations in behavior. Furthermore, much recent research has shown a connection between dissociative disorders and early life experience of sexual and physical abuse. This does not mean that everyone with a dissociative disorder was abused or that everyone who was abused will develop a dissociative disorder. However, as we come to better understand acute and chronic responses to traumatic stress, it has become clearer that the sudden discontinuity in experience produced by a trauma can result in discontinuity of mental experience as well. Physical loss of control is re-experienced as mental loss of control over intrusive thoughts, nightmares, flashbacks, numbing, avoidance, irritability, hyperarousal, amnesia, and, at times, dissociation.

Robert Rieber, a research professor of psychology at Fordham University and emeritus professor at City University of New York, has reviewed early and recent theories of dissociation, along with many classical case descriptions. He places the greatest emphasis on the widely known case of "Sybil," subject of the best-selling book *Sybil* by Flora Rbea Schreiber, written with Sybil's psychiatrist, Dr. Cornelia Wilbur. The book focused widespread attention on dissociation and its link to trauma. This book reviews the original account of the assessment and treatment of Sybil, along with a new perspective provided by a prominent psychiatrist and hypnosis expert who examined Sybil, Dr. Herbert Spiegel of Columbia University (in the interests of full disclosure, he is my father), and several transcripts of audiotaped interviews involving Schreiber, Wilbur, and Sybil. Dr. Spiegel examined Sybil's hypnotizability and determined that she was highly hypnotizable, and, therefore, highly suggestible. He considered her a "brilliant hysteric" and concluded from his interviews with her that her use of separate identities was done to please Dr. Wilbur. He saw the treatment as intensifying rather than resolving her dissociative tendencies, which he knew she had. Reiber concludes that the tapes make it clear that Wilbur and Schreiber concocted many of the more troubling aspects of Sybil's history to make the book more interesting, including witnessing the "primal scene," and memories of physical abuse by Sybil's mother. From my perspective, these questions are thoughtfully raised but not answered. The most damning line in the tapes is Wilbur's admission that memories of abuse did not emerge until she started using sodium pentothal. The doctor then played the results of these drug-influenced interviews to Sybil, which could certainly have had the effect of convincing her that these reports were true, whether or not they were the product of imagination rather than recall. Sybil wrote a letter to Wilbur, recanting her many horrific memories about mistreatment by her mother. This was interpreted by Wilbur as denial, an attempt to protect her mother at her own expense.

The picture is further complicated by more recent information that resulted from the "outing" of Sybil as Shirley Mason by Peter Swales. This enabled interviews with people from her hometown who knew Sybil and her parents. Apparently the family was considered somewhat strange. Sybil's mother accompanied her each day to school all the way through high school. Sybil never married or had children. So her upbringing and life course were not normal, if not proven traumatic.

Memories are always fallible, with or without dissociation and hypnosis. We are all vulnerable to social influence, and a highly hypnotizable individual who is socially isolated and in need of psychiatric help is dependent upon his or her psychiatrist and prone to comply with expectations. That confabulation is possible does not prove it happened. Much of what patients tell their therapists is a mixture of memory and fantasy. Many forget and then recover memories. Indeed, we process so much information that keeping most of it out of awareness is the *sine qua non* of cognitive functioning. We often divide elements of our lives and personae to function well—we are different at work than we are at play—but hopefully know it and are in control of the process.

The Bifurcation of the Self examines a fascinating problem: identity, memory, and consciousness, and adds some new information to the mix. You can read it and still be of two minds about dissociation in general and Sybil in particular, but that is what makes dissociation the problem that just won't go away. It intrigues us because we see flashes of ourselves that don't always seem consistent, giving us new opportunities to put the pieces together.

DAVID SPIEGEL, M.D.
Professor of Psychiatry and
Behavioral Science
Stanford University School
of Medicine
Stanford, California

Preface

Few disorders are so shrouded by myth and distortion as Multiple Personality Disorder (MPD), now known as Dissociative Identity Disorder (DID). That so many people are under the impression that the disorder, while a real one, is far more widespread than it actually is no doubt stems from the treatment it has received in the media. Those responsible for perpetrating the myth that this is a widespread disorder or exaggerating the implications of the handful of cases that have been documented do not only include writers of popular fiction or movie makers, who might be expected to shun science in favor of sensation, but also self-declared authorities, therapists of various stripes, and researchers whose methodology is, to be polite, rather questionable. This book is intended as a corrective, an attempt to set the record straight, offering as it does an examination of the best-known cases from the nineteenth century on as well as a discussion of how a few of these cases—notably Sybil—have been exploited to fuel some disturbing social phenomena. Were cases of MPD/DID solely the concern or the purview of psychologists and academics, or appropriated from time to time by enterprising novelists or filmmakers, it might not be necessary to revisit it now. However, because the publicity attending the disorder has led—however circuitously—to thousands of allegations of childhood abuse and court cases in which long-buried memories of traumas (real or imagined) are painfully dredged up,

MPD/DID has assumed an importance out of proportion to its documented occurrence. Two major themes, which are inextricably linked, will emerge in this discussion. One is the nature and function of memory; the other is the nature and construction of identity. We may consider memory and identity as two aspects of the same problem. Indeed, memory is a thread of our ever-emerging identity; it is the link that connects us from one age to the next, and from one moment to the next. A significant disruption in memory—temporarily (because of posttraumatic stress, for instance) or permanently (because of illness)—can wreak havoc on our sense of self. When the integrated function of our mentation is broken—when the unity of the self is bifurcated—a pathogenic process may develop. In our discussion we will consider just how this process occurs and at which point it develops a pathogenic cast.

It is interesting to observe, on the basis of the cases I will describe in this book, that in cases of MPD/DID, the primary or dominant personality usually has no awareness of the existence of the alternate or secondary personalities. By the same token the primary personality has no memory of the actions carried out while the alternative personalities were in control. During these states the primary personality experiences amnesia or in more colloquial terms, "blacks out." In this sense, the disruption of the unity of self results from an annihilation of memory. On the other hand, the cases that have been most widely cited in the literature typically feature trauma—usually, though not always, in the form of childhood abuse. Therapists treating these patients generally agree that the trauma was a significant factor in the development of the disorder, e.g., that the fragmentation of the self occurred in response to, or as an escape from, the trauma. By introducing the concept of repression Freud provided these therapists with the tool they needed to explain the process that culminated in the break in the unity of self. These therapists argued that only by recovering the memories of the trauma to the consciousness of the primary personality would it be possible to reintegrate the self. Of all the techniques that have been employed to extricate these memories none has proven so popular or successful as hypnosis. Hypnosis is a tool, and like any other powerful tool, it can be used for good or for ill. Accordingly, this book will examine the evolution of hypnosis—beginning with a discussion of Mesmer's pioneering work—and address the ways in which it has been used (or abused) in the treatment of cases of MPD/DID.

Memory is notoriously unreliable, as anyone who has ever witnessed a traffic accident or recalled a heated family dispute, can certainly attest. Memories wrested from the unconscious by hypnosis (or any other technique) do not acquire miraculous veracity simply because they have lain long dormant for years, even decades; on the contrary, they might not have any veracity at all but may represent false memories implanted either deliberately or unintentionally. It turns out that many of the individuals most vulnerable to these pathological dissociated states are usually the most suggestible or hypnotizable. So the very technique that is intended to resolve the disorder may, in fact, play a significant role in creating it. This issue will be the focus of another part of our discussion as well.

"He is not himself today" is such a cliché that we give little thought to it. We assume merely that the individual is moody, out of sorts, acting erratically, but not to worry: tomorrow he will revert to his old normal self—that is, his behavior will comport with our experience and expectations. I will demonstrate in the pages that follow that our fascination—even obsession—with multiple personality is a symptom of social pathology, an underlying anxiety about the coherence of our own identity. If we cannot rely on our memories to keep the self intact, or if we are forced to accept the fact that our sense of self is constructed on an elaborate illusion, then we cannot escape the unavoidable question that allows no easy answers: If I am not myself, who am I? Or to put it another way: Who is this self that I insist belongs to me?

ROBERT W. RIEBER

Acknowledgments

I am indebted to many individuals whose knowledge, support, and advice have contributed so much to my life and career, but I would like to mention in particular Zvi Lothane, Joe Jaffe, David Spiegel, Eugene Taylor, Alex Scheflin, the late David Bakan, and the late Ted Carlson. In addition, I wish to acknowledge the help of Leslie Alan Horvitz and Evan Podolok in preparing the manuscript. Thanks must also go to Sharon Panulla and Herman Makler of Springer for their assistance. There are others too numerous to enumerate here, but I am sure you know who you are.

Contents

INTRODUCTION 1

I. A BRIEF HISTORY OF MULTIPLICITY

CHAPTER 1. THE ROOTS OF MULTIPLE PERSONALITY
DISORDER/DISSOCIATIVE IDENTITY DISORDER 11

Seizures, Hysteria, and Dissociation: Making
  Sense of Mind and Brain 11
Early Case Histories: Looking for Ansel Bourne in
  All the Wrong Places 14
The Neurophysiology of the Inhibition-Excitation
  Continuum 18
Pierre Janet 19
F. W. Myers 24
Morton Prince 25
Boris Sidis 27
Conclusion 29

CHAPTER 2. "NOTHING BUT GOD AND THE BRAIN" 31

A Brief Look Back 31
Nothing but God and the Brain 34

What Did Gall Actually Believe	34
Faculties in the Brain: How Much Is Enough?	37

CHAPTER 3. PRYING OPEN THE LID: THE ORIGINS OF HYPNOSIS .. 43

Animal Magnetism and Its Links to MPD	43
Conclusion	51

CHAPTER 4. LOOKING INSIDE THE BOX, THINKING
             OUTSIDE THE BOX 53

Freud and Hypnosis: Uncovering False Memories	53
The Free Association Technique	56
Overdetermination	58
Repression	59
Sexuality	60

II. SYBIL: A CASE OF MULTIPLE PERSONALITIES AND THE NATURAL HISTORY OF A MYTH

CHAPTER 5. THE CASE OF SYBIL: THE WILBUR/SCHRIEBER
             VERSION 67

CHAPTER 6. THE PUBLICATION OF A "PSYCHIATRIC MASTERPIECE" 85

Prelude to a Mystery	85
Publication of *Sybil*	86
The Aftermath	95
The Book and the Movie: A Comparison	95

CHAPTER 7. THE MYTH EXPLODES 105

The Multiplicity of Multiples	105
The Forgotten Tapes	107
Flora	108
An Analyst on Park Avenue	109
The Criminal Illusion of an Experimental Principle:	
The Primal Scene	110
The Trinity of Affinity	111
What Hypnosis Is—and Is Not	112
The Crucible of the Sixties	118
Highlights and the Implications of the Tape Recordings	121
The Reaction	126

CONTENTS   xix

    Who Is Sybil and What Is She? 129
    Conclusion 130

       III: SEMINAL CASES OF MULTIPLICITY: A HISTORY

CHAPTER 8.   FOURTEEN SEMINAL CASES 135

    Mary Reynolds 135
    Rachel Baker 137
    Mollie Fancher 138
    Ansel Bourne 140
    Felida X 141
    Marceline 143
    Mary Beauchamp 144
    Helene Smith 150
    Thomas Hanna 151
    Doris Fischer 155
    Norma 164
    John Charles Poultney 165
    Bridey Murphy 171
    Eve White/Chris Costner 172

CHAPTER 9.   BIFURCATION OF SELF: RETROSPECTIVE AND
                PROSPECTIVE 183

REFERENCES 197

APPENDICES 203

    1. Three Tape Excerpts 207
    2. Excerpt from the TV movie *Sybil* 285
    3. Sybil's Letter of Denial to Dr. Corneila Wilbur
        and Sybil's IQ Report 289
    4. Schreiber's PR Bio and Dr. Ralph Allison's Letter ... 297

NAME INDEX 301

SUBJECT INDEX 303

Introduction

The standard dictionary defines dissociation as "the splitting off of certain mental processes from the main body of consciousness, with varying degrees of autonomy resulting." The word probably owes its origin to the nineteenth-century physician Benjamin Rush, who presented lectures on cases typified by difficulties in speech and rapidity of body movements (Wolleck, Carlson, Nowell, 1981). He later incorporated these lectures (with some changes) on "physiological psychology" into his classical textbook, *Medical Inquiries upon the Diseases of the Mind* (Rush, 1812). He devoted a chapter to what he called "dissociation," which may be the earliest medical use of the term. Rush applied the term to people who were mentally deranged and who had "an association of unrelated perceptions or ideas, or the inability of the mind to perform the operations of judgment and reason." In other words, Rush was using the term only to refer to pathological behavior whereas, as I shall show, dissociation can be a routine, everyday experience as well.

But of the various phenomena of dissociation large and small, normal and abnormal, the most spectacular examples are those associated with Dissociative Identity Disorder (DID), formerly known as Multiple Personality Disorder (MPD). My goal in writing this book is to trace the history of the theory of dissociation and related processes from the seventeenth century to the present. I will primarily use a case history methodology to illustrate the relationship between theory and practice from one decade to the next. I will proceed to do this in such a way as to illuminate the basic theoretical and epistemological issues that are necessary to understand the processes of dissociation—both normal and abnormal aspects—as well as the role of hypnosis and its relationship to organic and hysterical epilepsy. My discussion will draw freely on the theories of Pierre Janet, Morton Price, William James, Boris Sidis, Ernest Hilgard, Herbert Spiegel, and other influential thinkers in the field. Throughout the book I will attempt to illuminate the various ironies and paradoxes that emerge from the story of the history of dissociation and its disorders. This issue isn't new by any means. In fact, it has been with us at least since Aristotle. It comes down to the question of how to show the connections or integrative functions of different levels of knowing and existence without throwing the baby out with the bathwater. We will consider the biophysiological level, the self-forming experiential level, and the socially constructed level of life experience separately and in terms of their relationship to one another. Even to ask certain types of questions will require a reliance on data and explanations that give greater weight to one level or another.

On the one hand, our exploration will be scientific in nature—what is known, what is unproven, what is speculative, and what is sheer nonsense. On the other hand, we will try to understand the social construction of what I call the myth of DID (formerly MPD). I wish to make clear that I am not asserting that MPD/DID itself is a myth; rather I will try to demonstrate that a mythology has developed about this relatively rare disorder and, further, that this mythology has been propagated by several therapists as well as people in the business of fabrication for entertainment purposes for agendas of their own. The myth is perhaps best exemplified by the case history of Sybil which has made its appearance in various incarnations as book, as film, and as a popular cult.

I will elaborate upon how *Sybil* the book and *Sybil* the film can be understood as symptoms of social distress and the "psychopathy" of everyday life. (This thesis is discussed in greater detail in my books *Manufacturing Social Distress* and *Psychopaths in Everyday Life: Social Distress in the Age of Misinformation*). One of the major arguments will be that Sybil is best understood as a "social dream." Our objective here will be to analyze and understand the messages society obtains from these social dreams. Taking my point of departure from the book and film versions of Sybil as well as other related social events, I shall explore the extent to which our contemporary social dreamers unwittingly reflect the underlying problems of our society. The next step, of course, is to understand them.

The phenomenon of normalized psychopathy and social distress tends to feed on itself, driving out the "good." When bad moral currency is in circulation it brings out the dark side of human nature. In other words, an individual's crisis becomes a reflection of a larger identity crisis within our culture. When one breaks the connection of learning that takes place between the biological, psychological, and social levels of existence, one interferes with the healthy, creative aspects of human conduct and experience. Too many mirrors are dangerous because they reflectively distort and multiply the self. Therefore, one should hold the mirror up to nature in order to reflect upon the natural images of life rather than falling prey to the ostentatious self-righteousness of multiple selves. The book will conclude with a discussion and argument of the dangers inherent in fostering this kind of ostentatious, deterministic, and/or reductionist theory of consciousness.

In introducing the concept of dissociation, I believe it is essential to point out several important factors that will help us understand the nature of the concept. The most important aspect of this concept is that dissociation is a specific mental capacity or ability which *all* human beings utilize during the course of their lines. The second important fact is that dissociation is a mental process and cannot only be observed but also even to some extent measured, somewhat like a spectrum, with various quantities and qualities. Finally, we need to keep in mind that dissociation is a mental activity which can be utilized by the individual for both creative as well as destructive purposes.

One may describe dissociation metaphorically by saying that it is a kind of shifting of mental gears which results in a high degree of concentration so that a kind of separation or shift occurs in consciousness between the "internal senses" and the "external senses"— between one's imagination and reality.

All of us experience this kind of shift routinely as we descend into a deep sleep and awaken from it; there is an intermediate or transitory state in which we are neither fully unconscious nor fully conscious. While "waking logic and feeling of certainty" are not "altogether extinguished," Froeschels writes in his essay, "A Peculiar Intermediary State Between Waking and Sleeping," it is "interfered with by processes which went on in different spheres of the personality, namely, the sphere of a peculiar pseudo-logic, and the sphere of another feeling of certainty . . . which is localized within the domain of transition." That is, "two levels of the personality are in conflict with one another. . . . The logic and the joined feeling of certainty, as perceived in the state of being awake, rejected as wrong the corresponding processes that were going on in the state of transition" (Froeschels, 1949). Although Froeschels is referring here to a perfectly normal process of dissociation, he is also describing the type of process which, if the "interference" intensifies and becomes more frequent, can turn pathological.

Different types of dissociative activity can be observed which stem from different motivational factors in the life history of the person. Since dissociation is not an abnormal behavior but can be found in any kind of individual, both normal and abnormal, it might be of some value to simply mention the form of dissociation that is commonly found in normal people. It is called automatic writing. This is the execution of movement of the hand without the intervention of the will. The hand seems to act of its own accord, what appears on the page as much of a surprise to the consciousness of the writer as it would be to an outside observer. Analogously, some individuals can speak apparently without being aware of the source of their words, almost as if they were simply taking dictation. The great French psychologist, Alfred Binet, came to the conclusion that there may exist in the same person at the same time, not only two independent streams of activity, but also two independent centers of consciousness, which was commonly referred to as double consciousness. In the automatic writing condition, Binet would whisper instructions to his subject which were to be followed by an oral response. Thus, the writing and the oral response would go on independently, neither process consciously related to the other.

Morton Prince and others conducted experiments that demonstrated similar processes. For example, the hand that might be writing automatically could occupy itself with answers to mathematical problems, while the mouth and vocal cords would be occupied with reading aloud. Neither activity interfered with the other. If we grant that dissociation actually occurs, not only in the activity of the person, but also in his consciousness, we need to demonstrate evidence as to whether we are all able to dissociate in this sense. Then we will need a means of finding out if individual differences in dissociation differ in quality and quantity. Over the years psychologists and researchers have tried to test this hypothesis by assessing levels of hypnotizability. According to Dr. Herbert Spiegel, a pioneer in the field, hypnotizability is defined as the interaction of the individual's dissociative capacity and his suggestibility capacity. I will discuss this issue at greater length elsewhere in the text especially since the condition of hypnosis, be it self-hypnosis or hypnosis induced by another party, is essential to uncover the dynamics of the dissociative process.

The concept of dissociation is closely related to the concept of consciousness, particularly divided consciousness or double consciousness, as some German scholars prefer. The voluntary control of conscious activity of the human organism becomes a central issue in dealing with this subject. To the extent that direct control of human activity is split off from consciousness or is unconscious, as it were, we can say that the dissociative process is at work. The French term "désagrégation" was used synonymously with "dissociation" in English and became popular through the works of William James, Morton Prince, and Pierre Janet in both the United States and France. The central question at hand, when dealing with dissociative processes, is directly related to self-integration and self-autonomy. Put in slightly different terms, one may pose the question of whether an individual can have more than one autonomous self, and if this is indeed possible, then is it possible for this self-process to be both conscious and unconscious?

Most of the controversy related to the theory of the process of dissociation concerns this issue. If one can bifurcate or dissociate oneself, how does this process take place? A number of issues must be dealt with before we can answer this question. First, what systems or patterns of behavior are more or less coherent in this process? Is there a degree of structure that facilitates the integration and/or the disintegration of the skills, memories, perceptions, etc., that are involved in this process? Second, we need to ask to what extent do amnesic barriers (or, in Freudian terms, unconscious and repression processes) prevent the integration and interaction of these systems? In other words, how do we explain the ego-alien "state of mind"? Since the middle of the nineteenth century, psychologists have theorized that in some individuals, consciousness may become split into two or more parts. The split-off or dissociated portion may be a fragment of the whole self or it may be so complex and extensive as to be capable of fulfilling all of the functions of an individual's consciousness.

Ideas, feelings, and actions, which are associated in life experience, tend to become linked together into various processes in such a way that stimulation of one element of a particular process excites the activity of all the rest. This process is often referred to as a complex process. A complex formed in relation to some event that is accompanied by a great deal of affectivity may become dissociated from one's personal consciousness so that recollections of the event, as well as feelings and actions connected with it, become inaccessible. Such a complex process of dissociation does not completely disappear. In other words, it is still possible for the process to function in some manner. Various reports of normal and abnormal individuals have been described in the literature to illustrate this point. Thomas Mayo, for example, gave one of the earliest lucid recognitions of this process of the human mind in 1838 while describing what he called the moral cases of insanity. According to Mayo, there is a morbid state of the human mind in which the individual lives in alternate stages of two different beings. One is easily recognized as the person's normal state of mind. It exhibits the ordinary aspects of his or her character or behavior. In the second state, the person appeared to have undergone a remarkable change. He or she has forgotten things or else saw them in a different light. He or she may lapse into one or another of these states without any clear recognition of the subjects and objects experienced in the other state. For example, Mayo says, "This morbid state, to which the name double consciousness is usually given, has a considerable affinity to the intermittent form of madness—so much so that it seems not unreasonable to suspect that their laws of causation may have some common points." Mayo goes on to refer to the practice of mesmerism, which had only recently been brought to the attention of the British public, and concludes that "[W]e have here also a form of double consciousness, which those who have seen the experiment (using mesmerism) made during the Spring of 1838, at a London hospital, will admit to have exhibited this affinity in a high degree." Mayo contends that this form of double consciousness can be voluntarily brought about by an external agency. Mayo is referring to what we would now consider to be the process of hypnosis. The close relationship between the process of dissociation and the process of being hypnotized, putting the individual in a state of divided or double consciousness, thus becomes a crucial aspect of the story of how the theory of dissociation emerged and how it attempted to explain the normal and abnormal aspects of the normal mind.

In the next chapters we will explore a number of issues that Mayo's work raises:

1. How the explanation of the association and dissociation of ideas emerged in the seventeenth and eighteenth century to set the stage for the nineteenth century recognition of the concept of dissociation.

2. How is spiritual dissociation related to the phenomenon? Can it be understood the same way or does it represent a dissociative experience all of its own?
3. How is pathological dissociation related? Is a dissociative experience that results in double consciousness the same when it arises from a person's mental processes as it is if it stems from a medical condition?
4. How is the condition of double consciousness related to the dissociations of everyday life which we all experience and can be positive as well as negative?
5. How are neurophysiological processes of dissociation related to the reflexive actions of the brain and the mind?

I

A Brief History of Multiplicity

Proteus is an ever-changing melody.
HUGH SYDENHAM

Multiply sensitive minds and you will multiply good and evil.
DIDEROT (Paradox Comedian)

WONDERFUL WORKS OF GOD.

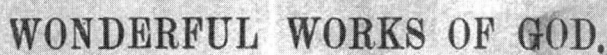

A NARRATIVE

OF THE

WONDERFUL FACTS

IN THE

CASE OF ANSEL BOURNE,

OF

WEST SHELBY, ORLEANS CO., N. Y.

WHO, IN THE MIDST OF OPPOSITION TO THE CHRISTIAN RELIGION, WAS SUDDENLY STRUCK BLIND, DUMB AND DEAF; AND AFTER EIGHTEEN DAYS WAS SUDDENLY AND COMPLETELY RESTORED, IN THE PRESENCE OF HUNDREDS OF PERSONS, IN THE CHRISTIAN CHAPEL, AT WESTERLY, ON THE 15TH OF NOVEMBER, 1857.

WRITTEN UNDER HIS DIRECTION.

FALL RIVER, MASS.
WM. S. ROBERTSON, STEAM PRINTER, 6 MAIN STREET.
1877.

1

The Roots of Multiple Personality Disorder/Dissociative Identity Disorder

SEIZURES, HYSTERIA, AND DISSOCIATION: MAKING SENSE OF MIND AND BRAIN

No disorder of the mind has captured the imagination of the public more than Multiple Personality Disorder (MPD). The phenomenon isn't new by any means. Multiple Personality Disorder, now known as Dissociative Identity Disorder, has been of great interest to the public for centuries. Case histories of MPD can be found in the literature as far back as the eighteenth century; nevertheless, it is in the literature of the latter part of the nineteenth century that we find the clearest descriptions of this disorder as we know it today.

Most of the nineteenth century literature regarding dissociative phenomena of both mind and brain shows a peculiar preoccupation with the possible connection between dissociative phenomena of various kinds, i.e., hypnotic states, fugue and other amnestic states, and various forms of hysteria—particularly hysterical fits as they may relate to organically caused epileptic fits. In fact, the etiology of any type of altered state of consciousness, such as a convulsive-like attack, was thought to be precipitated by organic malfunctions. This connection between epilepsy and hysteria seems to have come originally from Boerhaave (1745), and later elaborated on by his students, particularly George Cheyne and William Cullen.

The idea that dissociation is related to unconscious processes first finds its champion in a Scottish scholar and judge who is all but unknown today—Lord Henry Kames. In a book published in the late eighteenth century, he explores the phenomenon of dissociation which he describes as a routine experience with which anyone could identify. "In a dead sleep, we have consciousness of self," he writes in *Essays on the Principles of morality and natural religion in two parts*. But that consciousness of self can vanish in sleep, too: "We dream sometimes without this consciousness, and even from our waking hours pass without it. A reverie is nothing else, but a wandering of the mind through its ideas, without carrying along the perception of self" (Kames, 1751).

He then goes on to observe that while consciousness has a principal role in our personal survival, the state of dissociation that we experience whether in dreams or in daydreams diverts us from this all-important preoccupation: "This consciousness or perception of self is . . . of the liveliest kind. Self-preservation is everyone's peculiar duty; and the vivacity of this perception is necessary to make us attentive to our own interest, and particularly, to show every appearance of danger. When a man is in a reverie, he has no circumspection, nor any manner of attention to his own interest . . . ."

While he allows that the "perception, or consciousness of self, carried through all the different flavors of life, and all variety of action" is "the foundation of personal identity," he also asserts that people are mistaken to take for granted the idea that consciousness is contingent on "what is present in the mind, or passes within it." On the contrary, he argues "that we are conscious of many things which are not the impressions and ideas, within the mind" (Kames, 1751). He goes on to explain: "In some instances, we feel the impression and are conscious of it. . . . In others, being quite unconscious of the impression, we perceive only the internal object" (Kames, 1751). This is the first known use of the word "unconscious" in the English literature.

Kames was clearly ahead of his time although it doesn't appear that he understood the implications of the phenomena that he described; nor was there anyone to pick up the ball and run with it. The concept of the unconscious would lay dormant for another century before it was revived and its significance recognized.

Nonetheless, by the nineteenth century the groundwork had been prepared—especially during the first decade—for people to think about how the mind functions in terms of the notion of association of ideas. This expression of association of ideas was one of the more important theories advanced in John Locke's great and influential treatise, *An Essay Concerning Human Understanding*. Locke's concept was developed with greater precision by such pioneering scholars as David Hume and David Hartley. During this period, it was assumed that the basis of most mental operations was derived from the law of association of ideas. It is not surprising, then, that scholars would eventually be driven to deal with its opposite—the *dissociation* of ideas and/or consciousness.

One of the primary issues that emerged during the nineteenth century was the question of the relationship between the association and dissociation processes in the mind. Were they continuous processes or discontinuous processes? When and how did they function to produce healthy mental states, as opposed to disordered or pathological states, in the organism? During the last decades of the nineteenth century, however, some physicians raised a possibility that seizures or "fit states" and/or other altered states of consciousness with amnesia could be understood in nonphysiological terms.

These controversial issues remain with us today, and are for the most part unresolved. We will examine the contributions to the understanding of dissociation by three of the most influential and well-known scholars of the nineteenth century, namely Pierre Janet, Morton Prince, and Boris Sidis. (We will also take a brief detour to consider the contribution of Frederick Myers who was strongly influenced by Janet.) All three authors were primarily interested in disordered minds in various states of dissociation.

How these scholars tried to deal with symptomatology and possible causative factors linked to wide range of dissociative "brain-mind" disorders is perhaps best illustrated by numerous case histories from the beginning of the nineteenth centuries onward. What makes the clinical cases so intriguing was that they were reported before the three formed or published their own observations theories to explain such manifestations.

As we investigate the interesting and sometimes bizarre case histories, it is important to trace the influence and development of the nomenclature and taxonomy used in the description of these cases. Both the taxonomy and the meaning implied in the nomenclature set the stage for the theories of "alienists," as they were known, of whom we have few better examples than Janet, Prince, and Sidis.

EARLY CASE HISTORIES: LOOKING FOR ANSEL BOURNE IN ALL THE WRONG PLACES

The earliest case histories of multiple personality disorder coincide with the earliest literature on mesmerism, later referred to as animal magnetism and hypnosis. This is not coincidental since there is an intrinsic relationship between them, especially as they relate to the discovery of various altered states of consciousness. I will discuss Mesmer and hypnosis in more detail in Chapter 5 but for now you should keep in mind that most of the early case histories that have come down to us are anecdotal in nature and are saturated with overtones of "religious enthusiasm."

We begin in 1811 with the extraordinary case of Mary Reynolds. This case is one of the best known in the literature and it was described in detail contemporaneously by a number of physicians, particularly Samuel Mitchell (1816). Reynolds experienced a severe convulsion which left her unconscious. Upon recovering she was deaf and blind. It would take some time before she regained the use of either her sight or her hearing. Within a year, she went into a deep trance state, from which she could not be awakened for a considerable time. When she did emerge from her unconscious state—spontaneously—she exhibited a general state of amnesia which we now know to be typical of such cases. Reynolds seemed to have forgotten most of her skills and had to be reeducated. She appeared to relapse into these states sporadically for many years before returning permanently to an uninterrupted state of consciousness.

We can thank Samuel Mitchell for his description of another remarkable case involving a woman named Rachel Baker. Baker talked in her sleep, which is not so strange, but her sleep-talking took the form of sermons, which most certainly is. She would go into these trance states periodically, only to emerge with no recollection of the preaching she had done in them. In these states she was known to recite original poetry and perform original musical compositions in addition to praying and preaching. Eventually she was examined in New York City by a number of prominent physicians, all of whom were puzzled by her "strange form of madness." The sleeping preacher, as she was known, became quite popular and a source of lively speculation among many important people of the time who, no less than the physicians, wondered about what could possibly account for her condition (see Simpson and Carlson, 1968).

A third case involves Jane, a 17-year-old girl from Springfield, Massachusetts, whose case was described by L.W. Bilden in 1834. Like Baker, she was examined by several physicians and, like Baker, she displayed unusual behavior while asleep. Jane didn't talk, much less preach, in her sleep; she was a sleepwalker—a somnambulist—but one who could carry out complex household tasks while in this state. Her eyes were typically shut, but her senses seemed to be fully alert. This was the antithesis of Shakespeare's description of Lady Macbeth, whose state of mind was exemplified by open eyes and dulled senses.

Although these cases did not seem to exhibit full-blown alternate personalities, they nevertheless exhibited symptoms that suggested that condition. Two popular authors of the early nineteenth century—Abercrombie (1832) and MacNish (1835)—discussed the psychological aspects of disorders of perception, sensation, and consciousness in light of such cases, supplying elaborate anecdotal details to supplement their accounts. The cases they described dealt with memory loss, strange disorders of the imagination, and fugue states in which the individual temporarily loses the memory of his or her "real" self. Different systems of thought, feelings, and desires seem to determine their wanderings and appear dissociated from their personal consciousness. Kihlstrom, for instance, has written a paper discussing how the identification of self with memory has been viewed as an important criterion of self-identity. In his paper he emphasizes the dissociative symptomatology, such as depersonalization, derealization, fugue states, etc. (Kihlstrom, 1987).

It is important to clarify what is meant by fugue states. In fact, I don't believe that for the most part, it is a "state" at all but a developmental process which is characterized by the loss of memory of self. This loss can last for an hour or a day or even for months. Under such circumstances the individual understandably seeks to adopt some identity—any identity—to replace the one he's unaccountably mislaid. The classic case is represented by Ansel Bourne, a Rhode Island native who disappeared for months and lived under another identity until he recovered (see below). Like almost any other mental illness, these fugues tend to be episodic, which is why, colloquial use notwithstanding, a fugue is really a process and not a "state."

Dissociation was also seen as a result of the structure of the brain itself. One early researcher, Arthur Ladbroke Wigan (1785–1847), wrote a book, *A New View of Insanity: Duality of the Mind Ruled by Structures, Functions and Diseases of the Brain* . . . , which, as the title suggests, attributed mental disorders to the anatomy of the brain. He believed that the right and left hemispheres were two separate and complete organs, which resulted in a literal duality of the mind. Although he had no interest in making his theory the basis for a philosophical system, he did anticipate the work of Morton Prince in his use of case histories to give it weight. He described one patient who periodically entered a somnambulant state in which he could read, write, and speak without demonstrating any real comprehension. As soon as he emerged from these states, however, he had no recollection of what he had seen or done in them. Yet when he reverted to his somnambulant state he could recall what had happened the last time he'd experienced such a state. Wigan called the alteration of dissociated and conscious states an example of "double consciousness" (Wigan, 1844). It is worth noting that the late brain surgeon Joe Bogen, who performed operations to sever the corpus callosum to alleviate epileptic seizures, was familiar with Wigan's work. Alienist Forbes Winslow was another early researcher who championed the concept of dual consciousness; in his book *On Obscure Diseases of the Brain and Disorders of the Mind* he discussed what it meant to have two senses of identity, or two separated selves, relying on some remarkable case histories as examples to make its case (Winslow, 1860). Herbert Mayo, too, wrote about such cases, one of which was similar to the Beecham girl whom Prince treated (Mayo, 1837).

Nevertheless, it is virtually impossible to make a hard and clear distinction between fugue cases and typical multiple personality cases. No two multiple personality cases or fugue states, for that matter, are exactly the same. Furthermore, there is good reason to believe that multiple personality disorders can develop out of fugue episodes, especially when a subject is highly hypnotizable. This hypothesis is uniquely illustrated by the famous case of Ansel Bourne, a carpenter and sometimes preacher who lived in upstate New York and who was 61 years of age at the time of his fugue state experience. Some time in January 1887, he went to a bank in Providence to get money for a farm that he wanted to buy. But as he was on his way to his sister's house he disappeared. He didn't resurface until March 14. On that date, an individual by the name of A. J. Browne rented a small shop in Norristown, Pennsylvania. The next day, he woke up in a state of confusion. He asked the residents of the house what he was doing there. His name, he told them, was not Browne at all, but Ansel Bourne, and the last thing he could recall was being in Providence in January. He could not recollect anything that had occurred in the interim nor did he believe that he could have been living in Norristown for two months. Yet even in his second state he apparently carried out business in his shop without anyone supposing that there was anything wrong with him. Everything seemed absolutely normal. After recovering his original identity on March 14, Bourne was taken home by his friends and resumed his former life as if nothing had happened. No one else had any idea how to account for the missing months. Only once, years later, at a prayer meeting, was Bourne able to recall even a fragment of his mysterious life as Browne in Norristown.

The missing part of Bourne's life was not recovered until three years after this episode, when he was hypnotized by Professor William James (see Hodgson, 1891–92). Under hypnosis, he was able to provide a detailed account of his wanderings during the first two weeks of his amnestic state. Apparently, before settling down in Norristown, he had traveled to Boston, New York, Philadelphia, and various other places. It is quite clear that in the first two weeks of his secondary state, Bourne had acted in the characteristic manner of an ordinary fugue case. He was a wanderer who forgot his personal identity and having assumed a new name, subsequently enjoyed a quiet, respectable, but altogether different lifestyle. In his second state, he had no recollection of his former life, and when he recovered his identity, he had no recollection of his life in Pennsylvania. These lost memories, however, turned out to be recoverable during hypnosis. His only explanation for this strange experience was that he wanted to get away—somewhere, anywhere—so that he could get some rest.

The original description of this case was written by Richard Hodgson (1891–92), in a paper titled "A Double Case of Consciousness" (see Bourne, 1877). Hodgson made an interesting observation regarding this case and its relation to epilepsy. "I suppose that on January 17, 1887, he [Bourne] may have had a mild epileptic seizure," Hodgson wrote, "and that after the fit, he was a different person, although in the same skin; or as the popular phrase is, the post-epileptic patient was not himself." Hodgson (1891–92) makes reference to John Hughlings Jackson's 1884 Croonian lectures on the evolution of the nervous system, as well as Jackson's article on temporary mental disorders and epilepsy, published in *The West Riding Lunatic Asylum Reports, Volume 5* (Jackson, 1958). Over the ensuing years many authors discussed this case, but perhaps the most extensive treatment was written by Michael Kenny in his book, *The Passion of Ansel Bourne*. Kenny's assessment, however, suffers because he doesn't understand how hypnosis works (Kenny, 1986).

Cases involving similar disorders, though not necessarily so spectacular, were described by many alienists in books published between 1830 and 1850, notably by Abercrombie and MacNish. Herbert Mayo (1851), George Combe (1832), and Jerome Kidder (1869) also tackled these unusual cases. Kidder's work, entitled *Vital Resources* and heretofore unmentioned in the literature, offers over seventy pages of commentary on the plurality of personality and discusses both the mental and physiological aspects of these conditions.

If one took the time to look carefully enough for them, an exhaustive catalogue of all the cases during the nineteenth century would probably amount to close to one hundred.

These cases posed a dilemma for the alienists and psychologists of the day who not only disputed the nature of the disorder but couldn't even come to any agreement about the vocabulary that should be used to describe it. One writer used the term "multiplex" to characterize the various personalities. Skeptics vigorously carried out an argument with those who claimed that the disorder was real and verifiable. Even those who believed in the existence of the disorder differed about how many personalities were possible and at what point the number of personalities could no longer be considered plausible (*Journal of the Society of Psychical Research*, October 1889). These debates can be followed in the pages of *The Journal of the Society of Psychical Research* of 1888 and 1889. The letters to the editor column were filled with debates about the duality of the mind that were eerily parallel to the debates in the 1980s.

The literature of the latter part of the nineteenth century contained more sophisticated and detailed theories and case histories, which set the standards for twentieth-century psychiatric case history reports. The work of Charcot is well known, and was quite influential, especially in terms of the clear distinction made between organic epilepsy and hysterical epileptic fits. Although Charcot recognized that hysteria could assume various forms and that hypnotic phenomena could occur in seemingly normal individuals, he still refused to accept hypnosis as a normal phenomenon, calling it "sommeil nurveux," or nervous sleep. Indeed, he asserted that once a hysteric was cured he—or more likely she—would inevitably lose the capacity to be hypnotized, a hypothesis that research has long since disproved.

Eugene Bleuler (1924), in his famous textbook of psychiatry, offers a cautionary note about the relationship of epilepsy to hysteria:

> The marked dependence of the hysterical attack on external influences,1 and the slight dependence of the epileptic syndromes, can with a careful evaluation of circumstances often alone suffice for the diagnosis. In all other respects, it should not be forgotten that in epilepsy all hysterical symptoms may occur. (p. 462).

We now turn to some of the most prominent books of the late nineteenth and twentieth century and quote from the cases they mention.

THE NEUROPHYSIOLOGY OF THE INHIBITION–EXCITATION CONTINUUM

In stating that attention is dependent upon cortical inhibition, which acts to shut out activity within regions of the nervous system, Charles Sherrington was in agreement with the view of many psychologists during the latter part of the nineteenth century. The possibility of controlling the inhibitory capacity was an important preoccupation of David Ferrier as well as Ivan Sechenov during most of their careers. Ferrier's notion about the power of fixing one's attention during the constriction of consciousness depends ultimately upon the inhibition of movements (Diamond, 1963).

Théodule Ribot had similar ideas; so did William James. In his "Stream of Thought" chapter in *The Principles of Psychology*, James observed that consciousness consists of many factors, but especially the reinforcing processes advocated by G. E. Muller and the inhibitory agency of attention that was a major preoccupation of many authors during this period.

Sigmund Exner did much to advance our knowledge of the dependence of the attentive processes on both facilitation and inhibition. Exner was one of the first to attempt the difficult task of relating mental phenomena to their psychological correlates. He was engaged in this work even before Wilhelm Wundt (1874) formulated his ideas along these same lines in his *Principles of Physiological Psychology*.

The fundamental dilemma facing the authorities of the late nineteenth century was how to reconcile an alleged conflict between two opposing explanatory principles involved in the body–mind problem. This dilemma can be described as follows: how does one theoretically deal with the difference between the "hard rock of conscious matter" as opposed to the "free-floating bifurcating spirit of consciousness"? Pierre Janet, Morton Prince, and Boris Sidis all found themselves in this predicament; and they all attempted to resolve it in a similar, but not identical, manner. The solution was to marry the two approaches into a dynamic integrated whole and then explain how the process works. Of course, empirical evidence was always used whenever available. Let us now examine the view of these three late nineteenth-century scholars to find out how they tackled the problem.

PIERRE JANET

Of the three individuals whose ideas we will discuss in this section, Janet was clearly the one who made the earliest contribution and therefore in many ways was the most influential. Janet started out as a psychologist, but received a medical degree in 1893; however, he was never willing to completely abandon a nonphysiological explanation for the cases he examined and reported on over the years. In fact, he cautioned that reductionism, in terms of physiological explanations for psychological issues, had many problems and should be avoided at all costs. Janet's seminal work on psychological automatism published in 1889 is seen to contain both an automatic action (beneath awareness) and a conscious action—thus the term "psychological automatism." In other words, he was the first person to argue that people under hypnosis are not unconscious but rather have a kind of divided consciousness. Janet's case studies in hysteria illustrated that the hysterics could experience exceptional states of consciousness which were not really distinct from one another. In other words, these exceptional states of consciousness were continuous. However, it seemed as if they were different aspects of the person or "different personalities."

The basis of Janet's position with regard to Dissociative Identity Disorder is found in his book, *The Major Symptoms of Hysteria*. Janet makes the distinction between the epileptic and the hysterical fit, which will be elaborated upon later. Janet was fond of quoting Martin Charcot and, as it turns out, one of his teacher's favorite sayings was, "Nothing was left to chance, on the contrary everything happens according to rules, always the same, common to private and hospital practice, applicable to all countries, to all times, and to all races" (Janet, 1907).

Because there were different qualities as well as quantities observed in the process, Janet coined the term "monoideism." The term referred to a relatively simple condition in which a single idea dominates the consciousness while everything else is dissociated.

Janet's case history of a woman named Irene exemplifies this concept. For months Irene suffered from a tortured devotion to her dying mother. After the funeral, however, Irene proceeded to banish all memory of her mother's illness and death from her mind. Irene was a poor French girl whose troubles began shortly before the turn of the century. Raised in an impoverished family in Victor Hugo's Paris, Irene lived in a wretched garret with a mother who was dying of tuberculosis and a father who was drunk and argumentative nearly all the time. The strain on Irene evidently pushed her to the edge of hysteria, and her mother's death carried her over it. The mother's dying was a long, drawn-out ordeal which for Irene proved a harrowing experience. For nine weeks Irene hovered anxiously about the bedside, watching helplessly as her mother gasped ever more weakly for breath and vomited ever smaller quantities of blood. When the end finally came, Irene refused to accept it. She tried frantically to bring the body back to life, lifting it from the bed, only to collapse to the floor under its weight.

Evidently no one else in the family witnessed this act of desperation, but not long after the funeral Irene dissociated. During these dissociations, which sometimes lasted for several hours and which Janet considered an extreme form of sleepwalking, Irene would reenact the scene of her mother's death in one way or another. Sometimes she would merely sit in her chair and silently observe the scene as it took place in her mind's eye. She would sit in silence with her hands gripping the chair, her eyes filling with tears. At other times, though, she would describe the deathbed scene in a rushing flow of words and in meticulous detail. At still other times she would act out the drama while she described it, going through all the motions without any variations between one reenactment and the next. She would discuss things with her mother, carrying on what might have been mistaken for a normal conversation apart from the fact that her mother wasn't there. She began to contemplate suicide and enacted scenes in which she would end her life.

It was sheer exhaustion more than any other factor that seemed to restore her to normalcy—that is, her primary state. Afterwards she would remember nothing that had occurred during the dissociations. Indeed, she remembered nothing about her mother's death. She knew that her mother must be dead, she confessed, only because people had told her so and because her mother was no longer present. But she didn't know what had caused her death and admitted that she was troubled that she hadn't been there to take care of her mother in her final hours. In effect, she shut out or dissociated the memory of the events. Yet the memory could reassert itself and cause her to again assume the role of her mother's comforting daughter.

Obviously the mother's death had come as such a terrible blow to her that she couldn't consciously process it, and it was a long time before she recovered from it. In fact, there is no clear evidence or testimony from Janet that she ever really did.

As Janet described it, the case of Felida represents another type of dissociation: the fugue state (Janet, 1907). (It should be noted that someone in a fugue state does not necessarily have MPD/DID, but MPD/DID is almost always characterized by the occurrence of fugue states.) As the dissociation proceeds, the individual not only loses the perceptual and memorial elements, but also some of the time sequences that are involved in his activities. With this dynamic amnestic effect, a new functional whole is established. For example, Felida was both an exuberant and lively young woman and a solemn and despondent bereaved matron.

Dissociation theory, as we call it today, rests solidly upon the early work of Janet. He sometimes referred to these divided states of consciousness as alternative personalities which could be produced through hypnosis. This divided consciousness functions beneath the level of consciousness in an individual, and is still capable of complex mental operations. The hidden part of consciousness is capable of producing feelings, actions, and even hallucinations.

This approach, which stresses the amnestic effect, represents an important contribution to Janet's theory of narrowing the field of consciousness. But one should not misunderstand that the narrowing of the field of consciousness necessarily restricts the process of consciousness. Janet believed and demonstrated that extraordinary individuals (i.e., highly hypnotizable) may be able to take in many sensations and impressions at one time, so that they can both broaden and narrow the field of consciousness, especially under a state of hypnosis. In investigating the unconscious aspects of divided consciousness, as well as the origins of these states, Janet frequently used the technique of uncovering memories of events in the life of the individual that could not be integrated into the normal personality.

Another aspect of Janet's theory, particularly regarding hysteria, pertained to "fixed ideas." Although this was not a new concept in the literature, Janet endowed this concept with a new meaning and made it central to his theory of psychopathology. (I have elaborated on Freud's own interpretation of Janet's fixed ideas in Chapter 4.)

Janet's ideas were influenced by his teacher Charcot. Although their ideas differed, Janet expressed nothing but praise and admiration for his mentor, crediting him for paving the way to greater precision regarding our critical knowledge of hysteria.

Janet assumed that all cases of hysteria were examples of dissociation and that dissociation was its major characteristic. Furthermore, he believed that dissociation was a major characteristic of hypnosis. In this respect he agreed with Charcot's position, which assumed that hypnosis is "artificial hysteria."

As we have previously indicated, one of the best summaries of Janet's contribution to hysteria and related disorders can be found in *The Major Symptoms of Hysteria*. One can assume that such eminent people as Morton Prince, William James, and Boris Sidis attended these lectures. In fact, one of the lectures was entirely devoted to double personalities, in which Janet paid great tribute to the work of Morton Prince and cited Boris Sidis as well. We know that James and Janet were friends for many years and frequently corresponded with one another.

One of the most important contributions during these lectures at Harvard was what Janet referred to as "a very curious property known as hysterical accidents." Although he did not believe that these hysterical accidents were unique to the hysteric patients, he did believe that they were very important to consider while working with them. Janet stressed that these accidents or occurrences could be artificially produced. Like Charcot, he cites the case of a man who had been afflicted with epilepsy for several years, but cautioned that it was important to distinguish between *genuine* epileptic fits and *hysterical* epileptic fits. With a true epileptic condition, he wrote, one cannot artificially produce the seizure or fit, whereas in hysterical or pseudoepilepsy, one can easily bring about a seizure through hypnosis.

Janet went on to present another case about which he had written, that of Marceline. This case was molded by repeated hypnotism over a period of fifteen years. "She had really become a kind of artificial Felida," Janet explained, referring to the patient given to lapsing into fugue states, "and she shows us that double existence itself can be reduced by artificial means as well as occurring naturally."

Janet's disagreements with Freud regarding hysteria and hypnosis are well known. (I will discuss the conceptual rifts between Janet and Freud in further detail in Chapter 4.) However, one question that remains puzzling today (since the study of dissociative disorder has become of great interest and importance) is why Janet's contributions have been overlooked for such a long period of time, while Freud's theories endured great success. The reasons are probably multiple. One factor is the differences in personality between Freud and Janet. But it might have to do more with the prevailing social and political climate. Janet was a professor at the College of France in Paris, and therefore did not train students in a teaching hospital. He was also more the lone wolf type of scholar who had little interest in creating a school of thought, let alone an ideology or a system like Freud. He also lacked a nephew like Edward Bernays, known as the Father of Public Relations in America, who had done so much to help promote Uncle Freud and psychoanalysis for much of the twentieth century.

If one were to point out a major weakness in Janet's position, it would be that Janet basically saw dissociation and hypnosis as pathological processes. He did not realize that dissociation and hypnosis may be involved in both healthy creative activities of the organism as well as in unhealthy and destructive activities (Rieber, 1997). Janet also had a tendency to use spatial metaphors excessively. His conception of dissociation was described in spatial terms. His theory suggested, basically, that some mental elements were separated out from the greater aggregate of elements that constituted the totality of mind. In other words, his language suggested a literal splitting of the mind into separate fragments. Nevertheless, whatever the shortcomings in his theory, Janet's contribution to this field of study is certain to be lasting.

F. W. MYERS

At this point we should mention Frederick Myers. In many respects Myers followed in Janet's footsteps recognizing that Janet's work was closely related to his own and even used Janet's experiments to support his own ideas. Myers was a rather unique and important figure during the latter half of the nineteenth century. His work at Cambridge, which brought him in contact with Henry Sidgwick, led to the founding of the British Society for Psychical Research. His friendship with William James helped make it possible to establish an American branch of that organization in the early 1880s when the British society got off of the ground. One of the major beliefs that Myers was committed to during this period was the assumption that the human mind was capable of more than one type of consciousness in each individual person. In other words, there were multiple centers of consciousness, and because of this important assumption, the extraordinary manifestations that occurred during trance states, or what we now call altered states of consciousness, could be better understood and investigated. Myers, like James, believed that these personal "unconscious" aspects of consciousness did have physiological correlates that should be investigated, but that on their own they could not explain such extraordinary phenomena as mental telepathy, hypnosis, automatic writing, and other related altered states of consciousness. One of Myers's major assumptions, which certainly made his ideas compatible with William James at the time, was that an adequate theory of the human mind would have to take into consideration both normal and pathological aspects, and furthermore, that the study of the normal would enhance the study of the abnormal and conversely that the study of the abnormal would enhance the study of the normal. This belief was not unusual at the time. Such important scholars as W. Preyer, professor at Jena University, and Karl du Prel, of Leipzig, held similar views. Much of this work was stimulated by explorations into the physiology and pathology of the mind by prominent British alienists, such as Henry Maudsley, William Carpenter, and Thomas Laycock. Carpenter and Laycock debated the mechanism underlying unconscious reflex actions of the brain and the way in which these reflexes could operate unconsciously. Carpenter coined the term "unconscious cerebration" in his very popular book titled *Mental Physiology*. Considerable discussion centered around the related concept of the automatic action of the cerebrum in an attempt to explain how thoughts and activity of an intelligent nature did not have to be caused by thinking at the conscious level.

Morton Prince actually wrote his first book on this subject matter, before he had fully developed his dissociation theory. The existence of telepathic skills in certain individuals was not new in the late 1880s. Reports of such extraordinary phenomena were well known and popular in the 1840s and 1850s, especially in France and England. John Elliotson, J. Esdaile, and many others were involved in controversies having to do with the relationship between telepathy and animal magnetism. In 1885, Myers published an important article arguing for the existence of a bifurcated self or the existence of a secondary self within individuals. According to Myers, this secondary self was—or allegedly could be—entirely dissociated from the primary consciousness of the individual—so much so that the person could be totally ignorant of the consequences of this situation. What Myers was doing was forming the basis for a more fully developed theory of dissociative mental processes. This notion of a primary and secondary self, as far as Myers was concerned, was not the exclusive property of the mentally disturbed or insane. In this respect his opinion was at odds with Janet's. Myers preferred the term "subliminal self" rather than "unconscious self" that Freud and other German scholars of the time advocated.

Nonetheless, both Myers and Janet were interested in deriving an explanatory principle that could somehow bridge the gap between the mind and the body in accounting for the phenomenon of bifurcation. At the time automatism was used to explain everything from compulsive behavior to composing a symphony. They sought to get away from the purely physiological approach that automatism represented and construct a unifying theory that would explain MPD. Adam Crabtree in an illuminating paper describes this attempt by Myers and Janet, calling it a failure, but a profitable one insofar as it paved the way for dynamic psychiatry (Crabtree, 2003). I believe that Crabtree is too harsh in his judgment; Myers and Janet made a gallant effort which opened up possible solutions that we are still exploring today. While research has yielded more clues, we still don't know how to completely explain such a baffling disorder. Myers and Janet were pioneers and like all pioneers, they pointed the way for those who followed in their footsteps.

MORTON PRINCE

Morton Prince initially became interested in the problem of multiple personality disorder when he tried to relate the psychological and physiological aspects of MPD and hysteria, especially when it entails the use of hypnosis. Prince was particularly impressed by Janet's early work, although he felt that it was necessary to go beyond Janet by formulating a physiologico-anatomical basis for the psychological phenomena in Janet's work. His attempt, as he would be the first to admit, was purely speculative. He had no wish to oppose Janet's psychological theory but, on the contrary, hoped to strengthen it. Although his paper elaborating on Janet's theories was actually written in 1891, Prince only got around to publishing it seven years later in 1898 in the *Proceedings of the Society for Psychical Research*.

In Prince's view, the problems of hysteria and related disorders were so complex and so serious that in the study of individual clinical cases, one must search for more than a single psychological or physiological principle. For example, he believed that the phenomenon involved a variety of elements: problems with consciousness or subconscious "fixed ideas" in hysterical patients, for one; the problems involved in cerebral inhibition as it relates to association of neurological processes, for another; as well as the amnestic effects seen during conditions of hypnosis. All of these elements needed to be integrated. In other words, he contended that no single explanatory principle could account for all of the facts of the disorder. In order to remedy this situation, Prince utilized the well-known and highly respected theoretical position of John Hughlings Jackson.

Jackson's idea was based upon the dynamic interaction of levels based on the development and evolution of the central nervous system. He attempted to divide the mental processes into higher complex processes of thought and voluntary movements, on the one hand, and lower automatic subconscious processes, on the other. This theory of the mind–body process was based on "duality of personality." One aspect consisted of complex associated states of conscious memories, which made up the personality of the conscious individual in the waking state. The second aspect of this duality consisted of the more autonomous subconscious mental states (sometimes referred to as subliminal consciousness).

This theory advocated the correlation of the higher complex states of self-consciousness (the first aspect of the person or the organism) with the highest brain levels. The theory also correlated the more autonomous subconscious states with a second level, which corresponded to the middle motor and sensory region of the brain and central nervous system. This theory compelled Prince's interest because he wanted to know how this particular frame of reference agreed with or supported the observable phenomena in pathological cases, such as hysterical anesthesia and amnestic effects during hypnosis. Prince was working on these issues about the same time that he started to work on his famous Miss Beauchamp case (Prince, 1898).

Prince felt that his theory had great promise because it helped explain how and why a sensory impression is recorded but not perceived during the waking state, and yet remembered during the hypnotic trance state. He was less certain about the area of the brain in which hysterical symptoms were suppressed—a phenomenon which Prince referred to as inhibition or "going to sleep." He was, however, more positive and hopeful about this theory when it came to providing physiological explanations for the various forms of hysterical anesthesia observed by Alfred Binet. Prince assumed that an inhibition of the higher centers takes place while the middle centers continue to react in hysterical anesthesia. Nevertheless, the impressions received at the middle centers cannot excite the highest tactile centers, and therefore be perceived in consciousness. However, they may excite the highest visual centers, which are normally coordinated with tactile centers for the perception of one's hand. If the tactile sense fails, Prince hypothesized that the other senses may be excited by an impression in the middle centers. From this point of view, it is clear that Prince was pursuing a more integrative theory of mind–body functioning than was presented in many other cases of the period.

BORIS SIDIS

Boris Sidis was a Russian immigrant who came to the United States as a young man in the 1880s. He proceeded to pull himself up by his bootstraps and convinced Harvard University to fund him to study with William James and company. With James as his mentor he produced a thesis on the psychology of suggestion. Strangely enough, Sidis was such an eccentric character that James had to persuade him to write a book based on his thesis (Sidis, 1898). This book appeared in 1898 with James supplying a flattering foreword.

Sidis was a man who truly had the courage of his convictions, for he took his mentor James to task on several occasions in the book— and with great effectiveness, too. James took note of his criticism but made sure to insert a mild disclaimer in the forward in which he said that although the book was a fine piece of work he did not necessarily agree with all of the positions taken by its author.

Sidis's views about suggestibility and later dissociation and its disorders embodied a universally applicable integrative style of thinking, which is hard to classify as either primarily Anglo-American or Russian-European. Sidis had a highly individualistic way of deriving his own ideas that set him apart from any traditional school of thought. When he returned to New York he became the first experimental psychologist to work at the now-world-famous New York State Psychiatric Institute, then known as the Pathological Institute, located on Ward's Island in the East River. Since he was in charge of the experimental laboratory, he was in a unique position to administer a wide range of tests and conduct all kinds of experiments with a large variety of mental patients. Several more books relating to dissociative identity disorders and hypnosis emerged from the work he did at the Institute (Sidis, 1898, 1902).

In 1898, a multidisciplinary research program was initiated at the Pathological Institute which coordinated work in fields as diverse as neurology, psychopathology, psychology, bacteriology, and physical anthropology for the study of mental disorders. The laboratory was associated with the Columbia University College of Physicians and Surgeons, as it still is today. Dr. Ira van Gieson came to the institute as its first director with a background in neuropathology. Sidis's work with van Gieson put him in contact with other important people in the field of mental pathology. William Alanson White was one such person with whom he later collaborated on a book on the use of hypnosis in various dissociative hysterical disorders. Sidis elaborated upon this work with theoretical speculations regarding the manner in which one could understand the action of the "moment consciousness," to which each neuron contributed, and which in turn contributed to the total mental state. Together, van Gieson and Sidis refined both the neurological and psychological aspects of their theory, thus providing and accounting for clinical observations of normal and abnormal behavior on the basis of a dynamic model of neurophysiology. In 1898, they formally presented their ideas in an article entitled "Neuron Energy" (van Gieson and Sidis, 1898).

Neurons, they supposed, must possess a certain level of "dynamic energy" in order for them to maintain their position in a neuron aggregate, on the one hand, and the position of this aggregate in an associated cluster, on the other. To some degree this theory anticipated the work of Donald Hebb years later. When aggregates begin to dissociate from each other, they believed, the neurons separate from the aggregates in turn. Presumably, hypothetical changes in neuronal energy result in dissociation because the neuronal energy level is correlated with various states of consciousness. This separation, Sidis and van Gieson claimed, results in the degeneration and the destruction of the neurons, and their aggregates can be correlated with clinically observed symptoms.

In 1904, shortly before Freud came to Clark University to speak at the famous 1909 conference, Sidis published a book (with Simon Goodhart) entitled *Multiple Personality: An Experimental Investigation into the Nature of Human Individuality*. He dedicated the book to William James. In the book Sidis used his new physiological theory as a basis for explaining the various aspects of what he dubbed the Thomas Hanna Case. (A more detailed examination of this case can be found in the second part of this book.) It is of some interest to note Sidis's observations regarding epilepsy and multiple personality. He wrote:

> Double or multiple consciousness may be induced by many different causes, and epilepsy is but one of them. Epilepsy and the phenomena of multiple consciousness must be by no means identified when we find a case of amnesia in double consciousness without any typical epileptic attacks we're not justified to ascribe it to epilepsy simply because such phenomena are also manifest in this disease. . . . Epilepsy and multiple consciousness should not be confounded. One can exist without the other. (Sidis, 1904)

Sidis hypothesized that it was possible to discover the reproduction of the original traumatic event which brought about the state of multiple personality in the "hypnoleptic" state. He used the Hanna case to illustrate this hypothesis. Sidis believed that if integration were to occur the aggregation of neurons would have to proceed through two states: the primary state (representing the patient's consciousness and totality of his life experience) and the secondary state (the patient's unconsciousness). Only then could the primary state be reintegrated with the secondary state. This cyclical process was repeated time and again—and always in the same order.

Sidis continued to advocate this theory throughout his career and incorporated it into almost all of the writings he did until his death in 1922.

CONCLUSION

The basic problem one has to address with regard to how the human organism develops over time must take into consideration a basic bipolar process which has been called the "stimulative–inhibitory mental process." It is assumed that within the human organism, this bipolar process is essential in understanding how a given organism experiences and conceives of him- or herself in a particular social context. This experiential level of self-formation has long been discussed and debated in terms of both its healthy creative aspects (the light side) and its unhealthy disintegrative aspects (the dark side). In a more poetic vein, the great Gandhi once said, "In the midst of light, darkness exists, and in the midst of darkness light exists." Having said this, one still must consider the larger picture in which these processes function. And inevitably, this leads us to the "Gordian Knot" of psychology, which still challenges the inquiring scholar—namely, the problem of etiology. How can one explain the causative factors involved in human conduct and experience?

It has been said that the human organism does not simply experience what's out there in the world (external sensory stimuli) or simply what's inside himself (the internal sensory world or imagination), but rather as a negotiated transaction between the two. This transaction is mediated by a social construction of "reality," notwithstanding an enduring will to believe in something. To omit any one of the above-mentioned factors in an attempt to explain the organism's experience and conduct, one runs the risk of fostering a reductionist-deterministic view of the world (Rieber, 1998).

Undoubtedly, certain types of questions will require data and explanations that give greater importance to one or another of the different levels (i.e., the biophysiological level, the self-forming experiential level, and the socially constructed level of life experience). Disruption of the learning process that takes place between the biological, psychological, and social levels of existence also has the effect of interfering with the healthy, creative aspects of human conduct and experience.

Too many mirrors are dangerous because they reflectively distort and multiply the self. Therefore, one should hold the mirror up to nature in order to reflect upon the natural images of life rather than the ostentatious self-righteousness of multiple selves.

What, then, has history taught us regarding the dual actions of the brain and the multiplicity of minds? First, it teaches us that if we read more literature we will have less to discover. Second, it teaches us that the concept of dissociation should not be used in a deterministic or reductionist manner, or in a tautological way. The process of dissociation should not be misrepresented as dividing the mind into parts. Rather, it should be understood as a process of shifting gears producing functional units that act more or less independently and have different patterns of information, as opposed to completely discrete and different types of information. Furthermore, it should be understood as a process that produces a difference, rather than producing something entirely different, and this is a difference that makes a difference.

2

"Nothing but God and the Brain"

When we say that the exercise of the propensity of the soul and the mind depend on the natural condition, we do not mean that the faculties are a product of bodily structures. That would be confusing the conditions and the effective cause. We confine ourselves strictly to observation. We consider the faculties of the soul only in so far as they become phenomena for us through the medium of organic substances and without going beyond the material conditions, we neither deny nor affirm our theory except what can be judged from experience. We do not extend our reach to living bodies nor the soul taken alone, but to living man the result of the union of the body and souls . . . If we can demonstrate that a relationship exists between the exercise of the soul properties and the origination of their existence in the brain it would no longer be possible to doubt that it is possible to establish a doctrine which will enable us to know the noblest part of the organism.

F.J. GALL, 1811, *Des disposition innees (On innate dispositions) Paris: 1811, pp. 4–7*. Translated by Solomon Diamond from his *Roots of Psychology*

A BRIEF LOOK BACK

Before we proceed it might help to take another look at the territory we've already traversed. In our last chapter I chiefly focused on three seminal thinkers, each of whom had the courage (and presumption) to tackle the phenomenon of dissociation.

From his studies of hysteria Janet argued that individuals could experience "divided consciousness"—exceptional states of consciousness that made it seem as if they had different or alternate personalities which could be brought out under hypnosis. He categorized dissociation—and hypnosis—as pathological processes. Janet observed "that spontaneous dissociative reactions function as defenses to keep traumatic memories out of consciousness.

Furthermore, while memories of traumatic experiences were split-off from the mainstream of consciousness, they could still exercise effects and influences on thought and behavior, not consciously appreciated" (Calot, 1994). Janet advocated a therapy whose aim was the reintegration of traumatically dissociated aspects of personality (Janet, 1907). What Janet failed to recognize was that under other circumstances dissociation, far from being unhealthy, could be productive and creative. In fact, dissociation is an everyday occurrence. One only has to think of dreaming; the daydreamer and the dreamer at night will be dissociating but we do not consider ourselves abnormal for doing either.

Johann Friedrich Herbart (1776–1841) was one of the first psychologists to realize that dissociation occurs along a continuum and does not represent a pathological state. "The duplication of self-consciousness into different parts is one of the most remarkable peculiarities of the dream and its affiliated states," he writes. "The dreamer often ascribes to others his own thoughts, sometimes feeling ashamed that he himself has not perceived or has not known them. In changing states of dreaming and waking, of paroxysms and of intervals of quiet, there is often a double personality without that memory of a former state that it is retained on passing out of one into the other when waking from a dream. There are examples of violent fright after which people ask 'who am I?' and must be reminded again of their own name, position, calling, etc. by some circumstance. In the comparative study of the fundamental forms of mental disorders there seem to be excluded from the anomalous conditions only the facts of so-called animal magnetism, which are too little understood. These facts indicate a change in the bond of union between body and soul—a change which, however, may be quickly reversed and the former state reestablished." Later on in his text, Herbart makes reference to this issue in discussing the connection between body and mind. He observes: "If we wished however to attribute to man several souls in one body we should beware of thinking of mental activities as divided among them. The latter must be regarded as being entire in each soul. Secondly, the most exact memory among these souls would have been soon so that they might serve as identical examples of this same kind. This is, however, in the highest degree improbable and hence the whole thought is to be rejected. If in the contest between reason and passion it sometimes seems to mean that he has several souls this is a psychical phenomenon which cannot be considered in connection with the paradoxical thoughts just mentioned, that which will be explained later" (Herbart, 1891). Here we have one of the earliest if not the earliest recognition of the dangers of the bifurcation of body and mind as well as different cells or personalities in one body. Herbart's words of caution, however, failed to reverse the tide. Eighty years later William James had to reiterate warnings of the dangers of making such assumptions to another generation.

For his part, Morton Prince derived a theory intended to explain how—and why—a sensory impression could be recorded in the unconsciousness which does not register during the waking state, yet once under hypnosis, can be recalled with surprising vividness. Prince tried to determine in which part of the brain these impressions were recorded and why they were inaccessible to the brain in its waking state. Where, he wondered, did hysterical symptoms become suppressed? Why during sleep or hypnotic trances were the higher, conscious centers of the brain anesthetized while the middle centers of the brain—at least in his reading—were still active? Why, for that matter, was knowledge of what went on in the middle centers of the brain denied to the higher centers?

This brings us to the work of Boris Sidis who dug (metaphorically anyway) even further into the brain in search of the supposed "original traumatic event" that could explain the state of multiple personality in the "hypnoleptic" state. His investigation led him to propose his famous "law of dissociation" which proposed the controversial theory that neurons (i.e., nerve cells and their extensions) had an independent unity and that once in contact with other aggregations of neutrons could form new clusters or break apart and dissolve depending on the prevailing conditions. Mental disorders, Sidis contended, could be explained by such processes: a neuron disturbance could account for memory loss, hallucinations—or even a changed personality and dissociation.

We now come to Joseph Gall. He, too, sought to locate in the brain the locations for both sensory and cognitive abilities—and disabilities. Like Janet, Prince, and Sidis, Gall was eager to find physical analogues to mental states to explain how psychological disorders, such as hysteria, could arise. Gall believed that the brain had "organs"—and early in his career he set about equating these organs with aberrant states, finding, for instance, a brain organ for murder and thievery. Although the approach Gall took—known as "phrenology," a fad in the nineteenth century, a laughable superstition in the twentieth and all but forgotten in the twenty-first—has been discredited, it represents another step in the long, lurching odyssey scientists, psychologists, and scholars of all stripes have undertaken in their attempt to determine where in the brain our sense of identity and personality originates and why (and how) that coherent construct of ourselves can sometimes be shattered, spinning out of control in unpredictable directions.

NOTHING BUT GOD AND THE BRAIN

Homer told a story, Newton told a story, and so did Gall. Nevertheless, Franz-Joseph Gall's discovery of organology, later dubbed "phrenology," was destined to become one of the most important hallmarks in the history of neuropsychology. No matter how unconventional, the story of phrenology simply doesn't seem to be able to go away. Perhaps it is this "immortality factor" that helped make Gall (1758–1828) a master survivor.

But what was this new movement in the history of neuropsychology all about? It is well known that the function of the brain is responsible for particular human activities such as seeing, hearing, and specific movements of the body. This early form of localization of cortical functions was an outgrowth of Gall's ideas which purported that the physical characteristics of the skull are related to the propensities of the underlying areas of the brain. Gall believed that there were some 26 "organs" on the surface of the brain which affect the contour of the skull, including a "murder organ" found—not surprisingly—in murderers. These organs reflect various aspects of an individual's personality such as reasoning, agreeableness, inquisitiveness, self-esteem, etc. The Viennese physician's theory attracted many scholars, not to mention the general public, throughout much of the nineteenth century.

But it didn't take long for Gall's phrenological theory to spark a controversial debate. The theory was even dubbed a form of quackery, mainly due to the abuses in the hands of charlatan and commercial entrepreneurs. It gradually declined during the last quarter of the nineteenth century and was transformed into a more "modern" field of inquiry, namely, the localization of brain function (Finger, 2000). But before phrenology lost its appeal, we ought to ask what did Gall and his one-time disciple (and prodigal son) Spurzheim actually believe and why.

WHAT DID GALL ACTUALLY BELIEVE

Phrenology was opposed by leading figures of the time including Johann Friedrich Herbart (1891) who felt that it did not primarily stress the unity of the mind and Pierre Flourens (1846) who derided it because it ignored the unity of the cerebrum itself. Meanwhile, Gall admitted that he did not originate the idea of the brain as organ of the mind, but rather that he had provided new and specific empirical evidence for it. Nevertheless, Flourens was to Gall as Hamlet was to his mother; he had to be "cruel only to be kind." Flourens writes that the brain as an "organ of mind" was better described before Gall's description. He then facetiously put him down by saying "one can only say that ever since Gall, it reigns there." But who was all wet in this business? No matter, Gall said of himself: "I leave unsought the nature of the soul as well as the body . . . I confine myself to phenomena." This was Gall's statement about his methodology.

"The object of my research," said Gall, "is the brain. The cranium is only a faithful cast of the external surface of the brain, and is consequently but a minor part of the principle objects" (Gall, 1796, as cited in Hollander, 1920). What then was the principle object for Gall? The answer to this question lies primarily in how Gall envisioned a concordance between areas of the brain as it relates to personality.

Gall's objective was to discover *mind space* in the brain. He wished to deeply penetrate where no scientist had gone before. In order to understand why Gall was dissatisfied with the received view of his times, it is necessary to know whom Gall perceived as the enemy. The major source of enmity was the prevailing theory of physiognomy promoted by Johann Lavater (1741–1801, 1804). Gall expressed a much more passionate objection to the physiognomy theory and method than he did to the contemporary experimentalists such as Flourens (Gall, 1835, Vols. 5 and 6). This question becomes even more interesting when you take into consideration that one of Gall's mottoes was, as E.H. Ackerknecht (1958) clearly points out, "God and brain. Nothing but God and brain." Unfortunately, Ackerknecht does not provide an explanation for Gall's use of this contention. It is my opinion that Gall's use of this motto is within the pantheist tradition of religion of holding the mirror up to nature. He made Spinoza's philosophy biopsychological rather than just logical; consequently, it would be a mistake to simply characterize Gall as a modern day materialist, as many of his contemporary opponents and present-day historians have, such as Jerry Fodor (1983) and Antonio Damasio (1994).

Spinoza believed that matter and mind (that is, brain and faculties) are identical but different in the way they are manifest. Like Spinoza, Gall desired to explain the order of the whole of nature. Thus, Gall's motto "God and brain. Nothing but God and brain." For Spinoza what is in the body formally is in the soul objectively. Therefore, "to determine the difference between the human mind and other things, and its superiority over them, we must first know the nature of its object. That is to say, the nature of the human body" (Spinoza, 1910). For Spinoza both material and spiritual mind are "real" (i.e., "part of the intrinsic intellect of god"). Neither body nor mind is able to work alone, only together. Spinoza also went as far to indicate that man's judgment is a function of the disposition of the brain. It is important to distinguish the old use of the term "materialism" from the modern use. In H.C. Warren's *The Dictionary of Psychology*, materialism is defined as "the theory that matter is the only ultimate reality. The view which regards the body, more specifically the brain, as the substratum of the psychic processes which are ultimately material products" (Warren, 1934), The older definition of materialism, which fits Gall as well as Spinoza, fostered the notion that God is an infinitely perfect being. Therefore, God was the first cause—the cause of all things that exist and that all things in existence are a reflection of God, both spirit and matter being conceived as one unity. Catholic theology objected to this form of materialism because it wished to strictly bifurcate spirit and matter.

If Gall was a materialist, in the premodern sense of that term, to really understand his position we must deal with his doctrine of materialism as it was developing, and not with it as it was developed afterward. This difference makes a difference both theoretically and historically. Karl Lashley was searching for the engram for his answer, while Karl Pribram began to look at the hologram for his answer. Having said that, it should be recognized that it all started with Gall who was looking at the Cosmogram for his answer.

Now consider for a moment, Gall's position regarding the matter in his own words: "If outward accidental causes are the source of all inventions why have they not produced the same effects in brutes? Why does not the dog build a house to protect him from the inclemencies of the weather? Who invented the spider web . . .? The cause of these inventions therefore, lies in the organs, or in other words animals have received from nature, by means of organs certain definite powers, propensities and faculties which produce their habits. It is precisely the same with man. All that he does, or knows, all that he can do or can learn he owes to the author of this organization. God is the source, the cerebral organs his intermediate instrument. . . . the poet, the orator, the legislator, the minister of religion are the work of God. Thus God is everywhere the artist, and man only the instrument . . . Prostrate ourselves before the Creator, who has transformed such slight materials into the instruments of such sublime and numerous powers are we to cast a stone at the physiologist, who in the height of his astonishment exclaims; God and the Brain! Nothing but God and the Brain!" (Gall, Vol. 6, 1822–26).

Up to the present time most scholars considered Gall's famous quote, "God and the brain. Nothing but God and the brain," as a means of placating the church and the Austrian monarchy. It was alleged that Gall made this avowal to convince the authorities that he was not an atheist. This, I believe, is quite possible especially when one interprets this last sentence in context, i.e., "cast a stone at the physiologist."

Nevertheless, his accommodation of the church is not mutually exclusive to the position that I have taken that Gall held a neopantheistic worldview as exemplified by his statement about God and the brain. His position reflects Spinoza's; indeed, it elaborates upon it. For example, J.M. Baldwin in his *Philosophy and Science* characterizes Spinoza in the following way: "Spinozism is rightly considered the force that makes for pantheism" (Baldwin, 1901). If Baldwin is correct—and I believe he is—then Gall wished to take his ideas even further. The Catholic dogmatic theory had as much to fear from pantheism as it did from absolute skepticism or sensationalism—or, for that matter, from Gall himself.

When one takes the above-mentioned quote into consideration it is not hard to understand why both the church and the Austrian monarchy considered Gall as great a threat as they considered Mesmer. The mysteries of the cosmos according to the Catholic Church, which primarily embraced a Thomastic theory of causation, was diametrically opposed to any kind of pantheistic theory of causation. It was going just a little too far for Gall to embrace pantheism as opposed to a Catholic Thomastic theory of causation.

Furthermore, it is crucial to understand that Gall's theoretical position insisted upon the assumption that "living bodies are the result of the union of the body and the soul" (Gall, 1811). This position was in direct opposition to the church's long-held dogma which placed the soul above any material object. This was not only important because of its long, traditionally held dogma, but was also most important for its pragmatic consequences, which mainly pertain to the notion of free will. The leaders of the church in Vienna saw Gall's unified theory of mind-body as a threat to their notion of free will, especially as it related to their responsibility to inculcate in all Catholics a proper form of moral conduct. We may now be better able to understand why both Gall and Mesmer were forced to leave Vienna and flee to Paris.

FACULTIES IN THE BRAIN: HOW MUCH IS ENOUGH?

But why Gall and his disciple Johann Caspar Spurzheim (1776–1832) were dead set on discovering as many faculties in the brain as they could is another question altogether. (Admittedly, this was more the case for Spurzheim than for Gall.) Why didn't they know where to stop has never been adequately answered. It is my opinion that the source for this "faculty mania" of Gall and Spurzheim may be found in the early training that they experienced as medical students. During the later half of the eighteenth century, major developments took place in the fields of anatomy, physiology, and pathology. Galvani (1791), Haller (1767), and Morgani (1761) set the stage for these new areas of research into the central nervous system. At the same time a new nosology was inspired by the works of Sebastian Sauvage (1768) and William Cullen (1769). Both Sauvage's and Cullen's classification system were widely used when Gall was studying medicine. This new taxonomy was obsessed with finding as many diseases as there were symptoms so that, in the final analysis, for almost every symptom found there would be a disease to match it. It would be only natural for Gall to fit his brain taxonomy into the same paradigm used in the classification of disease entities. The difference, of course, was that Gall was primarily searching for normal propensities in the brain. Variation in structure that matched variation in function was Gall's objective. Charles Darwin pursued a similar objective many years later. One should keep in mind, however, that variation is another way of talking about individual differences in the human organism.

There is no question that Gall made some formidable contribution to both anatomy and physiology, pointing out, for instance, that damage to one side of the hemisphere would affect the homeostasis of both sides of the brain. But Gall never so much as hinted at the possibility of laterality—that one part of the brain might develop functions that the other did not.

It is my opinion that Gall was struggling, either consciously or unconsciously, to reconcile a holistic, monistic, theoretical concept of the organism, with an elemental brain–mind faculty type of psychology. Gall failed to recognize the element of self-deception that marred his discoveries—what we now call the Clever Hans Effect. He was additionally handicapped by the fact that he was ignorant of modern, statistical techniques of factor analysis. Like many pioneers, he was certainly onto something, it was just that he wasn't able to appreciate or understand the implications of his findings.

Even given the elegant symmetry of holism in terms of the organization of the brain we still have to ask: How are specialized faculty functions compatible with an approach based on Gestalt field theory using the concept of process as its major dynamic factor? In other words, can you have it both ways without throwing the baby out with the bathwater? This epistemological issue is still with us today; it takes the form of reconciling the solid rock of materialistic theory versus the ever-bifurcating stream of consciousness theory of brain–mind connections. Gall was trying to have it both ways but was not able to complete his formulation before he died in 1828.

It is a matter of dispute whether Spurzheim was a true disciple of Gall who simply had some minor differences of opinion with him or whether he was a self-centered opportunist who was reluctant to give Gall the credit he deserved for originating and promoting his brain localization theory. What is clear is that the two eventually had a falling out and that as time passed the conflict between Gall and Spurzheim became worse before it got worse.

After Gall's death Spurzheim seemed to take credit for work that Gall had done. As John Elliotson noted in *Anatomy and Physiology of the Brain*, "Yet, Dr. S. had the effrontery to claim the discovery of the true mode in which the brain unfolds in hydrocephalus" (Elliotson, 1982). Elliotson dismisses Spurzheim as little more than Gall's witness or assistant—the "hand man of the headman."

After Spurzheim's death in America in 1832, Elliotson (1982) had considerable difficulties of his own at the University Hospital in London with his work in mesmerism and clairvoyance (see Crabtree, 1993). Elliotson developed a new interest in merging mesmerism and phrenology during the late 1830s. Since George Combe had become the heir apparent to Spurzheim, and was the editor of the *Phrenological Journal*, it was quite reasonable for Elliotson to consider publishing his new findings on phrenology in Combe's journal. Most of the debates at this point had to do with the actual location of both the old and new faculties in the brain. Elliotson was more orthodox and favored Gall's locations. He was also quite pleased by the warm reception that Gall gave to Mesmer's concept of animal magnetism. The fact that Gall embraced Mesmer's animal magnetism is very important because it is not mentioned in any of the histories of hypnosis written up to this point. Elliotson (1982) quotes Gall as follows:

> We thus see that if ever a great truth was promulgated, it is the doctrine of predestination and pre-established harmony. Magnetism proves, in the preemptory manner that everything in the universe is not only concatenated, but completed. . . . Scientific discoveries still have to be made by the long and laborious method of experience not withstanding, the magnetized see all their internal structure in the clearest manner and magnetism has been practiced so long.

Furthermore, he points out that Gall was convinced that there was nothing "supernatural or contrary to nature" about Mesmer's animal magnetism. In writing about "some particulars respecting

Gall," Elliotson refers to several authors who disagree with Spurzheim's views particularly as they relate to Gall. He refers to a book by Joseph Selpert dealing with Gall's lectures. It quotes him as follows: ". . . after valuable remarks dreaming, somnambulency, clairvoyance, etc. is the following: 'can it not easily be imagined, that if there be a particular magnetic or galvanic essence (stuff) which could be discharged as something distinctly material on the separate organs of the brain, and could be so directed that one organ only at a time might be excited by it to the highest degree, whilst all others remained in sleep—persons thus excited would be able to discover things in nature (naturlich verhaltrisse) otherwise unknown to us?'" ("Some particulars respecting Gall," 1844). Gall even admitted the possibility of Mesmer's fluid theory and goes on to say:

> how often in intoxication hysterical and hypochondriacal attacks, convulsions, fever, insanity, violent emotions after long fasting, through the effects of such poisons as opium, hemlock, belladonna, are we not in some measure transformed into perfectly different beings, for instance, into poets, actors etc. (Elliotson, 1982)

During the late 1830s, Elliotson sent a paper for publication to George Combe, then editor of the *Phrenological Journal* in Edinborough; Elliotson's article favored Gall's system which differed from Spurzheim's version. Combe edited out the disagreement and sent it back to Elliotson. Elliotson complained that it was merely his opinion and that it should not be misinterpreted to reflect the editor's opinions. Both parties' opinions were politically motivated and there was no possibility of resolving the conflict. I believe this impasse between Elliotson and Combe resulted in the creation of a new journal in 1843 titled *The Zoist: A Journal of Cerebral Physiology and Animal Magnetism*. Elliotson devoted over thirty years of his life from the time he discovered animal magnetism to his death promoting and demonstrating the therapeutic and theoretical importance of mesmerism. He founded and edited *The Zoist* and also carried on a lively friendship with luminaries of the age such as Dickens, Thackery, and Wilkie Collins. *The Zoist* provides a detailed record over a thirteen-year period of contributions of scholars working in the field of animal magnetism particularly in England. Pointedly Elliotson omitted any mention of phrenology.

Phrenology just didn't disappear from the title of his magazine. Elliotson seemed to forsake phrenology for mesmerism, giving public demonstrations of mesmerism at the London University College Hospital and advocating mesmerism's use as an anesthetic in medical operations.

But what exactly was mesmerism, why did it capture the public fancy to the degree it did, entrancing scholars such as Gall and Elliotson, and why did it fall into such disrepute? To answer those questions we need to examine the place mesmerism occupies in the checkered history of hypnosis.

From Elizabeth Sibley, *A key to physic and the occult sciences.* London: Champarte & Whitrow 1795 (in the private collection of Robert W. Rieber)

3

Prying Open the Lid
The Origins of Hypnosis

ANIMAL MAGNETISM AND ITS LINKS TO MPD

During the nineteenth century, the problem of multiple personality was for the most part compatible with and influenced by a more romantic view of human nature than its eighteenth century predecessor.

The popular literature of the period flooded the minds of the public with fascinating macabre psychological novels that dealt with various aspects of mind brain stories about human beings' moral problems, including sanity and identity. The most popular of these novels, such as Mary Shelley's *Frankenstein*, Robert L. Stevenson's *Dr. Jekyll and Mr. Hyde*, and many short tales by Edgar Alan Poe, had a formidable impact on the reading public. Something was clearly in the air that would manifest itself straight through from the scientific literature to pop culture and back again.

What became known as "multiple personality disorder" emerged at about the same time as what was known as "animal magnetism," later dubbed "hypnosis".

Basic knowledge and practice of hypnosis may be traced back to the ancient Greeks and Romans, who used hypnosis for religious as well as therapeutic practices. Hippocrates, one of the founders of Greek medicine, recognized the importance of the role played by suggestion in the healing process; he would try to convince patients that they would soon become well. Not only this, but Hippocrates felt that a touch of his hand upon the subject would relieve pain, and that he could make an individual fall asleep by simply commanding him to do so.

In medieval times, hypnosis was used by wizards and sorcerers. The common people viewed hypnosis as being evil and dangerous. Those who practiced it were looked upon as agents of the devil who were anxious to place innocent people under their spell.

A more scientific approach to hypnosis and its use began in the sixteenth century with a man who called himself Paracelsus. Although he had many old-fashioned ideas and was greatly interested in alchemy and sorcery, Paracelsus is an important figure in the history of medicine, and, in particular, of hypnosis. He believed that the attitude that the patient had toward his own illness could have a powerful influence upon the course of a disease:

> It is not the curse or the blessing that works, but the idea. The imagination produces the effect. (Buranelli, 1975)

Paracelsus also made use of magnets to concentrate in his patients what he believed to be a cosmic fluid that possessed healing properties.

Later on, James Maxwell would elaborate upon Paracelsus's theory of a healing cosmic fluid.

Years later, the first great faith healer Valentine Greatrakes appeared. Greatrakes eventually became famous as the Stroking Doctor for his success in healing by touch. He is reported to have cured, by the laying on of hands, fever, palsy, hysteria, and convulsions. Greatrakes's powers were explained by the passing of invisible entities from his own body to that of the patient.

Yet while hypnosis may be traced back many centuries, it is popularly thought of as originating with an eighteenth-century Austrian physician, Anton Mesmer—indeed, an earlier term for hypnosis still occasionally used today is that of "mesmerism." Mesmer felt that medicine could be turned into an exact science by extending cosmological laws to the physiology of the human body, and in this sense, his views were strangely foreshadowed by Valentine Greatrakes. In particular, Mesmer hypothesized the existence of a universal fluid within the individual, that, together with the indirect influence of the stars and planets, would act to make the person healthy or ill.

Mesmer was intrigued by the many psychosomatic illnesses of his time, seeing how often conventional medicine failed to cure the likes of paralysis, chronic nightmares, panic, depression, hysteria, and convulsions. In the cases of these maladies, Mesmer felt that classical medical diagnoses were inadequate. He believed that many of his patients suffering from hysteria were being bothered by the effects of a universal fluid, or animal gravitation, ebbing and flowing through their bodies. Mesmer felt that it was his job to find an agent that could be used to control this ebb and flow motion.

Mesmer found this agent in magnets. In their polar attraction and repulsion, magnets set up an ebb and flow that could be comprehended as one version of the general tidal effect, of which the gravitation of the heavenly bodies was another version. One of the first patients successfully treated with magnets was a woman who had been suffering from recurring hysteria, with convulsions, vomiting, depression, hallucinations, fits of blindness, and paralysis. The startling results of her treatment may be seen in the following statement written by Mesmer himself:

> It was on July 28, 1774, that my patient having suffered another of her attacks, I placed three magnets on her, one on the stomach and one on each leg. Almost immediately she began to show severe symptoms. She felt painful volatile currents moving within her body. After a confused effort to find a direction, they flowed downward to her extremities. Alleviation followed and lasted for six hours. A repetition of the attack on the following day caused me to repeat the experiment, with the same success. (Buranelli, 1975)

Mesmer now felt that he had learned how to channel the universal fluid into his patients, and what he had earlier referred to as "animal gravitation" he now called "animal magnetism". According to Mesmer, the proper balance of animal magnetism in the body of the individual makes the difference between health and illness. Vast psychical and many physical disorders were due, then, to the abnormal distribution of these fluids within the body, and cures could be brought about by having the ill person become "harmonized" with his fluids. This was achieved through the use of magnets and by bodily stroking or passes over the afflicted area. It was later found that many things other than magnets could be used to conduct the universal fluid. These included objects such as paper or wood, which, although not magnetic in the sense of mineral magnetism, are strongly magnetic in the sense of animal magnetism. Such objects became "magnetized" upon being touched by Mesmer.

Over the years, Mesmer's theory of animal magnetism was almost constantly being refined and modified. The female hysteric mentioned above was likely Mesmer's first classic "mesmerized" patient, although Mesmer himself was not aware of it. When he first began her treatment, Mesmer mainly relied on magnets to direct the flow of animal magnetism. Soon afterwards, though, Mesmer saw that he only had to touch the patient in order for her to receive beneficial effects. Magnets, or magnetized objects, were not at all necessary (Buranelli, 1975).

Mesmer further experimented with different techniques and found that he didn't even have to touch the patient in order for effects to be seen. He dramatically demonstrated this phenomenon to the respected Dutch physicians, Jan Ingenhousz, hoping to convince him of the reality of animal magnetism. Although Ingenhousz admitted that he was impressed by the demonstration, he remained skeptical, an example of the poor responses that Mesmer typically received from the scientific world.

Nevertheless, today it is clear to us that Mesmer had, in fact, discovered how to put a patient into a hypnotic trance. While he still believed that the patient's behavior was due to the effects of animal magnetism, Mesmer did recognize the important role played by suggestion. He made sure that he instilled the proper attitude in the patient, and usually told the patient ahead of time how he would behave during treatment. Today it is widely agreed that subjects have a strong tendency to behave under hypnosis as they expect a hypnotized person acts, or as they are told they will behave when hypnotized.

As Dr. Herbert Spiegel noted, as a precursor of modern hypnosis, mesmerism was dismissed for many of the same reasons that hypnosis is dismissed today. "[I]t is as if many clinicians and behavioral scientists not only reject Mesmer's 'fluid' concept," he writes in his paper "Hypnosis: Myth and Reality" in *Psychiatric Annals*, "but also reject the observable data as well" (Spiegel, 1981). "By simply substituting the concept 'imagination' for 'fluid,' the observed behavior of Mesmerism becomes understandable in modern behavioral terms. In fact, the French Royal Commission... studied Mesmerism then intensively dismissed it with the astute critique that it was nothing but 'overheated imagination.'" He also notes that Mesmer's theory of fluid, which was based on a hypothesis about an invisible world, was conceived at a time when Newton was deriving his theory of gravity, Lavoisier was coming up with his theory of calories, Franklin was discovering the marvels of electricity, and Priestley and others were experimenting with heated gases, all in their way explorations of invisible worlds (Spiegel, 1981)

In spite of the skepticism he generated among scientists Mesmer became quite popular with the general public as a healer. Not having the time to treat all of his patients privately, he arrived at a method of "group therapy" that he called the baquet. This was a circular tub filled with magnetized filings, and equipped with projecting iron rods that patients could touch while sitting around it. By holding hands around the baquet, the patients would set up a "current," and by holding on to the baquet's rods, the patients would receive a magnetic flow directed to the pain areas. Eventually, Mesmer would abandon the use of magnets altogether, because he felt that their use was damaging to his hopes of scientific acceptance; having a reputation as a "magnetizer" was little better than being labeled a charlatan.

Mesmer unexpectedly found that he was able to throw his subjects into a state between sleep and wakefulness. In such a state, they would obey commands "even though their faculties had stopped functioning in the normal manner" (Buranelli, 1975). The state that Mesmer had discovered was the hypnotic state. Realizing the importance of this form of trance, Mesmer made increasing use of it, until it became the essential component of his method of treatment.

Mesmer began to use the hypnotic trance to bring on what he called the *crisis*. The crisis had been a critical feature of a patient's therapy since early in his career when Mesmer still relied almost totally on magnets. Unfortunately, however, many people were more afraid of the Mesmerian crisis than they were of their illness, and so avoided Mesmer entirely. Members of a French royal commission, investigating a follower of Mesmer by the name of Deslon, declared that they were "astonished and appalled by the sight of patients going suddenly into agonizing contortions" (Buranelli, 1975). They described these convulsions as being

> Marked by violent, involuntary movements of the limbs and the whole body, by constriction of the throat, by throbbing in the chest and nausea in the stomach, by rapid blinking and crossed eyes, by piercing cries, tears, hiccups and uncontrollable laughter. These are preceded or followed by a state of languor and daydreams, a type of abatement or even slumber. The slightest sound causes a startled shuddering; and it has been observed that a change of tone or beat in music played on the piano influences the ill, so that a rapid composition agitates them and throws them back into convulsions. (Buranelli, 1975)

Although the commission could not deny the occurrence of cures, the members felt that the crisis could hardly be considered a desirable element in the treatment process. Once again Mesmer was denied scientific acceptance.

Government investigations, while noting Mesmer's success in the treatment of his patients, refused to accept his explanations of just how his cures were brought about. They carefully studied Mesmer's techniques, including his magnets, the baquet, the crisis, and the trance, and concluded that all cures were simply due to the individual's imagination, and not to any actions of Mesmer. Mesmer was officially declared a charlatan; his reputation was hopelessly destroyed, and he eventually was forced to give up his practice.

Fortunately, however, Mesmer's work was not forgotten. Several men carried on his research, and through it became quite well-known. The Marquis de Puysegur, although an amateur, was a dedicated follower of Anton Mesmer, and, as Mesmer himself had done, relied heavily on the presence of the trance in his practice. While unable to account for it, Puysegur noted the phenomenon of posthypnotic amnesia. Mistakenly, he referred to the trance state as "somnambulism," which really means "sleepwalking," but his most important accomplishment was being able to achieve, in his patients, a form of the Mesmerian trance that did not involve the crisis.

When in the trance, subjects would answer questions and offer suggestions, always coherently and intelligibly. Upon awakening from the trance, the subject would only remember what he had been told to remember. Puysegur also became familiar with the phenomenon of regression. His patients would recall and relive childhood events that had previously seemed forever forgotten. The Marquis also clearly showed that the methods and apparatus that Mesmer had relied upon, such as the séance, baquet, and eerie music, were not necessary, for the same results could be obtained without them. Puysegur had, in fact, achieved a true hypnotic state in his subjects, although scientists remained unconvinced.

In 1819, a Portuguese priest by the name of Abbe Faria published a work entitled *On the Cause of Lucid Sleep*. In it, he replaced the phrase "animal magnetism" with the term "concentration." As Puysegur had done, Faria recognized that the séance and baquet were unnecessary; he called the trances he induced in his patients "lucid sleep." To induce this sleep, Faria would have his subject sit in a comfortable position, and instruct him to relax, lean back, close his eyes, and concentrate on sleep. This approach, Faria felt, required some confidence on the part of the subject. Then he would issue the final command of "sleep," and the subject would fall off into a lucid sleep, or, as it would be called today, a hypnotic trance. Faria also experimented with posthypnotic suggestion.

We owe the word "hypnotism" to James Braid, another important psychologist of the mid-nineteenth century. Braid decided that "hypnotism," a word coined from the Greek word for sleep, should replace "mesmerism." He also established that the true basis of hypnotism is psychological rather than physical, and that the power of the trance lay in suggestion. Stressing the role of concentration, Braid said that the patient must clear his mind of everything else, focusing only upon the concept of sleep.

As Braid's views diffused across Europe, the nature of hypnosis was further defined in France by Ambroise-Auguste Liébault (1823–1903), who wrote:

> The characteristics of active somnambulism are what the hypnotist makes them by mobilizing the nervous energy accumulated as a usable power in the mind through suggested ideas. (Buranelli, 1975)

Liébault emphasized his belief that suggestion plays the major role in any effective therapy. Together with his student Hipolyte Bernheim, Liébault led the Nancy school of hypnosis. The rival Salpetriere school, led by Charcot, considered hypnosis to be a neurosis, a form of abnormal behavior. Charcot referred to the hypnotic state as an artificially caused "morbid condition," and discussed what he felt were strong similarities between hypnosis and hysteria (Buranelli, 1975). In fact, Charcot said, only those people displaying hysterical symptoms could be hypnotized.

The Nancy school, on the other hand, maintained that hypnosis belonged to normal psychology, believing that

> hypnotic sleep is not a pathological sleep. The hypnotic condition is not a neurosis, analogous to hysteria. No doubt, manifestations of hysteria may be created in hypnotized subjects; a real hypnotic neurosis may be developed. . . . But these manifestations are not due to the hypnosis—they are due to the operator's suggestion, or sometimes to the autosuggestion of a particularly impressible subject. . . . Catalepsy, transfer, contracture, etc., are the effects of suggestion. To prove that the very great majority of subjects are susceptible to suggestion is to eliminate the idea of a neurosis. (Buranelli, 1975)

The controversy between the Nancy and Paris (Salpetriere) schools continued, but the superiority of the Nancy school emerged more and more clearly, as tests in hospitals and in consulting rooms were seen to support Bernheim's claims that there was nothing at all abnormal in hypnosis.

In Germany, too, hypnosis began to make inroads in academia. In a series of articles published in *The Nation*, an important American periodical, Stanley Hall set down his observations about such German phenomena as the cult of war and its idolization of Kaiser Wilhelm as well as trends in German science, psychology, spiritualism and recent studies in hypnotism based on his experiences in Berlin and Leipzig between 1878 and 1880. These reports were subsequently collected in his book *Aspects of German Culture*.

Hall was a great believer in Germany, convinced that it was in the forefront of a new science that would prevent a relapse of the world into barbarism of the Dark Ages. He opposed the admission of students into universities who were not prepared to accept this new scientific method and raised a vigorous protest against the threat of "Americanisms," a term he used to apply to ultramaterialistic tendencies—e.g., making money as the all-consuming goal of life and the corruption that greed can lead to—that he associated with the United States. His objective was to promote a humanistic scientific culture for its own sake, putting aside all considerations of profit or personal advantage. It was an ideal that he found best exemplified in Germany.

In his reports Hall noted the differences between Germany, on the one hand, and the United States and the United Kingdom, on the other, in terms of what was then called "mental philosophy" (an early nineteenth-century term for "psychology") that concerned the essence, constitution, seat, origin, and future state of the mind, i.e., metaphysical questions that psychology is based upon. Unlike sciences such as physics and chemistry, which used the old deductive method, various forms of mental activities, or mental powers or faculties loosely connected with the ideas of Fichte, Schelling, and Hegel, were not quantifiable since these were phenomena that were thought impossible to be observed or controlled.

However, Hall noted, the new German research on psycho/physic methods didn't feel obliged to honor the limitations established by their American and British counterparts by experimentally studying sensations and relating them to neurophysiological processes. Hall discusses some of the results of time reaction studies, especially the work of Wundt.

Hall also cites a very popular book by Rudolph Heidenhain, professor of physiology and director of the Physiological Institute at

Breslau, Heidenhain and his colleagues, Hall wrote, were able to hypnotize one half of their subjects' brain and body. When the right side is hypnotized, they found, it produces aphasia, but not when the left side is affected. This is, of course, in agreement with pathological observations that locate the speech center in, or near, the left cerebral hemisphere. Hall goes on to explain how hallucinations can be induced, as well as other interesting phenomena.

Although Sigmund Freud practiced in neighboring Austria his views about hypnosis were shaped more by the Frenchman Charcot as well as through his associations with Liébault and Bernheim. As we've seen, Charcot had a great interest in the study and treatment of hysteria which he believed was caused by the congenital degeneration of the brain. To counter charges that hysterics were simply malingerers Charcot would hold public demonstrations in which he employed hypnosis on young women who had been victims of rape and other forms of violence (Dillain, 1959). Sometime around 1885 Freud attended one of these demonstrations and was sufficiently impressed to consider the idea of using hypnosis on his own patients. But it was from his colleague Joseph Breuer that he learned how to use of hypnosis as a means of uncovering memories of traumatic events that were inaccessible in the normal waking state.

CONCLUSION

Scientific interest in hypnosis over the past few centuries has waxed and waned in a cyclic manner. Changes in its popularity have arisen as a result of a number of very concrete situations. For instance, even though there was intense interest in hypnosis in late 18th Century France people became understandably distracted by the outbreak of the French Revolution. The investigations into the practices of Anton Mesmer served to discredit Mesmer while causing people to lose interest in animal magnetism. (Pattie, 1967, Ellenberger, 1974), For a number of years, through the beginning of the twentieth century, hypnosis—which took over where Mesmerism left off—was considered a remarkable new therapeutic tool, advocated by no less of an authority than Sigmund Freud. And yet its usefulness began to wear off and finally Freud himself abandoned it, certain that he'd been forging out in a fruitless direction. Why he found hypnosis such a dead end—and what he chose to substitute in its place—is the subject of our next chapter.

From George Cruiskshank's *Table Book*, ed. by Gilbert Abbott Beckett. London: Punch, 1845 (in the private collection of Robert W. Rieber)

4

Looking Inside the Box, Thinking Outside the Box

FREUD AND HYPNOSIS: UNCOVERING FALSE MEMORIES

"But Doctor, I'm not asleep, you know! I can't be hypnotized." Those half-apologetic, half-taunting words hung in the ears of Sigmund Freud one afternoon in 1909. They had just been uttered by one of his patients, whom he knew he could cure of her symptoms if only he could induce her to enter a state of deep hypnosis. To bring that about, Freud, then thirty-six years old, had repeated over and over again, "You are feeling drowsy; your eyelids are getting heavier; soon you will be asleep."

The patient suffered from hysteria, a condition which baffled and irritated most nineteenth-century physicians, since its major symptoms were peculiar physical complaints which had no discernible physical basis. Some patients complained of paralysis, but thorough neurological examination revealed no organic damage. Equally baseless were other hysterics' reports of blindness, deafness, anesthesia (numbness), lameness, and numerous other sensory and physical symptoms. Many physicians were understandably tempted to dismiss hysterical patterns as malingerers and fakers, since the bases of their complaints seemed so obviously imaginary.

Freud knew the situation was more complicated than that, however. He had studied with the French neurologist Jean Charcot, who taught him that hysteria was to be taken seriously. As one of the few Viennese doctors who would deign to accept hysterical patterns, Freud had learned that the symptoms had a subjective reality for the patients, even if objective physical causes were not evident to their physicians. Most patients were sincere in their complaints, and if they were malingering they themselves were unaware of the fact.

When Freud began his practice there were few established therapies for hysteria. The most fashionable treatments bore the impressive-sounding names "hydrotherapy" and "electrotherapy." The former consisted of various kinds of baths, the latter of passing mild electric currents through the afflicted body areas. Freud quickly realized that the beneficial effects of those treatments were produced largely by suggestion, so he next sought something to make use of suggestion even more directly. He knew that members of the Nancy school in France had been using hypnosis as a therapy for hysteria, and he visited their clinic to learn their techniques. These were very straightforward: patients were hypnotized and then given direct suggestions that their symptoms would disappear. Sometimes they did, and although relief was usually partial or temporary, hypnosis was clearly an improvement over hydrotherapy and electrotherapy.

It was becoming increasingly apparent that certain individuals were especially suggestible and could be hypnotized rather easily. Stanley Hall was of the opinion that people could be persuaded to believe almost anything; for proof he didn't have to look far. Mediums were enjoying great popularity, hoodwinking the credulous into thinking they were hearing from the spirit world. Hall was eager to analyze and hypnotize mediums such as the famous Mrs. Piper and others like her, though he was never able to realize his ambition. Nonetheless, he remained convinced that these mediums were either schizophrenics or hysterics.

Freud began using direct hypnosis on his own patients, with some success. Still not satisfied, however, he sought a more complete and permanent cure. In the course of his search he remembered a remarkable case that had been described to him several years previously by his older friend, Joseph Breuer (1842–1925). Breuer was a prominent Viennese physician who seldom treated hysterics, but during the years 1880–1882 he had worked intensively with a single hysterical patient. After much experimentation he developed a technique that seemed to cure her completely.

The patient suffered from a whole array of hysterical symptoms, and Breuer discovered that he could remove them, one by one, if after hypnotizing her, he asked her while under hypnosis to try to recall the first time she had ever experienced a physical sensation similar to that produced by the symptom. Invariably she gradually remembered a "forgotten" memory of an emotion-laden experience. For example, one symptom was a contraction of the muscles around her eyes, forcing them into a perpetual squint. When the patient was asked under hypnosis to recall the first time the squint had occurred, she proceeded to recount an emotionally painful experience that had taken place while she was keeping a tearful vigil beside the bed of her desperately ill father. Suddenly her father roused himself into momentary consciousness and asked for the time. Not wishing to betray her concern, the patient choked back her sobs and tried to look at her watch. Because of the tears it was necessary to squint.

As she recalled this painful scene, she reexperienced the entire emotional impact of the incident. Further, in the therapy she allowed herself the previously denied luxury of expressing the emotion openly. Following this emotional catharsis, the symptoms disappeared. Breuer discovered that he could treat each of the other symptoms in the same manner, which he came to call the cathartic method. Gradually the patient was restored to health. Ironically, however, Breuer never treated another hysteric.

Thus in his own practice, Freud attempted to widen the zones of consciousness through hypnosis by "making the patient revert to the psychic state in which the symptoms had appeared for the first time" (Freud, 1953, cited in Wolberg, 1967; Freud and Breuer, 1907).

It was Freud who carried on with the cathartic method several years later, after recalling Breuer's case. When he tried it on his own patients he had generally good results, and concluded that a cure for hysteria was close at hand. It was clear, as he and Breuer phrased it, that "hysterics suffer mainly from reminiscences"—not ordinary reminiscences, to be sure, but reminiscences of emotionally charged experiences that have been somehow forgotten and placed beyond the reach of normal consciousness. With hypnosis these memories could be recovered and the emotions associated with them fully expressed. It seemed that the emotional energy had been bottled up or "strangulated" as long as the memory was out of consciousness. Denied the normal path to conscious expression, the emotional energy had been converted into physical energy, and expressed itself as a physical symptom. When permitted access to consciousness, it expressed itself in the normal way and then dissipated.

The remarkable discovery that Freud and Breuer had made was that physical symptoms could be created by mental states. Accordingly, the two men gave the name "pathogenic" (disease-producing) to those unconscious but emotion-laden memories underlying hysterical symptoms. And those mystifying symptoms, which had defied rational analysis for so long, were now shown to have a comprehensible cause and a straightforward cure. All the physician had to do was hypnotize his patient, and then . . .

But there was a problem: while hypnosis offered a key to the cure of hysteria, not all hysterical patients could be hypnotized. Many patients did not respond to Freud's hypnotic induction by falling into a state in which their memories were exceptionally fluent. Instead, they remained puzzled, anxious, or even defiant: "But Doctor, I'm not asleep, you know. I can't be hypnotized!"

But according to Louis Wolberg (1967), Freud's efforts in hypnosis went largely unrewarded. Failing to obtain the results he had hoped for, Freud concluded that a very deep hypnotic trance was necessary in therapy. But many people appeared unable to be hypnotized at all, and very few could reach a deep trance level. Besides this, he felt, in most instances, any beneficial results appeared to be only temporary.

Freud's eventual solution to this problem led directly to his most fundamental discoveries—and to the most revolutionary psychological system of the twentieth century. The solution did not emerge suddenly, however, nor was it simply the product of Freud's isolated genius. Developing over a period of several years, it owed a great deal to Freud's extremely rich intellectual and personal background. This is not to say, however, that by giving up hypnosis he was changing the objective of his treatments—on the contrary. "In abandoning the hypnotic technique, Freud never abandoned the hypnotic aim—that of relieving symptoms of mental illness by recovering lost memories of the painful experiences out of which the symptoms had arisen; psychoanalysis, as Freud conceived of it, was simply a more effective technique for achieving the aim" (Rieber and Salzinger, editors, *Psychology: Theoretical Historical Perspectives*, 1995).

THE FREE ASSOCIATION TECHNIQUE

Freud took the first step toward solving his problem by recalling an almost casual observation he had made on his visit to the Nancy Clinic. A subject had been hypnotized, made to experience a number of the common hypnotic effects, and then wakened from the trance. Upon awakening, the subject had no recollection of what had occurred in the trance—a single case of posthypnotic amnesia. Freud had been surprised, however, when the hypnotist placed his hand on the subject's forehead and said, "Now you can remember." Immediately, the subject recalled the entire hypnotic experience in minute detail.

In reflecting on his experience, Freud reasoned that if such a simple technique could work to help a subject overcome posthypnotic amnesia, it may also work to help his hysterical patients recall their forgotten pathogenic ideas. To test his idea, he experimented with a pressure technique and had patients lie on a couch with their eyes closed, but in a completely normal waking state. Freud would then ask them to try to recall symptoms. They would begin to articulate trains of recollections that inevitably stopped somewhere short of the goal. At these points Freud pressed his hand on the patient's forehead and confidently asserted that important new memories did emerge, and the chain of reminiscences could be continued. Often, after repeated applications of this new technique, pathogenic ideas were recalled, with subsequent emotional catharsis and symptom relief.

As time went by, Freud became increasingly subtle in his use of the pressure technique. From the first it had been clear that patients did not always respond to the pressure with obviously relevant memories; instead, they sometimes reported only vague and apparently irrelevant images or ideas. Initially Freud dismissed their reports as unimportant, and felt he must start the procedure all over again. Gradually, however, he learned that even these vague responses were significant, and ought to be listened to and used.

One crucial experience occurred when a patient responded to the pressure on her forehead by reporting flickers and flashes of light with a starlike quality. Freud was disappointed, and assumed that she was simply experiencing phosphenes, those flashes of light that often occur when pressure is placed on a closed eye. He was almost ready to give up, when the patient said that the images had begun to assume geometrical shapes—crosses, circles, triangles, etc. that resembled Sanskrit figures. Now intrigued, Freud asked the patient to recount any ideas that came to mind in association with the figures. She said that the crosslike figures represented "pain," and a circular, sunlike figure symbolized "perfection." This led to an emotional description of her feelings of pain and lack of personal perfection. She said that she had been made to feel especially inadequate recently by reading an article, translated from the Sanskrit, in a spiritualist magazine. The experience of recounting this proved cathartic and therapeutic for her. Thus her response to the pressure technique turned out to have been highly significant after all. After several similar experiences like this, Freud learned to pay attention to everything his patients said, even if it seemed unimportant at first.

Trial and error gradually convinced Freud that he did not really have to apply physical pressure to the forehead at all. He had only to encourage his patients to begin by thinking about their symptoms, letting their thoughts run completely free, and reporting to Freud everything that came to mind. The only essential rule was that nothing must be held back, even if it seemed stupid, irrelevant, embarrassing, or obnoxious. Everything was of potential importance.

Freud called this new technique "free association," and discovered that it could be just as effective as hypnosis in recovering pathogenic ideas. Freud now felt that, through free association, memories and pent-up emotions could be reliably and wholly released, which was not the case in hypnosis.

Since it did not require hypnosis, to which some people were resistant, it could be used on anyone. Freud abandoned hypnosis altogether, convinced that he'd wasted his time experimenting with the practice, and began to rely exclusively on free association in his treatment of patients. The change was to have far-reaching implications, since the added subtlety of free association enabled him to see features of hysteria that had been masked by hypnosis. Among these were the phenomena of overdetermination and repression, and the importance of sexuality as a causative factor.

OVERDETERMINATION

From his patients' free associations, Freud quickly learned that the relationships between symptoms and their underlying pathogenic ideas were usually not simple. Instead of there being a single pathogenic idea for each individual symptom, a whole series of emotion-laden scenes associated with a single symptom was far more common. One of his patients, for example, suffered from hysterical twitching of her hands. Analysis revealed three strong pathogenic ideas associated with this symptom: memories of being badly frightened while playing the piano, of receiving a disciplinary strapping on the hands as a schoolgirl, and of being forced to massage the back of a detested uncle. As each of these previously forgotten memories was recalled, the symptom diminished somewhat in intensity. Freud's term for this phenomenon was "overdetermination," since the symptom was not determined by a single pathogenic idea, but overdetermined by several of them. Freud noted that the overdetermined symptom conveniently symbolized the three pathogenic ideas, which all had to do with the hands. He discovered that most symptoms were simultaneously overdetermined by, and symbolic of, several different pathogenic ideas.

REPRESSION

Even more important than the discovery of overdetermination was Freud's gradual realization that unconscious pathogenic ideas had not been simply "forgotten" in the sense that unimportant details of experience are forgotten. He found that the pathogenic ideas had been actively and willfully—though perhaps not consciously—repressed by his patients. Pathogenic ideas were not so much a matter of patients' not being able to remember as of their wanting to.

The evidence leading Freud to this conclusion has varied in nature, but unmistakable in its implication; patients often manifested resistance to the free association process and the uncovering of pathogenic ideas. The most obvious examples of resistance occurred just at points when the therapy seemed to be going most smoothly. The patient would be free associating, and Freud would feel sure that the important pathogenic material was about to be recalled. Suddenly the patient would stop and say that his mind had suddenly gone blank or engage in some other behavior that served effectively to end the train of associations. He might say, with visible signs of anxiety and embarrassment, that what he had just thought of was too ridiculous to mention, or too personal to be shared. Another common example of resistance was a sudden shifting of the subject to Freud himself, perhaps a questioning of his medical credentials or the usefulness of his strange therapeutic technique. In short, patients used many different devices to avoid the uncovering of their pathogenic ideas. This behavior protecting the repression tended to occur automatically when the free associations got too close to the pathogenic ideas. Freud also noted that much of the resistance seemed to be unconscious as well as automatic; patients often did not realize they were avoiding the issue.

Freud's discovery of unconscious resistance taught him an extremely important lesson because it indicated that his patients' true attitudes toward their illness were far from simple. On the one hand, they experienced real discomfort and distress from their symptoms, and genuinely wanted to be rid of them. The very act of seeking therapy was a sign of that. On the other hand, however, their resistances tended to undermine the progress of their therapy. It was as if one conscious part of each patient wanted very much to be cured, while another unconscious part resisted therapy out of fear that the pain involved in a successful cure would be too great to bear. This was one of the first situations where Freud saw the importance of conflict in determining human behavior, where different aspects of an individual clamored for mutually exclusive goals. By the time he had fully developed his theories, Freud saw conflict as characterizing much more than just hysterical conversion symptoms.

The presence of conflict greatly complicated Freud's therapeutic task. He now had to try to ally himself with the positive, health-seeking attitudes of his patients against their unconscious resistances. In practice, this meant that he constantly had to warn his patients to be on the lookout for resistances and to try to combat them. The patients were explicitly told that while sometimes they would not want to continue their associations, those were precisely the times when it was most important and useful to do so. Usually the resistance could gradually be overcome and significant pathogenic ideas revealed if Freud worked hard and patiently to win the confidence of his patient.

SEXUALITY

As Freud gathered more experience in combating resistance, he began to gain a clearer understanding of why it existed, and what it was really directed against. He found that patient after patient began eventually, after much resistance had already been overcome, reluctantly to provide associations of a sexual nature. Particularly frequent were recollections of sexual experiences dating from childhood, often of sexual mistreatment at the hands of parents or other close relatives. The patient with the hand twitch, for example, eventually revealed that the uncle whose back she was forced to rub had attacked her sexually afterward. Freud gradually concluded that all of his patients had pathogenic ideas of a sexual nature, which were the deepest and most important causes of the hysterical symptoms. As long as those sexual ideas remained repressed, the patient always remained at least potentially hysterical. Any therapy short of bringing the ideas to consciousness was destined to be imperfect at best.

At first Freud incorporated these ideas—prematurely, it would turn out—into the seduction theory of hysteria, which asserted that all hysterics had undergone sexual mistreatment as children. The memory of the event was supposedly so painful and embarrassing as to become repressed. Then, in later life, events which would normally have called the memory to consciousness were incapable of doing so because of the repression, and the patient experienced a symptom instead of the memory. Thus the patient with the hand twitch experienced an intensification of her symptoms whenever she came into contact with her uncle. Instead of remembering the childhood seduction she experienced a symbolic physical pain. According to the seduction theory, the symptom was a defense against consciously recognizing a sexual pathogenic idea. Symptoms appeared in consciousness as the lesser of two evils, an unpleasant but less anxiety-arousing substitute for the repressed ideas themselves. The defensive function made symptoms valuable to the patient, and explained the presence of resistance in therapy. Hysteria thus came to be regarded by Freud as a neurosis of defense. Freud hoped that repressed memories and impulses would be able to return to the patient's consciousness, and that, once released, the symptoms, which had been caused by the repressed emotions, would disappear. He concluded that the central clinical features of his hysterical patients were dissociation (Standard Edition, 1907) and double consciousness. In 1896 Freud published *The Aetiology of Hysteria* (Standard Edition, 1907) in which he asserted that the accounts his patients gave of their recovered memories of abuse and neglect were based in fact and that these memories were thus the cause of their symptoms. Taking a circuitous route he discusses the concept of dissociation but gives it his own interpretation, quite at odds with that of Janet. Specifically he writes: "If in psychoanalysis, one group of ideas remains in the unconscious, psychoanalysis does not infer that there is a constitutional incapacity for synthesis, which is showing itself in the particular dissociation."

It's quite clear that Freud accepts the assumption of dissociation as a psychological process, but finds it important to differentiate his use of the term from the concept of dissociation that he appropriated from Janet. Freud and Breuer wish to interpret Janet and criticize him for not having a sufficiently dynamic theory to account for how conflicts in ideas in the unconscious are in an associative relationship with one another. This directly relates to Janet's use of the term "fixed ideas," but Freud does not understand or wish to understand what Janet meant by fixed ideas. What Janet was referring to was the way in which a particular hysterical patient had developed an obsession (or a fixed idea) or a somataform disorder which he (or more often she) suffers such as hysterical blindness or hysterical deafness. One can find added support for this view from Ellenberger who also argued that Freud wished to make use of Janet's concept of dissociation even while he was in the process of trying to work his way away from it (Ellenberger, 1970). Further corroboration—and clarification—can be found in Hilgard's discussion of dissociation and repression. Hilgard points out that the concept of repression is similar to amnesia because it involves once available memories that are no longer accessible. These memories are recoverable only by means of free association, a technique Freud invented. The concept of repression implies repressive forces that reduce and maintain inhibition of the capacity to recall noxious ideas—a process that forms the core of psychoanalytic theory (Hilgard, 1977). In his discussion of the method of hypnosis in relationship to amnesia Hilgard makes the

Pierre Janet   Sigmund Freud

following point: "Because, in a dissociation interpretation, the barrier between separated activities is essentially an amnesiac barrier, preventing the interchange of memories, whereas in psychoanalysis, the barrier is based on repression of unacceptable impulses . . ." (Hilgard, 1977).

Freud's willingness to use Janet's concept of dissociation before 1911 might be characterized as an affair with dissociation which—as many affairs do—began with flirtation and culminated in abandonment for after 1910 Freud had dropped the use of the word "dissociation" altogether and substituted the concept of repression in its place. One can assume that Freud hoped by engineering this substitution he could dissociate himself from dissociation and Janet's use of it, very likely because of the threat to psychoanalysis posed by the school of thought that Janet represented. Freud believed that the concept of repression might be more theoretically useful since it gave a privileged position to repression as a part of a dynamic process of conflicting emotional ideas in the unconscious that directly relate to his psychosexual stages of development and later to other aspects of his meta-theory. In short then, however much Freud might invite the confusion between the two terms, dissociation and repression should not be considered synonymous.

When Freud published his seduction theory of hysteria, its implausibility caused it to be regarded derisively in medical circles. His colleagues ostracized him and stopped sending him patients. What was worse, Freud himself began to have doubts about certain aspects of the theory. In spite of the regularity with which his patients reported childhood sexual traumas, and the sincerity with which they believed in the reality of those events, often their stories did not quite ring true. Sometimes Freud was personally acquainted with the alleged seducing relatives, and he felt that they would never have actually done such things. Besides, the theory, if correct, indicated a much higher rate of perversion among parents in the general population than one might reasonably expect. In general, then, Freud came to suspect that the "memories" of sexual mistreatment produced by his patients were not true memories at all.

But what were they, if not memories? This question was to haunt Freud for several months. He could not believe that his entire theory of hysteria was useless. His therapy still was the most effective one available, and it still made sense to regard symptoms as defenses against pathogenic ideas of some type, even if they were not actual memories. Furthermore, sexuality must have been important in some way, or else why would so many patients report those scenes of childhood seduction in their free will associations? The seduction theory was obviously wrong in some of the details, yet right in others.

There was, of course, no way that Freud could have imagined to what pernicious and twisted uses his theories of repressed memories and seduction would one day be put. And the way in which these repressed memories would be wrested from the subconscious where they lay submerged was by means of the very practice that Freud himself had abandoned as impractical years before—hypnosis.

Admittedly, the revival of hypnosis as a therapeutic tool did not happen all at once but rather gradually. Renewed interest in hypnosis was sparked by a phenomenon of "shell shock" suffered by soldiers in World War I which would now be called "posttraumatic stress disorder." The symptoms of shell shock very much resembled those of hysterics treated by psychologists of the preceding century and indeed, shell shock was seen as a kind of male hysteria. After World War I Clark L. Hull established the first experimental hypnosis laboratories and in 1933 wrote a book entitled *Hypnosis and Suggestibility: An Enlightened Approach*. But it wasn't until much later in the century that the term "posttraumatic stress disorder" was legitimized in that "the psychological syndrome seen in survivors of rape, domestic battery, and incest was essentially the same as the syndrome seen in survivors of war" (Herman, 1992).

This type of trauma can develop into dissociation by a path that by now has been fairly well charted and described by David Spiegel et al. in a paper entitled "Dissociation and Hypnotizability in Postraumatic Stress Disorder": "Along with the pain and fear that are associated with rape, combat trauma, or natural disaster comes an overwhelming and marginally bearable sense of helplessness, a realization that one's own will and wishes become irrelevant to the course of events; this leaves a view of the self that is damaged or contaminated by the humiliation, pain, and fear that the event imposed or a fragmented sense of self" (Spiegel et al., 1988).

The preexisting personality, the authors contend, pretends as if nothing is wrong and tries to carry on like normal but that means that the painful truth must be pushed aside. Of course, the truth doesn't disappear; defenses have to be mounted against it just as Freud had described. And it is this defensive process, the authors suggest, that may result in dissociation.

For even if the defense is successful it comes at a price; the dissociation "becomes an entrenched part of the overall view of self." And this division of self has the effect of disrupting "the experience of unity" where "ordinary self-consciousness is no longer synonymous with the entirety of self and personal history . . . " The self feels inauthentic even as it continues with the routine tasks of everyday life. Meanwhile, "the unconscious, warded-off memories exert censorship on conscious experience." In this way "the process of dissociation becomes part of the patient's identity . . ." (Spiegel et al., 1988).

So we can see how trauma, whether it occurs to a child or an adult in combat or anyone else under exceptionally trying circumstances, can produce memories so painful that the mind forms defenses to blot them out, setting in motion a process leading to the fragmenting of the self and causing dissociation.

It turns out that individuals who are dissociated are more suggestible, which is to say more highly hypnotizable than other people.

This raises an intriguing question in the authors' minds: "Does the experience of stress enhance hypnotizability or are the highly hypnotizable individuals more sensitive to the aftereffects of . . . trauma?" Not enough research has been done to satisfactorily answer this question.

All of the elements we have discussed—childhood trauma, repressed memories, sexual abuse (real or imagined), and dissociation—are present in most, if not all, cases of MPD/DID. Similarly, in many of those cases hypnosis has been used—and misused—to recover the memories, reveal the personalities that have been created as a result of the dissociation, and effect their reintegration. There is probably no better example of how all of these elements come together (for better but mostly for worse) than in the case that we are now about to examine, the most famous multiple personality case of all, that of Sybil Dorsett.

II

Sybil

*A Case of Multiple Personalities
and the Natural History of a Myth*

FASCINATING*
SPELLBINDING**
ASTONISHING***

Over Six Months a National Best Seller!

SYBIL

by Flora Rheta Schreiber

The True and Extraordinary Story of a Woman Possessed by Sixteen Separate Personalities

* Chicago Tribune ** Time Magazine *** Doris Lessing

5

The Case of Sybil
The Wilbur/Schreiber Version

Rome had to wait for the coming of Greek artisans in the second century B.C., at which time the Sibylline Books also arrived from Cumae in the south: an ancient holy site...founded by the Greeks as early as the eighth century B.C., and celebrated particularly for its oracular cave, where the Sibyl prophesied of whom Virgil wrote in Ecologue IV. The old woman incumbent visited the city with a bundle of nine prophetic books of which three were purchased and buried for safekeeping in the temple of Jove, where at intervals they were consulted until they perished in the fire of 82 B.C. . . . And as we may judge from Virgil's celebrated words, the Sibylline round, declining to its end, was to be followed—as everywhere in such mythic cycles—by a golden age of rebeginning.

JOSEPH CAMPBELL, *Occidental Mythology*

This is a story about a woman who couldn't make up her mind. She called them "blank spells"—they were Sybil Dorsett's secret and they made her ashamed and frightened. As she grew older the blank spells occurred with ever greater frequency and they lasted anywhere from a few minutes to several days. One of them—which took place in her childhood—lasted almost two years. While she had no idea what happened during these spells her family was aware of them, though they had no idea what to make of them. Sometimes they punished her for misbehavior of which she had no recollection whatsoever. Sybil couldn't figure out what she'd done wrong but realized that she must have done something. She became withdrawn, timid, and unsure of herself.

Her story has been told quite eloquently by Flora Rheta Schreiber in a fascinating, controversial book, *Sybil* (Regnery, 1973). Sybil is portrayed as a case of multiple personality carried to unprecedented extremes. From about the age of three and for about forty years thereafter, Sybil's body was intermittently inhabited by sixteen different people. That at any rate is what Schreiber said—and presumably believed. As we shall see, there are several versions of Sybil's story and Schreiber's, while the best known, is only one of them.

Different people? Surely, even if Schreiber was correct and Sybil did have MPD, the existence of sixteen people inhabiting a single body seems a bit much. Sixteen different aspects of the same person, perhaps, but not sixteen people! The answer to this is less than crystal clear because it all depends on how one defines "person"—and no one can, at least with any precision and finality. Yet it's significant that the psychiatrists who have treated cases of multiple personality—and who have had wide experience with the vivid but clearly imaginary personalities created in daydreams and hallucinations—often have little or no inkling about which of the personalities was the "real" one.

It has become a cliché in psychiatry that pathological behavior in an adult will most probably have its roots in some childhood experience or experiences, and Sybil's case proved no exception. To give readers some grounding—no mean feat in this case—it might help if we begin our investigation with Schreiber's portrait of Sybil. (Sybil is a pseudonym, used by Schreiber to protect her subject's identity, but even though Sybil's real name—Shirley Mason—has been known for some time, I will continue to use Sybil in this discussion for the sake of convenience.)

Sybil was an only child, born when her parents were in their forties. Her mother had already had several miscarriages so one might expect that the child would be welcomed. But that was not the case at all.

Dodge Center, the Wisconsin town of her childhood—called Willow Corners in the book—could have come right out of the pages of a novel by Sinclair Lewis. A Bible-fearing town, Willow Corners was a place characterized by a rigid morality and a deep suspicion of outsiders. At least some of Sybil's problems—especially the religious hang-ups that plagued her throughout her life—can be attributed to the American Gothic atmosphere of the town.

Sybil's mother, Hattie, had four brothers and eight sisters, all of whom suffered from the neglect of their overworked mother. (Many of the children developed psychological and psychosomatic problems as adults.) Perhaps in compensation, Hattie devoted herself to her schoolwork; she was a consistent A student and displayed such musical talent that her teachers enthusiastically urged her to continue her studies at a music conservatory for training as a concert pianist.

But Hattie's dream of becoming a rich and famous concert performer was never realized. When she was 12 her father, who owned a prosperous music store, informed her that she wouldn't be going to school the next day. Instead he insisted that she go to work in the store to replace an older sister who was getting married. Hattie didn't protest even though she knew that her father could very well afford to hire another employee. She couldn't even cry since crying was practically forbidden in the household. Her response was to laugh shrilly and hysterically. Thereafter when people recalled Hattie they always spoke about her wild laugh. A neighbor interviewed many years later described it this way: "She had a witchlike laugh. She didn't laugh much but when she did it sounded like it was a screech."

Not long afterwards she became afflicted with a case of St. Vitus dance so severe that the least little disturbance could send her into a frenzy. Even though she eventually recovered from the disorder her resentment of her father never abated. While he was alive she expressed her derision (if only occasionally) by whatever mischief she could contrive: cutting up his favorite smoking jacket, for instance, embarrassing him in church, and tattling on his efforts to ease the pain of a terminal illness with liquor. Yet after his death she idolized him. She cherished the smoking jacket he'd bought as a replacement for the one she'd cut into shreds. When she was feeling nostalgic she'd remove it and sit there fondling it for hours. She couldn't very well have admitted to herself that she hated her father; that would have been sinful, a violation of God's word.

Hattie was just as sentimental about her mother. Hattie's siblings were also emotionally stunted and throughout their lives they exhibited various degrees of neurotic behavior. By the time Sybil was born, Hattie, now 40, had been diagnosed as schizophrenic at the Mayo Clinic.

Sybil's father, Willard Dorsett, was also raised in a household dominated by the father. His father was a strict fundamentalist who feared Roman Catholicism and insisted that his three children always smile (for smiling was Christian) but forbade them from laughing (for laughing was a sin). As a boy Willard was both sensitive—and sensible—enough to be embarrassed by his father's Christian hostilities and idiocies, but he was weak enough to embrace them as an adult. He became an interesting mixture, for part of him—perhaps from his mother—was quite humanistic; he exhibited an interest in music and other arts and even embarked on a successful career as a small-town architect. Even though he broke with the church for fourteen years he could never quite overcome the influence of the religious dogmatism which dominated his childhood.

Perhaps it was this ambivalence that made him so indecisive when it came to dealing with the way Hattie treated Sybil. By no means was he aware of everything that went on between Hattie and Sybil, but his ignorance was willful; it was easier to ignore the physical evidence than to investigate it or risk a confrontation. After all, this was some forty years before the "battered child" syndrome was officially recognized, and he could hardly be expected to accept evidence that flatly contradicted his bedrock beliefs about motherhood.

According to the book, Hattie was a very sick woman who subjected her child to frequent punishments which left the child with black eyes, large bruises, fractures, and dislocations. But these beatings paled in comparison to far more sadistic punishments which made her daughter's life a living hell. Hattie would bind the little girl in various ways and shoot cold water up her urethra and into her bladder. She administered enemas meant for adults and forced her to retain water until she was in agony. The child was obliged to drink milk of magnesia and then forbidden to use the bathroom. She even went so far as to insert any number of objects including bottles, knives, buttonhooks, and her fingers into Sybil's vagina with such force and frequency that her injuries left permanent damage. Many years later a gynecologist told Sybil that as a result of her mother's brutality she would never have children. Soiling the bed would invite a beating as well. To such routine torment the frenzied mother added variations—filling the child's bladder with cold water, for instance, often as a prelude to tying her fast to a piano leg before proceeding to further torture her with the heavy vibrations of a Chopin polonaise. In addition, she made sure that Sybil suffered regularly from little "accidents," tripping the child and causing her to fall downstairs, dropping heavy objects on her—a rolling pin, a hot iron—and slamming a drawer on her hand. Some of these tricks were quite dangerous, putting the child's life at risk; after reading the book, one is astonished not only that Sybil survived but that she did so without completely losing her mind. She seems to have had a great deal of inner strength. Hattie doubtless would have accounted her resilience to the fact that the child came from good stock. The whole time Willard remained on the sidelines, pretending not to notice that there were any problems.

In such a troubled household it's hardly surprising that Sybil's hysteria went untreated. There was a heavy price to pay. By the time she was about three years old her personality split in response. Three personalities emerged, though neither Sybil nor her mother recognized their appearance. The daughter's suppressed rage against her mother was expressed in the personality of Peggy Lou, a rather aggressive young lady who treated Hattie with much less respect than the dominant personality, even going so far as to show open hostility. (Hattie had recently taken to calling Sybil by the name of Peggy, or Peggy Louisiana, more often than not.) Peggy Ann, on the other hand, was the fearful personality. But by far the most interesting of the three newcomers was Vicky, or Victoria Antoinette Scharleau, a cool little blonde who airily dismissed the idea that Hattie and Willard could possibly be Sybil's parents. That Vicky was blonde was no coincidence, at least in the view of her therapist Cornelia Wilbur, the third member of the triumvirate that also included Sybil and Schreiber. In a letter to Schreiber many years later she noted that several of the personalities Sybil manifested were blonde. That was because Sybil's mother's family had children who were beautiful blondes, Wilbur believed, and since Hattie was always criticizing Sybil's looks and made her feel ugly the personalities responded by adopting her mother's ideal of beauty (C. Wilbur, unpublished letter to F. Schreiber, July 26, 1966).

Vicky might have convinced Peggy Lou and Peggy Ann to deny their parentage; the two girls were careful to call themselves Baldwin, taking their name from a teacher Sybil had liked named Miss Baldwin. So where then were Vicky's "parents"? According to Vicky, they were off in Europe, living mostly in Paris, Vicky claimed, and they would return before long and make sure that Sybil had all the love, security, and comfort she needed. Meanwhile she would enjoy life whenever Sybil's circumstances would permit. Indeed, as time passed Vicky gradually came to realize that she held an advantage over Sybil and the Peggys.

Because Sybil knew nothing of the other personalities their existence was a complete mystery to her; they emerged only during her blank spells. Hattie was as mystified as her daughter: "Honestly, sometimes she just acts like another person!" The Peggys, however, were well aware of each other while their acquaintance with Vicky was more distant. Their emergence generally occurred only when Sybil was experiencing an intense emotion—anger, for instance, or fear. Vicky, however, knew everything about everyone (including all the personalities that would later appear). Unlike the Peggys, she seemed capable of emerging whenever she wanted and on her own terms. She also exercised considerable power over the other alters. Vicky wielded so much control that years later, while Sybil was undergoing analysis, it was Vicky who often seemed to be the "real" dominant personality instead of Sybil.

By the time she reached the age of 21 Sybil had accumulated eleven more personalities. They were all quite distinct not only in character but, at least in their "eyes," even in appearance. About a year after Vicky and the Peggys had emerged, Marcia Lynn Dorsett appeared on the scene. Like Sybil, she was a painter and a writer as well and, like Sybil, very emotional. A year later, in 1928, four additional personalities emerged: Sybil Ann Dorsett, a shy, colorless ash blonde; Marjorie Dorsett, a happy, mischievous, lithe, and lively little brunette; Mike Dorsett, a rather swarthy young carpenter who shared Willard Dorsett's fascination with building things; and Sid Dorsett, a more Nordic version of Mike, who was more interested in repair and maintenance than in construction. Both of these personalities were male chauvinists who dealt with their obvious genital incapacity by ignoring it.

In 1929, Helen Dorsett appeared. She was a brunette with hazel eyes who wavered between resolve and fear. Mary Lucinda Dorsett appeared in 1933; she was chubby and matronly with strong religious convictions. The redhead Vanessa Gail Dorsett made her debut in 1935; prettier than the others, she had a flair for the dramatic. Next came Nancy Lou Ann Baldwin who resembled the Peggys but seemed to have inherited Grandfather Dorsett's religious fervor; she was followed by Clara Dorsett, who was even more of a religious zealot; and then by Ruthie Dorsett, who displayed infantile behavior and was the least developed of the fifteen personalities. The years in which these three emerged is unclear; however, it is known that the sixteenth and last personality, a nameless blonde teenager, appeared in 1946.

Sybil's first dissociation occurred in September 1926, when she was three, which was when the personalities made their initial appearance. It was Sybil's MO, as Schreiber put it, to fall ill as an unconscious protest of her mother's abuse. In this case, the illness was a painfully sore throat

Her parents took her to the renowned Mayo Clinic in Rochester, Illinois, where the doctor diagnosed tonsillitis, prescribed some drugs, and then told Hattie that her daughter was disgracefully thin and undernourished, and needed to be put on a more nutritious diet. Of course, Hattie said nothing about the beatings, laxatives, and enemas.

Sybil had never met anyone quite as kind and personable as the young doctor who called her "honey" and "my big girl" and who let her look down his throat as a reward for letting him look down hers. She looked on him as a surrogate parent and would have done anything if he would only take her home with him. She even asked him if he would like to have a little girl in his life, but to no avail. He said he had good news—her tests turned up negative; she could go home. The doctor had no way of knowing that for the little girl the "good news" was terrible.

For Sybil the Mayo Clinic was practically a vacation. When she learned that she would have to leave she became distraught. As Schreiber described it, "this poor little girl could not have been told anything worse had he [the doctor] said, 'We're putting you in the gas chamber tomorrow . . .'" (Sinason, 2000). In rebellion the Peggys and Victoria appeared. Sybil receded into the background, unable to deal with the blow and so it was the three personalities who went home in her place.

Over the next several years Sybil suffered from ever more frequent blank spells. Hattie treated her daughter in wildly inconsistent ways—beating her one day, showering her with gifts the next (at one point she had upwards of 50 dolls). Even as she was being steeped in a fundamentalist creed that viewed sex with horror the little girl was forced to sleep in her parents' bedroom where she witnessed torrid sexual couplings—a classic instance of the primal scene. Sybil (rarely) and her surrogate personalities (usually) were exposed to other lurid tableaus in which Hattie would molest other kids who lived nearby and openly defecated on the lawns of neighbors whom she'd taken a disliking to. In addition, she took the poor girl along on excursions to the grocery store where she freely engaged in shoplifting. Sybil was instructed never to breathe a word. Hattie instilled her with the fear of God, warning her of the terrible consequences that would ensue if she tattled on her mother.

The battering that Sybil was obliged to endure wasn't only physical. She also had to put up with Hattie's incessant criticism. If Sybil did something, it probably was done wrong; and if anything went wrong, it was probably because of Sybil. In 1927, for instance, when Sybil was four, Hattie subjected the child to a particularly traumatic experience. Invited to dinner at the home of relatives, Hattie sent her daughter to play with her cousin Lulu in the kitchen. As they were washing the dishes after dinner, Lulu held up a dish for Sybil to admire. Then, before Sybil knew what was happening Lulu flung it against the French doors that separated the kitchen from the dining room, shattering both the dish and one of the doors.

In the pandemonium that followed, Lulu lied and blamed Sybil. Hattie naturally assumed that her daughter was responsible and accused her of breaking the dish deliberately. At this point Peggy Lou emerged and vehemently insisted on her innocence—to no avail. Hattie ordered Sybil to stand in a corner. The beating would come later.

The Great Depression that began to settle over the land in 1929 reduced the Dorsetts from affluence almost to destitution. They lost their home in Willow Corners and had to move into a one-room house five miles out of town. To Hattie this experience must have been one of unbearable humiliation. Whether the change in circumstances was responsible or some other factor accounted for it, Hattie fell into a catatonic state. Utterly passive and helpless, she had to be fed and clothed and kept clean by Willard and Hattie. Though her care represented an additional burden for the parents, Sybil looked on this period almost as an extended holiday because it was the first time that her mother let her alone. It was only a brief interlude, however. The catatonia lifted abruptly in a melodramatic scene, with Hattie suddenly appearing at the crest of a snow-covered hill. With her hysterical laugh ringing in Sybil's ears, she came sledding down, barreling into a furrow and almost breaking her leg. Not long afterwards, though for reasons unrelated to the bizarre incident, the family's fortunes improved. The Dorsetts returned to town, and gradually life settled back to what Sybil considered normal.

The only source of succor in young Sybil's life was her paternal grandmother, Mary Dorsett, who lived in a large bedroom upstairs. While unaware of what Hattie was doing to Sybil, she was nonetheless able to offer the child the refuge and affection she was unable to obtain from her own parents. When Sybil was nine, however, Grandma Dorsett died. Just as the attentive young doctor's departure from her life had come as a devastating blow, her grandmother's death was nothing less than a catastrophe. Her grief was sharpened by rather shabby treatment from her parents, who thoughtlessly left her in her room during the funeral service and neglected to make sure that she was seated in the right car for the trip to the cemetery. After the coffin had been lowered into the grave, she had to be restrained from jumping in with it. At that moment she dissociated again. That in itself was not unusual, but this was no ordinary blank spell. It lasted almost two years.

When the spell began Sybil was in the third grade. One day when she was eleven she found herself in a class that was familiar yet somehow strange. The last class day she could recall was the one just before her grandmother's death. She was not aware of any lapse of time. Yet when she returned she found that the room wasn't the same nor was the teacher and while she recognized her classmates they seemed bigger and were dressed differently. Indeed, she felt that she'd become bigger as well: she was wearing a dress that she had never seen before, much less remembered putting on. When she went back home she found many strange things, too, none more surprising or delightful than her discovery that she now had her own bedroom upstairs. She was afraid, of course, to confide in anyone about her bizarre experience. She kept it bottled up, and as time passed she adjusted well enough to keep anyone from suspecting her secret. She even managed to catch up on her fifth-grade class work sufficiently to pass her exams. She was a quick study, too, with an IQ of 170 in Schreiber's telling. (See Appendix 3 for a more accurate appraisal of Sybil's cognitive abilities.) Her greatest weakness (ironically) was multiplication, which she had never been taught. Luckily she had help from Vicky and Peggy Lou, who had conveniently memorized the tables.

Sybil managed to juggle the blank spells and personalities well enough to make it through high school and the first year or so of college. It was a struggle, though, since she had no idea when she'd be overtaken by a blank spell. Nor could she predict how long it would last when it did occur or what kind of mess she'd discover when she came out of it. Moreover, she was having a harder time keeping her problem a secret from outsiders. In June 1945, at the end of her freshman year, the college administrators urged her to drop out and not return until she had received psychiatric attention and her nerves were settled enough for her to resume her studies without further imperiling her health. By this point she only weighed 79 pounds.

With no alternative she returned to Willow Corners. At home she was as lonely as ever, although Hattie insisted on her daughter keeping her company almost every moment of the day. But being forced to live in her mother's shadow had an unexpected benefit; otherwise Sybil might never have seen a doctor who recognized that something was seriously wrong. The encounter with the doctor came about quite by chance. Shortly after Sybil's return from college, Hattie had an appointment in Omaha with her doctor and took her daughter along. As she waited for the doctor to finish examining her mother Sybil began to harbor hopes that this doctor would show as much solicitude and warmth as the doctor at the Mayo Clinic who had treated her for tonsillitis.

When at last the doctor appeared with Hattie in the waiting room, he looked directly at Sybil and asked if he could see her for a moment—alone. Her prayers had been answered. Once they were in the privacy of his office he remarked on how unwell she looked and asked if he could be of help. She admitted that she was having trouble and had suffered a nervous breakdown which forced her to leave college. While she mentioned nothing about the blank spells she did say that she'd been advised to see a psychiatrist. "Well," he said matter-of-factly, "if you like, I'll arrange an appointment with Dr. Cornelia Wilbur. She's right here in Omaha, and she works well with younger patients."

Relieved, Sybil agreed. She was pleased that the doctor had been so reassuring and expressed neither surprise nor disapproval. It had all been so easy.

Sybil saw Dr. Wilbur about a week later. She listened to Sybil's story without judging her. Until then Sybil had known only criticism, censure, and disdain. She had always feared that there was something radically wrong with her, and here this doctor was telling that her condition wasn't all that serious and that she could be helped. Not that the doctor was making light of the situation: after a few visits, she suggested that she arrange to have Sybil spend some time in a local psychiatric hospital.

The idea of hospitalization was coolly received by the Dorsett household, a bastion of dim views on the subject of psychiatry in general and Dr. Wilbur in particular. No doubt Wilbur smoked and probably even drank. After brooding over the prospect of allowing their daughter to be sent to the hospital, Hattie and Willard consulted their pastor, a narrow but not unregenerate man. He persuaded the Dorsetts that they should take the psychiatrist's recommendation. Meanwhile, though, Sybil had fallen sick with pneumonia and was unable to go to the hospital on the day scheduled. Hattie agreed to phone Dr. Wilbur to arrange a postponement. It was all an act. Sybil was allowed to listen in under the impression that her mother was talking to Wilbur, but the whole time she kept her finger on the cradle button. It wasn't until three years afterwards, when Hattie was close to death that she confessed the truth to Sybil.

Not surprisingly in view of her poor health, Sybil's bout with pneumonia was a long one. When she finally was well enough to call Dr. Wilbur, she discovered that the psychiatrist had left Omaha for New York where she would eventually open her own practice as a psychoanalyst. In spite of her disappointment she felt so encouraged by her few visits with the doctor that she decided to go back to college. This time she stayed at school, leaving only once in mid-1948 to make the trip to the Dorsetts' new home in Kansas City to nurse Hattie during her final illness. Sybil received her bachelor's degree in June 1949.

Over the next five years she kept house for her father, taught school, worked as an occupational therapist, and saved her money for a move to New York. She had two reasons for wanting to settle in New York: to take graduate courses at Columbia University and to reestablish contact with Dr. Wilbur. She was still having her blank spells.

She made the move in September 1954. After enrolling at the university, she phoned for an appointment with Dr. Wilbur, which she kept a few days later. Wilbur had no trouble accepting Sybil's explanation for the missed appointment years before. Nor did she seem particularly surprised by the story of Hattie's deception. The two agreed to resume the sessions, especially now that the doctor was an analyst. This was to be the first of more than 2300 sessions that ended up extending over the next eleven years.

Sybil still couldn't bring herself to reveal her secret. She didn't want the analyst to know about the blank spells, not only because she feared the implications, but because she thought that Wilbur might disapprove or even abandon her if she found out. The other personalities, however, were not so inclined to keep her secret and within a few months Wilbur knew more about Sybil's problem than she did herself.

The revelation came during a session late in December 1954. Wilbur and Sybil had been having a tense discussion about some letters Sybil had in her handbag. With no warning Sybil took them out and tore them into shreds, then tossed into a wastebasket. As Wilbur watched in astonishment, Sybil ran to a window and beat against it with her fist until she cracked the windowpane. In alarm the doctor escorted her back to her chair and tried to calm her down. Wilbur was relieved to see that Sybil's hand was only bruised and not bleeding.

Such a solicitous response immediately evoked the attention of Peggy Lou. If this had happened in Willow Corners her parents would have had a conniption. They would surely have expressed more concern for the broken window than for any injury she'd sustained and would have severely punished her. But not here. Wilbur was more worried about Sybil's injured hand. Indeed, the broken window didn't seem to bother Wilbur at all—the handyman could easily repair it, she explained. As for punishment, it clearly hadn't entered her mind.

Relieved, Peggy Lou relaxed a bit and began to talk. Wilbur was puzzled; she couldn't understand with whom she was now dealing. This was a much different person from the Sybil Dorsett she'd gotten to know; she was much more energetic in speech and gesture, much more open and forceful—and much less inhibited. And she was less attentive to her diction. She also seemed younger, less mature. At this point Wilbur was only distantly acquainted with the literature about MPD, but suspicion was growing that this was what she was seeing. Finally she summoned the courage to ask her patient who she was.

Peggy Lou Baldwin, the girl replied, surprised that it had taken all this time for the doctor to grasp the difference in personalities. She went on to say that while she lived with Sybil her home was in Willow Corners. She said that she liked to paint and do charcoal sketches, although she admitted that she wasn't as talented as Sybil. The doctor asked if Hattie was her mother. The question seemed to terrify her. No! No! she protested. In a flash Sybil was back, a quiet, prim young woman just as she was before.

Sybil immediately realized that the doctor must suspect her secret. Recognizing that she had caused a commotion she spotted the crack in the window. Embarrassed, she offered to pay for the repair but Wilbur told her not to worry. The doctor tried to put her at ease, explaining that Sybil had experienced what psychiatrists call a fugue. Sybil was relieved. Just knowing that there was a name for her blank spells reassured her that they weren't so unusual as she'd imagined. Moreover, Wilbur said, the condition was treatable. Sybil was gratified to hear this, of course, though she could hardly suspect how much time and work would be required for the treatment to resolve the problem. Wilbur left it at that for the time being, seeing no point in mentioning Peggy Lou's existence to Sybil.

Much later, in her correspondence with Schreiber, Wilbur recalled her initial reaction to the emergence of the various personalities. "The personalities were named before I got into the case. I discovered this quite by accident and followed up on it. One day Peggy was in the office and I called her Shirley and she said, 'You always call me Shirley.' In surprise I asked her what her name was and she said Peggy Lou. That was when I found out that she was a multiple personality. They were named as they emerged by the personality that emerged" (Schreiber Archive, Box 37).

Wilbur avoided any mention of the subject of Peggy Lou for the next several months. Then in March 1955 she met Victoria Antoinette Scharleau. Unlike Peggy Lou, Vicky didn't emerge in the middle of an interview. When the doctor opened her office door she found Vicky sitting in the waiting room, reading a copy of *The New Yorker*. She smiled up at the doctor and then sauntered into the office with a grace totally uncharacteristic of either Peggy Lou or Sybil. Sybil wasn't feeling well, Vicky explained, and so she'd decided to come in her place. And who, asked the doctor warily, are you? Vicky apologized for not introducing herself, and immediately did so.

Vicky talked freely with the doctor, regaling her with stories about her imaginary family in Paris and boasting how she knew all about Sybil and the other personalities. She noticed the look of surprise on the doctor's face. Oh, yes, she declared with undisguised pride, there were quite a few others. The doctor asked how much Sybil knew about them. Not a thing, Vicky answered—"to her we are just blank spells." There was Peggy Ann, for instance—but the doctor decided against allowing Vicky to go on, seeing that they only had a few moments left of their hour. Instead, she asked Vicky to let the personalities all know that they would be welcome in her office. Vicky agreed to pass the word along, for she was in a hurry to be on her way: she had an appointment to meet a friend for lunch and a visit to the Metropolitan Museum of Art.

Over the next five years Dr. Wilbur got to know the various personalities as they took advantage of her invitation. They were, she found, quite a mixed bag, especially if one took into account their own perceptions of themselves. They ranged in age from near infancy to adulthood. Although they all were tainted and troubled by a strain of Willow Corners morality, some suffered less than others. They all had their own philosophy of life. Most were artists of varying talents, but only one could play a musical instrument (Vanessa played the piano). Vicky had told the doctor in an early interview that all the personalities, including Sybil, were neurotic with the sole exception of herself. After several additional sessions Wilbur came to the conclusion that Vicky was correct in her assessment in spite of her delusion about having rich parents in Paris. Wilbur looked on Vicky as a kind of ally or accomplice. As early as 1955, she asked Vicky for help in getting the various personalities to cooperate in the healing process. Wilbur finally revealed to Sybil that she harbored several different personalities though what help Sybil could provide was more problematic; at this point there had yet to be any contact between Sybil and the alters.

Although Vicky had agreed to encourage the other personalities to cooperate with Wilbur, she had some difficulty in delivering. Several of the personalities—especially the Peggys—could be quite rambunctious and eager to escape the constricted prison that Sybil represented for them. As a result, Sybil continued to dissociate repeatedly—and she continued to get into trouble. Peggy Lou tried to break into a car, which she mistook for her father's. Then she broke some $2000 worth of glass bric-a-brac in various Fifth Avenue shops in a single year, saddling Sybil with the bills. Mary almost bought a house in her name. The two boys built a partition in the apartment she shared with another girl. One day Sybil found herself standing in front of a hotel in Philadelphia and looking at a newspaper dated January 7, 1958. It struck her that the last thing she remembered was being in class in New York on January 2 and hearing a glass break in the hall or the lab nearby. This wasn't the first time that she found herself in a strange place without having any idea how she'd gotten there. She'd had similar experiences in San Francisco and elsewhere. The trips left Sybil in a state of confusion but Peggy Lou had a ball!

When Sybil & Co. returned from Philadelphia, Dr. Wilbur interviewed Peggy Lou, and her inseparable companion Peggy Ann, about the trip. With their permission she recorded their account. For the first time Wilbur had an extended taped account of a dissociation which she could offer to Sybil as concrete evidence of the personalities.

Sybil was deeply troubled by the prospect of listening to the tape. She was torn. Even though she had an abiding trust in Dr. Wilbur's honesty she had a hard time coming to grips with the possibility that the doctor was right about her having "other selves." She resisted listening to the tape. Wilbur tried to change her mind. The ultimate goal of her treatment, the doctor explained, was to integrate all the personalities into one. Then Wilbur pointed out that that goal was as distant now as it had been three years ago when they'd begun their association. But if Sybil agreed to listen to the tape and became acquainted with at least a couple of the other personalities and shared their memories, progress might be possible. The tape would be a first step toward integration. The only alternative would be to remain stuck where they were now.

Sybil finally agreed, less because of the irresistible logic of the doctor's argument than because of her fear that she would alienate Wilbur by a flat refusal. She was still full of trepidation. But she was caught off guard as soon as the tape began to play. The first voice she heard could have been a ghost. She thought she was listening to her mother. The doctor had to stop the recorder and then spent several minutes trying to convince her that it wasn't Hattie but rather Peggy Lou although Sybil found this news only slightly more reassuring. After a good deal of starting and stopping, Sybil managed to get through the entire tape.

It was a sobering experience. But perhaps the last thing Sybil needed was a sobering experience. Sybil continued to dissociate, and in the fall of 1958 she even attempted suicide though Vicky intervened in time to save her life. Whether the attempt was really a determined effort is questionable, but a suicide attempt of any kind by a patient is hardly a source of comfort to her psychiatrist. Up to this point Wilbur had felt that analysis would be the gentlest and ultimately most effective type of therapy. But in view of the lack of progress she began considering alternatives. Three ideas occurred to her in order of their likely success: electric shock, sodium pentothal, and hypnosis.

When the electric shock treatments proved futile Wilbur opted to try the next alternative on her list—sodium pentothal. The drug had a marked effect. For a day or so after each shot Sybil was in a state of blissful euphoria such as she had never known before. Further, the drug showed some signs of producing integration: under its influence she could remember some of the things that had happened during a few of her blank spells. Wilbur was enthusiastic about the results—at least initially. "We'll have some pentothal sessions as Sylvia," Wilbur noted in one session, "and see if we can't get why guilty feelings." But by early 1959 it was clear that she was becoming psychologically addicted. She wasn't alone, either. The other personalities, who had to some extent shared her euphoria, were now also to some extent sharing her growing addiction. Sybil recognized that she had a problem. In her journal she wrote that she would like to give up the pentothal. Well, not quite; she felt that it would still be permissible to take it when she became depressed. Wilbur, however, decided that her patient would be better off going cold turkey and called a halt to the treatment. In a conversation with Schreiber Wilbur discussed her fears related to the drug:

> W: And it worries me because I had the feeling she was getting addicted. At least psychologically and I didn't want to go from a multiple personality to an addiction.
> F: And not paying for it apparently . . . (Schreiber Archive, Box 37)

The response by the personalities to the withdrawal came as a shock. Only Vicky expressed any sympathy for the doctor's concern about addiction. Without the drug, though, Sybil barely showed any sign of improvement. Just the opposite—she often seemed to lose more ground than she could ever regain. By the fall of 1959, the doctor was ready to try the last resort.

Early in their relationship, Wilbur had promised Sybil that she would not hypnotize her. Now she asked to be released from that promise. When she had made it, she explained, she couldn't possibly have suspected the kinds of problems that she was going to encounter. In the intervening years she had read accounts of other cases of multiple personality including Christine Beauchamp's and Eve White's—and she was struck by the evident effectiveness of hypnosis. This success seemed to confirm her strong opinion that the multiple-personality syndrome was a form of hysteria rather than of psychosis, since hysterics are characteristically susceptible to hypnotic suggestion. After listening to Wilbur's reasoning, Sybil consented, but more in resignation than with any enthusiasm.

For Wilbur, though, the experiment seemed to open a door that had previously been bolted shut. Under hypnosis the various personalities were much more accessible to the doctor, who now had to put this opportunity to good use. It occurred to her that a major obstacle to integration was the broad range of ages and levels of maturity exhibited by the personalities. How, for example, could Ruthie, who talked and behaved like a two-year-old, be successfully integrated with Vicky, who talked and behaved like (to use her term) a femme du monde in her twenties? And how were any of these disparate personalities going to be integrated with Sybil herself? A first step, thought the doctor, might be to induce them all to grow up through hypnotic suggestion. At least it was worth trying.

Wilbur started with Ruthie, naturally enough—she was the most childlike. With Sybil in hypnotic trance, she called Ruthie out and asked her if she'd like to be three. Ruthie said she would, especially since she could then color with crayons. The doctor aged her the additional year through hypnotic suggestion, giving her an imaginary couple of months to enjoy being three, before asking her if she'd like to be six. Ruthie agreed. And would you like to continue growing older? Wilbur asked. Oh, yes, replied Ruthie—she wanted to do all the things that the others could do.

Using variations of this technique with all the surrogate personalities—sometimes in what must be called group-therapy sessions for want of a better term—Wilbur slowly, patiently encouraged the growth process in each. By early April 1960, when they were all 18 or older the doctor decided to take the final plunge. On April 21 she induced them all to consider themselves 37 years and 3 months old, which was Sybil's age. The immediate results were spectacular. On the following day Sybil, under hypnosis, met Ruthie and Vicky. Ostensibly at least the three of them integrated on the spot. This session marked the first time Sybil had "met" any of the others, as well as providing the first positive signs of integration. The doctor's spirits rose considerably. Until this point, Wilbur later remarked, Sybil seemed to have known the other personalities as if in a dream and acknowledged them when she heard their voices on a tape only if it "felt right."

Nonetheless, Sybil's progress was uneven and she continued to suffer relapses. That summer Peggy Lou joined Vicky and Ruthie in Sybil. The triumph was brief; only weeks later Sybil was in a state of almost suicidal depression. In January 1962, in a very emotional interview, Sybil finally admitted her hatred of Hattie to the doctor—and to herself. If this acknowledgment accelerated the process of integration, her treatment nevertheless proceeded in fits and starts, with the remaining personalities proving reluctant to participate in what they viewed as their gradual demise. Happiness is integration, the doctor kept telling them, but it was a proposition that they found hard to accept.

Sybil had been too ill to continue her studies, but in August 1964, she managed to get and keep a job as a receptionist at a large hotel. Here she met Ramon Allegre, a Colombian national. He was a widower who was left to care for small children. He asked Sybil for a date, and she consented. Later he asked for something more—and she refused. But in October, undaunted, he proposed marriage, saying that his children needed Sybil as a mother as much as he wanted her as a wife. Sybil found both aspects of his proposal attractive, but she was much too uncertain of her condition to accept. Unfortunately, Wilbur was in Europe at the time, and Sybil had no one to go to for advice. And so Ramon, puzzled and hurt by her rejection, departed from her life as abruptly as he had entered it.

Sybil was disconsolate, but she didn't break down as she would have in the past. When Wilbur returned home, Sybil realized that her memory of the three months since the doctor's departure was unimpaired. She remembered everything that had happened. In all that time there had not been a single dissociation. And indeed this was the beginning of the end. Although other personalities were still in the wings, they were weakening, and they could emerge on stage now only under hypnosis.

It was around this time that a new person came into Sybil's life: the indefatigable journalist Flora Schreiber.

A clever, talented writer, who had written a pop book on child development and language and innumerable articles for magazines, she inspired admiration, envy, and resentment.

For Schreiber Sybil was a godsend.

The climax of Sybil's case (as it proved later) came in June 1965. One evening, at home in her apartment, Sybil had a sudden and severe seizure. Luckily, she managed to telephone her new friend Flora, who rushed to her apartment and found her lying sprawled on the floor. But in spite of her state of collapse Sybil hadn't lost consciousness or suffered a blank spell. On the contrary, she told Schreiber that she was proud that she had come through the ordeal intact. Schreiber instantly got on the phone to Wilbur. It was only after Wilbur arrived that Sybil experienced her last dissociation. This time it was as the nameless blonde teenager, who vaguely identified herself in a strangely cadenced recitation before reassuring Wilbur and Schreiber that she had no intention of interfering with Sybil's recovery.

The blonde was as good as her word. By mid-July Sybil felt well enough to tell the doctor, for the first time and with unprecedented confidence, that she was sure that she had dissociated for the last time. In a series of "test" interviews the doctor found that her patient indeed gave every indication of being one person. The other personalities, questioned under hypnosis, proved not to be in possession of a single memory that Sybil didn't have access to as well. The memory bank was finally complete, and in one place. In September 1965, the doctor made an entry in her office diary, "All personalities one."

The following month Sybil left New York for Pennsylvania, where she had been engaged by a hospital to work as an occupational therapist with emotionally disturbed children. She never did dissociate again.

6

The Publication of a "Psychiatric Masterpiece"

Spelt from Sibyl's Leaves

For earth her being has unbound, her dapple is at an end, as
tray or aswarm, all throughther, in throngs; self in self steeped and
   pashed—quite
Disremembering, dismembering all now.
. . .
Let life, waned,
Ah let life wind
Off her once skeined stained veined variety upon, all on two
Spools, part, pen, pack
Now her all in two flocks, two folds—black, white; right,
Wrong; reckon but, reck but, mind
But these two; ware of a world where but these two tell, each
Off the other, of a rack
Where, selfwrung, selfstrung, sheathe- and shelterless, thoughts
Against thoughts in groans grind.

GERARD MANLEY HOPKINS

PRELUDE TO A MYSTERY

We don't know what we don't know, said Wittgenstein. But nobody seems to know that—and there's a concerted effort to prevent anyone from finding it out. Most cases of multiple personality appear essentially to represent the organism's efforts to live, at different times, in terms of different systems of values.

   In the 1960s when this social dream was created there existed a mood of manic desperation, which eventually gave rise to the countercultural revolution. Authorities in psychology, such as Thomas Szasz and Ronald Laing, made the usual outrageous statements such as that mental illness is a myth (Szasz) and society is more schizophrenic than the schizophrenic (Laing). This was the spirit of the time that gave birth to *Sybil* the book as well as the motion picture. In this chapter I will tell how the real story about Sybil was "manufactured" as well as the story of how phony facts produce phony problems, which in turn create phony solutions. Furthermore, in this chapter we will see how the polluted results of this process caused experts as well as the general public to be "hooked, booked, and cooked." In other words, this is a tale of the natural history of a myth.

How influential was Sybil in her various incarnations? Well, before 1973, there were fewer than 50 known cases of multiple personality disorder. But by 1994 over 40,000 cases had been diagnosed. Some therapists contended that there were at least two million more. Most of the "victims" were women. In all of these cases one of the "personalities" was a slut or a prostitute, noted Sherryl Connelly in a February 1999 column in the *Daily News* cleverly entitled "The End of Sybilization." "In other words, multiplicity offered good girls a respectable way to go bad. Which was another aspect of Sybil's massive appeal to the broader female culture in the early years." If women were intent on "having it all," Connelly wrote, then that meant "doing it all." "They realized they couldn't survive their times if they didn't have multiple selves. Society made Sybils of us all. Except Sybil, that is."

Were thousands of multiples (as they're known) wandering around, undiagnosed and untreated until 1973? And what happened in 1973 to bring so many others to light?

What happened was *Sybil*, the best-selling book by Flora Schreiber. When it appeared some called it "a psychological masterpiece." *The American Journal of Psychiatry* declared that it was "destined to stand as a significant landmark both in psychiatry and in literature." It became a landmark all right, but not exactly the kind that the *Journal* anticipated.

PUBLICATION OF *SYBIL*

Until the publication of *Sybil*, the best-known modern account of a multiple was The *Three Faces of Eve* by Corbett Thigpen and Hervey Cleckley. It was a successful book when it appeared in the late 1950s and had a second life as a film in 1957. But the phenomenon of popularizing MPD as embodied in a spectacular case actually extends back much further to the early years of the twentieth century. In 1905 Morton Prince published a book that, like *Eve* and—even more sensationally—*Sybil*, enjoyed enormous success and captured the imagination of a (mostly) credible public. His book, *The Dissociation of a Personality*, was based on the case of a young woman, Miss Beauchamp, whom Prince had treated over a period of seven years. During the course of her treatment, which had included hypnosis, suggestion, and sedation, his patient manifested four different personalities, a relatively modest number compared to Sybil's sixteen. Prince was not, however, especially forthcoming about the details of treatment and readers were left to surmise the details of his methods from what he had set down. Prince was more explicit about the goal of his therapy which he defined broadly as the integration of the personalities. Initially only two personalities expressed themselves. Miss Beauchamp, a proper lady by all accounts, very pleasant if a bit frail, had to share her body with Sally, who displayed a "naughty, whimsical, disruptive personality." Prince took the side of the ladylike Miss Beauchamp and most of his narrative is replete with details of his contentious relationship with the irascible Sally although two additional personalities later emerged. Prince succeeded in arousing public interest in psychopathology. The book was an immediate sensation and it stirred considerable interest in psychology among the general reader, as evidenced by the response in the popular press. But it is clear from the reviews that even at this early stage the public was at least acquainted with MPD. In December 1905 a reviewer for the *New York Sun* pointed out that "[t]he irreverent layman as a rule does not approach the entertaining neurasthenic 'subjects' with the proper respect and awe and usually is in doubt as to whether the 'subject' is humbugging the investigator or the investigator is humbugging himself." The comment suggests that the reviewer was referring to public performances of hypnosis—recall the scandal that Mesmer caused—but he hastens to assure his readers that in this case "there can be no doubt about Dr. Prince's sincerity in his observations." Yet he also notes that "the readers' belief in them [Prince's observations] will depend on his willingness to accept the theories of 'abnormal psychology'" (Marks, 1970).

In March of the following year the magazine *Academy* weighed in with its opinion, calling the book "more interesting than any novel." Most reviews couldn't help remarking on its similarity to *Dr. Jekyll and Mr. Hyde*. A reviewer for *The New York Times* with a fondness for puns called it "a chronicle of facts, and in certain features, a realization in actual life of the old fairy tale of the bewitched, long-slumbering maiden who was awakened by a Prince." The *Boston Herald*, on the other hand, didn't consider Prince's patient so unusual at all: "Miss Beauchamp is simply ourselves 'writ larger'; ourselves passed on to a stage of chronic mental disease" (Marks, 1970).

On the other side of the Atlantic a reviewer for the *London Daily Mail* took the opportunity to render a social observation: "To a nerve specialist, she [Miss Beauchamp] must have presented a type common enough in big cities. A diligent student at her college, morbidly shy, a lover of books, unwilling to 'inflict' her personal affairs upon strangers." Miss Beauchamp's odd tale was so compelling that any number of aspiring playwrights flooded the offices of New York theatrical agents with no less than five hundred plays based on the case. One effort, entitled "The Case of Becky," actually made it to the Broadway stage and became a hit. It was reprinted seven times, the last time in 1957. The medical establishment of the day, interestingly enough, didn't share the public's enthusiasm for Miss Beauchamp. *The Medical Journal* of New York City, for instance, called it "a curious borderland study in the shadowy realm of the subconscious, hypnotic suggestion and scholarly research so evident in the book, might not have been bestowed with more valuable results upon a more important subject." The reviewer seemed not to have appreciated the impact the book would have on people avid for accounts of "ourselves, writ larger." "Prince's work," the reviewer concluded, will "bore the ordinary reader" (Marks, 1970).

Boring the ordinary reader is not a charge that could conceivably be leveled against *Sybil* by any stretch of the imagination. *Sybil*, which appeared in 1973, was grabbed up by an eager public—and quickly moved to the top of *Time* magazine's bestseller list. Paperback rights were acquired for $300,000, an enormous sum at the time. The TV movie shown two years later, with Sally Field as Sybil and Joanne Woodward as Wilbur, introduced the story to millions more.

Wilbur was very familiar with Prince's own study of MPD. In a conversation with Schreiber she refers to it directly in a scathing commentary on colleagues who fail to appreciate the significance of the disorder. "There are people all through our intellectual strata who are undereducated, uncurious and arrogant," Wilbur says. "They read [Moravia's] *Two Women*, but they've never read anything on multiple personalities, dissociation of personalities, etc., and that's all they've read, so that's all there is to it. Here is this kind of undereducation and intellectual arrogance. I would be inclined to say—do you think so—well how does that fit in with Morton Prince's *Dissociation of Personality*? And then if he said I haven't read that,—you'd say—well, that's probably one of the most famous cases of all."

Perhaps, though, Wilbur might have given more thought to another, though less famous case of MPD that Prince treated several years after Beauchamp. This was the case of Nellie Parsons Bean, a middle-aged Bostonian woman, known in the literature as BCA, which is notable among other things for "the formation of a clinical entity that evolved out of the therapeutic world shared by doctor and patient" (LeBlanc, 1993). Bean sought Prince out in 1907 for the treatment of neurasthenia and remained under his care until 1913. "BCA" stood for her different personalities: B is a vivacious and adventurous woman in her early twenties, while A is her opposite number—a priggish, morbid, depressed woman—with C representing the mentally balanced synthesis of the two after treatment has successfully integrated them. Prince regarded her as Exhibit A in support of his thesis about dissociation in his battle against Freudians who had abandoned dissociation for repression. Therapist and patient developed such a close relationship that it blurred the lines between personal and professional. Prince eventually hired her as his research assistant. In a paper on BCA, Andre LeBlanc observes: "In short, her experience as a reflective multiple personality, witnessing the battles over the theoretical survival of her disorder, placed her in a unique position to mirror the battlefield that surrounded her" (LeBlanc, 1993). In a dream recorded by BCA on April 12, 1912, Prince appears supervising the construction of "a temple of psychology." In the dream BCA brings Prince precious stones that cut her hands and "required enormous effort to carry and deliver." BCA interpreted these stones as "the facts of my own life of which he [Prince] has made use in experimenting . . . and the sacrifice of personal feeling which it required to relate these intimate facts" (From a typewritten manuscript of a dream by BCA, April 12, 1912, in the Morton Prince Collection). In the dream Prince exhorts her to build a temple of her own which she does though not without protest. On the one hand, LeBlanc states, the dream is "seen to reflect Prince's own perceived place in psychopathology as a builder . . . of the temple of psychology." On the other, it symbolizes BCA's attempt "to model her illness according to Prince's theory of multiple personality." He goes on to say: "Not until she had learned to see things as he did, to speak his language, to find the 'stones that he would like,' did a temple grow up that would stand for her past, present and future" (LeBlanc, 1993). "BCA's dream teaches us . . . that in cases of this sort a therapeutic entity cannot be separated from the therapy itself. Therapy and its clinical object, be it a dream or MPD, become inextricably linked under the dissociative gaze of the therapist" (LeBlanc, 1993)

In many ways, the intense involvement of the therapist and patient exemplified the symbiotic relationship by Prince and BCA echoes down the years in the increasingly intimate relationship that formed between Wilbur and Sybil, in which one's theory received immediate support and elaboration from the other. The danger inherent in such an association should have set off a warning bell, but evidently Wilbur wasn't thinking of BCA; it was the earlier case of Miss Beauchamp that she had in mind when she began her collaboration with Schreiber. And we must imagine that both women were acutely aware of the enormous popularity that Prince's book about the case had enjoyed. Surely, they must have thought, they could produce a book about Sybil that would earn them the same kind of fame and fortune.

Now that we've sketched a portrait of Sybil as she emerges in the pages of the book it might prove illuminating to see exactly how the collaborative team of Wilbur and Schreiber went about conveying her story. Like every author, whether of fiction or nonfiction (or something in between), Schreiber was worried about having a "hook"—something that will grab the reader right from the start. At one point early on in putting together the book Schreiber expresses her concerns to Wilbur. "Well, in this first chapter, what do we have?" she asks. "Do we have something to make us care . . . really care about this girl? Do we have it in Chapter 1?"

Wilbur is reassuring. "Boy, you sure have!"

From the way the book would go on to sell there is little question that Wilbur was right.

A story does not convey its meaning by its contents alone, though, but also by the way in which it is told. "We have to establish uniqueness," Schreiber writes to Wilbur as the two were trying to determine how to decide on who should be narrating the tale. "As I have inferred from our earlier conversations, where are other cases of multiple personalities? After examining these cases, what do we say, by way of selling the idea, that establishes uniqueness, that makes a publisher feel that this is sufficiently different from Eve to justify its interest?" (Schreiber Archive, Box 37).

To achieve this "uniqueness," the two women hit upon the idea of conveying the story from the inside rather than by the therapist (Wilbur) or an outside but concerned observer (Schreiber). Sybil is told from the point of view of the pseudonymous Sybil Isabel Dorsett herself, now known by her true name Shirley Mason. The story shifts in and out of her personalities—sixteen in all. Among them the elegant and sophisticated Vicky, the assertive and eager Peggy Lou, the more fearful Peggy Ann, the religious Mary, and the dramatic Vanessa who scorned religion. There are even two boys—Mike and Sid. As the story goes on, the reader begins to discover how each personality was formed in turn and why. Peggy, for instance, was created as a result of one of Sybil's earliest dissociations in order to cope with the anger which she felt toward her mother but was never able to express.

(To confuse matters—and identities—further, Schreiber and Wilbur first intended to call Shirley Mason "Sylvia" and only later settled on the more evocative and mythically resonant name "Sybil.")

According to the book, the breakthrough in the treatment—which began in the early fifties—comes when Wilbur finally understands the reason for why her patient had developed a multiple personality disorder—her mother. "You don't love your mother, your mother was wicked, bad, cruel, painful and you really hated her," Wilbur harangues Sybil. "If you don't hate her, you ought to and there is something a matter with you if you don't hate her. Because a normal response to this kind of treatment would be hatred. Bitter Hatred." She later repeats these sentiments in a conversation with Schreiber: "I was pushing her in terms of, you don't love your mother. Your mother was wicked, bad, cruel, and painful. And you really hated. . . . If you don't hate her, you ought to. And there is something the matter with you if you don't because a normal response to this kind of treatment would be hatred. Bitter hatred. And she couldn't figure . . . to say I hate her. So . . . after she wrote the letter that came through with I hate her, I hate her, I hate her" (Schreiber Archive, Box 37).

And what did her mother do that was so abominable? According to Sybil's recovered memories (which supposedly started from when she was six months old and lasted until she was about seven), her mother shoved spoons, knife handles, and buttonhooks up her vagina, copulated with her husband in front of her, defecated on the neighbors' lawns while her daughter was forced to watch, sexually molested her, and engaged in lesbian orgies with young girls in her presence. Nonetheless, even Schreiber must have suffered from the occasional twinge of doubt. Writing to Wilbur, she asks: "But have you, to your own satisfaction, established cause and effect between the brutal experiences the patient [Sybil] had with her mother and the emergence of the personalities? Have you established the approximate dates of their appearance?" (Schreiber, unpublished letter to Wilbur, July 23, 1965). Wilbur writes back to assure her: "There is a direct connection with the development of the personalities and the battered child syndrome. . . . We have all the material on the appearance of the various personalities, when they emerged and why and what reinforced them" (Wilbur, unpublished letter to Schreiber, July 26, 1965).

In another letter to Wilbur, Schreiber writes about her visit to the real Dodge Center, an excursion apparently intended to find some hard evidence to back up Sybil's accounts of her mother's cruelty: "Well, the evidence I have is enormous, she was tied to the table, she was beaten, she was given these enemas, these foreign bodies were inserted in her vagina, she was made to witness her mother's homosexual incidents, with the girls in the woods, and now actually having been to Dodge Center, I want to know where the hell the woods were. I didn't find any."

Schreiber's failure to locate the woods in question, where so many abominations were alleged to have occurred, did not, of course, deter her from pressing forward with the indictment of poor Hattie. Several years later, not long before her death, a British interviewer asked Schreiber about the evidence she'd compiled to substantiate her assertions of childhood abuse. "Well, through Sybil's recollections. . . . But a gynecologist Sybil visited in her adulthood told her that because of the internal injuries she would not be able to bear a child so that is certainly testimony to the fact that these injuries took place" (Sinason, 2002). That was the sum total of the evidence that Schreiber was able to cite. She never found anyone who would corroborate Sybil's accounts of her mother's maltreatment. Schreiber had an explanation: "the neighbors were strangely silent, although they knew what was going on. . . . There were teachers in her school who knew she came to school bruised, and mangled. And the local family doctor saw these bruises . . . " (Sinason, 2000).

Why this strange "silence" would have persisted for decades, long after Hattie had died and her daughter had left town, is something that Schreiber fails to explain and the interviewer doesn't press her. But the idea of childhood abuse was central to Schreiber's take on Sybil as it was later in her assessment of Joe Kallinger, the subject of her next book, *The Shoemaker*: "I think the important point to stress . . . is that without the abuse, both physical and emotional, Sybil would never have become a multiple personality and Joe would never have become a murderer" (Sinason, 2000).

Nothing apparently was going to persuade Schreiber or Wilbur that the personalities hadn't formed as a response to these early traumas resulting from her mother's abuse, providing Sybil with a way to escape her pain and humiliation. Wilbur might have had another motivation in turning Sybil against her mother. In my view Wilbur and Schreiber had become the surrogate parents for Sybil and as a consequence they must destroy any competition including her real parents. "I don't need to look for any missing woods to find evidence for my belief." In many of their sessions Wilbur would take Sybil's hands in her own to soothe her. And on one occasion, when Sybil assured her therapist that she was feeling okay—"No, nothing to cry about"—Wilbur begged to differ: "Oh. Yes you have. Dad, money, the neglected you. Only child, and he let you starve" (Schreiber Archive, Box 37).

Obviously it wasn't only Hattie who was a competitor for Sybil's affections. The feeling was mutual. In one of her innumerable letters to Wilbur, Sybil wrote, "When I was in Omaha I had a crush on you like I had on other women in other places."

In one particularly illuminating session in March or April 1960—Wilbur's note on the transcript isn't specific—Wilbur insists that she loves Sybil in a way that her mother never did:

Sybil says that she feels like "nothing." Wilbur indignantly tells her that she's insulting her "heart" and "intelligence." "Sweetie, do you see how?" Sybil says no. "Well, look, I'll tell you how you are insulting me and my intelligence. I love you. Consequently, you cannot be nothing."

"No," Sybil retorts. "You don't love me."

"Why do you insist upon it, dear, you know your mother was wrong? Wrong, wrong, wrong, wrong. Always."

Sybil is unconvinced. "Just look at me, just look at me, that's what you've got to do."

"I love looking at you and I looked at you now for a number of years, I looked at you in Omaha, I know what you looked like. I would look at you in my mind. All those years that you struggled on by yourself, and you came back to me and I looked at you. I look at you every day. I see you. You have just finished telling me that your mother looked at you over and over again, and didn't know you were there, now how the hell can this woman's opinion mean anything to you? When she didn't even see you."

Sybil replies uncertainly. "I don't know, but she is my mother, she is the only one around."

"That, dear heart, was a biological accident."

"There wasn't anyone else there."

"And your mother made damn sure there wasn't."

Sybil evidently feels she needs to defend her mother. "She dressed us, she got us something to eat."

Wilbur is having none of it. "She made damn sure there wasn't anybody else there, too. She made damn sure that you didn't find out for years that mothers were any different than she was."

Not long after that session Wilbur elaborates on her feelings for Sybil, referring to a colleague who asked her, Wilbur, why she was extending herself so much for her patient. ". . . of course, sweetie, you know what you are to me, you know what I have been through in not having children, and you are such a satisfaction to me, as far as I'm concerned, that you should be perfectly able to comprehend, since you are only fifteen years younger than I am, and I haven't had a chance to really be your outright mother." She proceeds to remind Sybil that she wanted to take her on a trip. "You will see things that I don't see," Wilbur says, "and I will see things that you don't, so that we both will see much more."

At that point Sybil again insists that her therapist look at her and tell her what she sees.

Wilbur proceeds to do so, describing "a young woman, with a nice trim little figure" who, however, could "use a little more weight." And she has "well-constructed hands." And, Wilbur says, Sybil dresses well with one exception: her coat, which Wilbur pronounces as "unbecoming." "It cuts you in all places," she says.

And where did that coat come from?

"Daddy bought it for me," Sybil says, but then hastens to assure her therapist that she shortened it. "I did the best I could with it."

Wilbur is eager to placate her. "You did very well. I'm not going to tell you anything that I don't feel is true. . . . Of course, you have small feet and small hands, and I like that" (Schreiber Archive, Box 37).

The relationship that the two formed was clearly one that crossed many lines and one that endured many years after treatment had ended.

The story—at least in the book—has a happy ending. In 1965, Wilbur declares Sybil cured, having "integrated" all of her personalities (just as her once famous precursor Miss Beauchamp had), finished her college degree, became a successful artist, and stopped having blank spells and memory lapses. The subject of the book pronounced herself eminently satisfied with the result. "Every emotion is true," she said. Wilbur agreed: "Every psychiatric fact is accurately represented."

Readers embraced the book with unrestrained passion. Women especially identified with its protagonist. One wrote, "I always wonder where she is now, and if she ever married. My sincere wish for Sybil is that she has peace of mind and a happy life." A California woman weighed in with this comment: "Fascinating study into the inner workings of the mind. Shows how past torments create future mental nightmares. Parents like Hattie and Walter [Schreiber's aliases] do exist daily, and they create a concentration camp atmosphere for a child to grow up in, as did their parents before them."

THE AFTERMATH

The book's astonishing success brought all three principals money and fame even if Sybil herself remained anonymous. Schreiber was now a celebrity at John Jay, more powerful—and more envied—than ever. Publishers began to court her. She was contracted to write a third book entitled *Shoemaker: Portrait of a Psychopath*—for a $600,000 advance—this time focusing on a Philadelphia cobbler named Joseph Kallinger, a serial killer whose crime spree was reputedly the result of child abuse.

Wilbur, too, was now a celebrity in her own right. She practically became a matriarchal cult figure. Adopting the theory that childhood abuse causes multiple personality disorder, some therapists began to talk about "the Wilburian revolution" and "the post-Wilbur paradigm." Her disciples in the psychiatric community would even give copies of *Sybil* to their patients as if it were an instructional manual.

Several years later after its publication in 1973, the book was made into a television movie of the same name starring Sally Field. The story of Sybil reached millions more with the broadcast of this movie, telling the story of DID to laypeople across the United States. It is speculated that with the airing of this movie, the publishing of the book *Sybil*, and the *Diagnostic and Statistical Manual of Mental Disorders IV* (DSM-IV) adoption of the term MPD, rates of diagnoses of MPD skyrocketed in the early 1980s and onward. At one point experts estimated that the number of those affected could constitute one percent of the population, a very large number indeed.

THE BOOK AND THE MOVIE: A COMPARISON

Predictably, the stories told in *Sybil* the book and *Sybil* the movie are somewhat different. The reasons for the contrasting views may be due to theatrical and artistic differences, as well as the author's and director's wishes to portray a specific story. Although few of these changes significantly affected the overall story they shed some light on the different ways in which this tale was spun. Before I describe some of the similarities and differences between the book and the movie I should mention a conversation that I had with the producer of the TV drama that took place many years after the movie was broadcast.

The producer had called me after he'd seen articles about a talk I'd given in San Diego in which I'd disclosed the existence of hitherto unknown tape recordings of conversations between Wilbur and Schreiber. (How I came to discover these tapes and what they revealed will be discussed a little later on.) The producer asked for copies of the transcripts of the tapes. Although he'd already seen the transcripts of the tapes that Flora had provided him several years previously, he'd known nothing about the ones that I'd found. I told him that I would be happy to forward a copy of an article I was writing about the tapes but I made it clear—politely as possible—that I had no intention of supplying him with the transcripts themselves. (Curious readers now have the opportunity to read them in their entirety by turning to Appendix 1.) As we talked he said that he'd exhaustively studied the case before making the movie and had become convinced that his version of Sybil was the "truer" one—more accurate than the book's. The irony was inescapable; everyone involved in the case was claiming Sybil for him- or herself. It was a little like a quarrel over the correct interpretation of Scriptures.

There are many basic similarities between the stories in both the book and the movie. The names and identities of the major characters and events are the same in both versions. Sybil is the pseudonym of the patient who is afflicted with sixteen personalities—which makes sense since she'd become something of a brand name for MPD—and the names given for each of the personalities remain the same in the movie as well. Wilbur is identified by her real name.

The importance and magnitude of Sybil's childhood relationship with her grandmother is poignantly described in both versions of the tale. Sybil, for instance, is shown in ways that suggest an idyllic life that was soon to be shattered; in one scene, for instance, we see her making Christmas ornaments with her beloved grandmother. Later we see her mother tripping her just after she left her grandmother, causing her to fall down the stairs. As this scene illustrates, Hattie comes off no better in the TV version than she did in the book. In both Hattie seizes any opportunity to mistreat the child; in one case, she crushes Sybil's crayons with her feet while her daughter obliviously continues singing to herself and coloring.

The account of the crayon incident comes from Peggy in a session in 1962 for which no month is given. "I was drawing pictures," says the alter, "and I had the paper on the seat of the chair in the kitchen, and I was singing . . . it was a song my daddy taught to me . . . . And I was making a picture . . . . And mama said, 'Stop that infernal noise!' And I said I was singing a song daddy taught me. And she said she didn't care where it was that I learned it . . . and she did like that [starts to cry] my colors—she threw them all over the floor . . . ." A few minutes later she adds that her mother stepped all over them. In her tears she later says, "But I don't want anybody to take the colors away, and take the music back."

Wilbur assures her that Sylvia/Sybil—that is, the dominant personality—will always have "colors" for her.

"But I'm afraid," Peggy says, "It's not like that. It's not all sunshine and colors when you grow up. Mother said there was always thorns in the rose."

Scenes of other traumas occurring outside of the home are also depicted in the same way in both the book and the movie although there are obviously things that cinema can do more effectively—the forced tonsillectomy at Dr. Quinoness's office, for instance, but it differs from the book only insofar as it's more graphic; the incident is the same in both media. Like the book, the TV version vividly—and touchingly—conveys Sybil's desperation as she pleads with a doctor to be saved from her abusive mother.

Most scenes based on the therapeutic sessions are portrayed in relatively the same way in both the film and book versions of Sybil. Wilbur coaxes one of the personalities out from under the piano in the movie the same way she does in the book. Both versions of Sybil also show Wilbur trying to convince Sybil of her ability to play the piano, a talent already exhibited by one of her alter personalities, Vanessa. When Wilbur first comes face-to-face with one of Sybil's alters, Vicky, her response is more or less the same in both versions.

Not surprisingly, given the constraints of time, there are some scenes which appear in the book that are not in the movie. I have identified some important parts of the book that are not shown in the film which I will describe below.

Several pages at the end of Chapter 11 are devoted to the experience of Dr. Wilbur speaking to two alters occupying the body of Sybil at the same time. It is a very interesting scenario that, while described in depth in the book, is not at all mentioned in the movie. I suspect that its absence is simply explained by the inherent difficulty of showing on screen a body being occupied by two separate alters simultaneously and more difficult still to make it clear to audiences that both alters are aware of each other. Indeed, as the book recounts, the two alters were able to converse with each other as well as hold conversations independently with Dr. Wilbur, as if there were simply two separate people sitting beside each other. Even with very creative camerawork and talented actors, this scene may have proven too challenging to achieve in a relatively low budget television movie.

A second scene missing from the movie is Sybil's exposure to the primal scene in which as a very young child she witnesses her parents having sexual intercourse. In fact, the entirety of Chapter 12 is devoted to this traumatic experience; the chapter also intimates at certain incestuous feelings that her father may have harbored for Sybil or that at least was how Sybil seems to have interpreted his behavior.

In a book, as Schreiber well knew, sex sells. But for a primetime movie of the week sex can also be problematic. So it is understandable why the director may have decided to omit the primal scene from the movie. Even if the events being shown are based on reality, a TV movie can't be aired unless it's approved by network censors, and primal scenes generally are usually considered too graphic or taboo to be shown, especially in prime time. Therefore, the director may have thought that it was a lot easier to delete the scene altogether rather than risk a fight with the folks at Standards & Practices.

Similarly erased from the film was any evidence of Hattie Dorsett's paranoid schizophrenia or her catatonic episodes. Chapter 13, for example, describes Hattie's psychotic break that caused Sybil to fear any outburst of laughter but the movie barely alludes to it nor does it trouble to show the troubling scene of Hattie barreling down the snowbank on a child's sled. One can look in vain, in fact, for much exploration of Sybil's mother's illness in the movie version. It is touched on briefly in some places, but not in anywhere as much depth as it is in the book. Time constraints, as I said before, are no doubt one principal reason why these scenes, if they were ever shot, remained on the cutting room floor; the other has to do with the very focus of the movie. The movie is about Sybil, not about her mother, and so the director decided to relegate Hattie to the sidelines in favor of her daughter even at the cost of depriving viewers of an explanation for why Sybil developed her dissociation.

By the same token, the problems of living with DID are also not explored in the movie. Chapter 27 explains the difficulties of many personalities being forced to share the same body, as well as the problems the personalities encounter when they are obliged to deal with other people. The problems these personalities encounter are as basic as choosing what clothes to wear and what food to eat, since each personality has different preferences. The movie leaves such mundane but vexing details to the imagination, probably because they didn't appear especially relevant to the story of Sybil's disorder and treatment. Those people with DID or their family members could presumably turn to other sources for pointers about how to address these problems; the movie had other business to tend to.

In the book Wilbur puts Sybil through an age progression process on the younger of Sybil's alters. Using hypnosis, Dr. Wilbur encourages the very young alters to "grow up" to the age of the other alters, which are closer in age to Sybil herself. Chapter 29 describes how the therapist used this method as a means to confront the traumas that were keeping the alters "stuck" at the ages they were when the experiences originally happened. The age progression, however, is absent in the movie. Most likely, the scene was omitted from the movie because it is a rather insignificant part of the therapeutic process to the layperson, although to someone in the field of psychology it bears further analysis.

Sybil's two male alters are barely touched upon in the movie version. The male alters embodied Sybil's own confused sexuality because after all, they were male but they were living within the body of a female. They had mixed feelings about females and they were afraid that once they were integrated they would lose their masculinity. Their main concern was that they would not "be able to give a girl a baby" and therefore assert their masculinity. The movie doesn't address the problems confronting the male alters, possibly because the director wanted to avoid a touchy, if tantalizing, issue. Focusing on the other female alters instead was a safer bet.

Sybil's relationship with her father is also given fairly short shrift in the movie; there are only two scenes in which her father is even present. He is portrayed as aloof and unconcerned while Hattie is the ogre. The depiction of him in the book is little different, but he is fleshed out more. In the book we learn that Sybil has had a dream about her father and some attention is devoted to the analysis of her relationship with him. His death, which she discussed in therapy, goes unnoted in the movie. Of course, with the primal scene gone, the movie never touches upon intimations of repressed incestuous longing that were raised in the book. However intriguing her relationship with her father might be, it is understandable why the movie would marginalize him and concentrate on his daughter's illness and treatment.

In addition, there are several events and scenes that appear in the book and the movie but are portrayed very differently. I will discuss these discrepancies briefly and then offer a hypothesis to account for why they might have occurred.

One example is Dr. Wilbur's first meeting with Peggy. In the book, it occurs during a therapy session during which Peggy makes reference to the personalities, calling them "the people." She then expresses her need to break glass, as well as her fear of music. She also talks about her life in Willow Corners as if she was still there even though Sybil was living in New York. Peggy discusses the same subjects and voices the same fears in the movie, too, but not at a therapeutic session. Instead the scene occurs in a hotel room when Sybil is on the verge of a suicide attempt. The difference here may be one of dramatic license. While it's true that suicide attempts are mentioned in the book, it is likely that the director combined those scenes with Wilbur's first encounter with Peggy both to save time as well as to draw attention to the changing of alters and the drastic difference between the alter Peggy and Sybil herself.

A second scene that is treated differently in the book and the movie is the trip Wilbur and Sybil take to the country where it is hoped Sybil will be inspired to paint. In the book, this incident happens fairly early in the course of the therapy and it is not described with very much detail; we learn simply that the two went on an excursion in order to help Sybil work on her art. In the movie, by contrast, this scene doesn't occur until the very end of the movie. It is also a very integral part of the film, because Sybil's renewed interest in her art takes place just before Wilbur uses hypnosis one last time to integrate all of her personalities. Again, the major difference between these two portrayals may be explained by the need to save time by combining scenes and perhaps more importantly to underline Sybil's "rebirth" by means of her art after her alters have been successfully integrated.

The movie and the book also part ways in their depiction of a confrontation between Wilbur and one of Sybil's more temperamental alters—that would be Vicky—when Wilbur probes her to find out what she knows about the other alters. In both media, Wilbur tries to reason with Vicky, making the case that although the personalities may have independent minds and personalities, they still share the same body and must, on some level, be aware of each other's presence. Vicky responds the same way in both versions, too, finding herself unable to admit that the personalities are part of the same person and therefore part of herself. The difference again is where the scene takes place. In the book Vicky resists Wilbur's argument within the context of therapy, whereas in the movie, this happens when Wilbur takes Vicky to her house and makes her lunch. The movie version is clearly more intimate. By setting the scene at Wilbur's home an intimate relationship is established between patient and therapist. This way the viewer knows that even if disagreements arise during a therapeutic session their personal relationship is not in any jeopardy.

Both the book and movie show Sybil confronting her fears that her therapy hasn't been productive. These fears express themselves in two ways. In the book, Sybil sees her "multiplicity" as unnatural and her personalities as a type of possession. She doesn't feel that she is getting well after three years of therapy, especially since her personalities are monopolizing even more of her time now than they had been previously. In the movie, Sybil goes further; she not only states that she thinks the therapy is going nowhere, but she declares that she has fabricated her personalities *and* her stories of abuse. She accuses Wilbur of lying to her. This confession happens in the book, too, but with far less drama—in the form of a letter rather than occurring in the middle of a session and it comes much later on. At no point in the text does Sybil level the accusations at Wilbur that she does in the movie. Again I suspect that the director took the direction he did to save time by combining scenes and to heighten the emotional impact.

The scene in which Wilbur must tell Sybil that she is a multiple personality is also portrayed very differently in the book than in the film. In the book, Wilbur asks Sybil to listen to the tape recordings of their sessions together and to get a better sense of the other personalities by listening to what they have to say. Wilbur has already explained to Sybil that she is a multiple and tried to impress upon her exactly what that means, and now she feels that Sybil is at a point in therapy where she needs to "confront" the other personalities in a more active way. After some coaxing, Wilbur persuades Sybil to listen to some of the tapes. As she listens, Sybil is shocked to hear Peggy's voice because it sounds to her so much like the voice of her mother. That's how the scene plays in the book. In the movie, though, Wilbur has an entirely different motive in persuading Sybil to listen to the tapes. In the movie it's to show Sybil that one of her personalities, Vanessa, can play the piano. Wilbur then accidentally fast-forwards the tape too far and plays an excerpt in which Peggy speaks. As soon as she hears Peggy's voice, Sybil mistakes it for the voice of her mother just as she does in the book and becomes so panicked and traumatized that she dissociates into a preverbal, infantile personality, presumably Ruthie. That's not what happens in the book. I suspect that once again the director made the changes to conserve time and to reveal—more dramatically—the existence of a personality that neither Sybil nor the viewer had been introduced to before.

Then there is Sybil's dream about the cat and the kittens. In both instances, the dream is the same, more or less. In the book, the dream starts off with Sybil riding a subway train, which stops because of some construction that her father is doing. The train cannot continue until her father finishes his project. Then Sybil finds herself inside of a warehouse where she discovers a decapitated cat and some abandoned, starved kittens. After disposing of the dead cat, she takes the kittens home to care for them. In the movie, Sybil also encounters the kittens and the dead cat, but she finds them in a field and in a macabre twist, is subsequently chased by the dead cat, desperate to save herself and the kittens cradled in her arms. Dramatic license surely must have played a part in making the dream so horrific. In the book Wilbur interprets the dream in terms of what it says about Sybil's life and the progress she is making in her therapy. The movie is much less subtle; the cat is Sybil's mother (even dead, a powerful presence), and Sybil must run as fast as she can from her to save herself; the kittens merely symbolize her own feelings of helplessness.

The book and movie also differ in other respects where Hattie is concerned. In the book, Sybil grapples with her feelings about her mother in a meeting with Wilbur. Wilbur notices that Sybil seems a bit depressed and hazards the opinion that it may be because Sybil hasn't dealt with her feelings toward her mother. Once Sybil is able to do so, we, the readers, discover she can actually verbalize the hate and anger she feels toward her mother and as a result, is able to heal more fully and cope better with her emotions. In the movie, the moment of confrontation is put off until Sybil "relives" the episodes of sexual abuse that she dredges up from her childhood in her therapy sessions. This confrontation does not occur until near the end of the film. The differences here I suspect are due mostly to a matter of artistic license and choice.

Sybil's suicide attempt is also given a different spin in the movie as compared to the book. In the TV version, Vicky calls Wilbur just after they first meet and warns of Sybil's wish to die, recalling a previous attempt to throw herself out of the window of a hotel. Later on in the film version, Sybil again threatens suicide through one of her alters, Marcia, by threatening to jump from the roof of her apartment building. In the book, however, Sybil's suicide attempt doesn't occur until she has been in therapy with Wilbur for some time. In the book, though, Vicky calls Wilbur and implores her to help talk Sybil down before she can throw herself into the Hudson River. Evidently a leap from a building was seen as a more threatening scenario than a short dive off a dock. Once again, the differences are probably due to the time constraints of the film, dramatic impact, and the need to introduce an alter without going through the trouble of an introduction.

Perhaps the most important difference between the versions is the way in which the two media depict the process of integration that Sybil undergoes. In the film, Wilbur takes Sybil into the countryside to paint, and while on their trip, she puts Sybil under hypnosis and completes the process of integration by introducing Sybil to each of her alters one by one. As she meets her alters, Sybil is able to accept them and integrate them into her own personality with the result that she eventually forms one whole personality in the end. The film speeds up the process, for one thing, and takes it out of Wilbur's office where it really happened.

In the book, the integration process is done more slowly as well. Sybil meets one personality at a time as opposed to all of them emerging in a single session. As she meets one, she is able to adapt to that personality and fully integrate it before moving on to the next. As the integration process progressed, the personalities began an integration of their own, maintaining their separate identities but "joining forces" of a sort as they grew closer to becoming one. In both versions, Wilbur begins by integrating the younger personalities. Again, the discrepancies between the two stories are likely due only to time constraints and the demands of storytelling and do not detract from the story as a whole.

There are a few differences, too, in the way in which Sybil's relationships with men are treated. In the movie, Sybil has a romantic involvement with her neighbor who is named Richard Lumis. The two of them date off and on but eventually break up when Richard finds out about Sybil's personalities and is unable to handle the stress of the situation. In the book, Sybil dates a man named Ramon. They get along well—to a point. When Ramon proposes to Sybil, she rebuffs him and he ends the relationship without ever knowing about her illness. The details about the relationship with Richard/Ramon are only incidental to the story, but they illustrate the difficulties that can affect people with dissociative identity disorder. Because this man played such a minor role in Sybil's life the differences in the way they are portrayed have little significance.

There is one further discrepancy between versions that should be cited which relates to one of Sybil's personalities called memorably The Blonde. In the movie The Blonde doesn't make an appearance at all, nor is she ever referred to, even when all the personalities are being integrated in the climactic scene. In the book, The Blonde is mentioned toward the end, when the integration process begins. The Blonde seems to be an iatrogenically created personality. This means that the personality was created as a result of the therapeutic process. While integration was taking place, Sybil may have felt increased anxiety and stress because she feared that the relationship between her and Dr. Wilbur was ending. Therefore, The Blonde arose as a sort of block to ending the therapeutic process. That's because the appearance of another personality would have to be dealt with in therapy and would therefore stretch it out; it was, in effect, a delaying tactic. But to convey the significance of The Blonde's last-minute appearance to a viewing audience was probably thought to be too difficult and a needless complication.

How a book and a movie depict the same events almost invariably differs and that's true for fiction as much as nonfiction; there are technical factors—time, for one—and cultural factors–network censors, the FCC—and there are creative differences. These differences emerge in almost every book that Hollywood brings to the big screen. However, in a case so fraught with emotion, so shrouded in confusion, and so subject to interpretation, the differences between book and TV movie take on greater importance. The movie re-created Sybil just as Schreiber did in her book and Wilbur did before her in her sessions; each version had something interesting, however suspect, to say about Sybil; even the real-life Sybil, Shirley Mason, didn't have an exclusive right to her story. On the contrary, she had no one story, she had many, depending on which personality was telling it. The closer we try to get to the real Sybil, the more we strive for the real story, the more confused we become. How Sybil was created, how Shirley Mason was transformed into Sybil, is the subject of our next chapter.

7

The Myth Explodes

Who Is Sybil and What Is She?

Who's the real me
Am I a person
One, Two, or Three
Who can it be?
Bring on the clowns.
Am I really sick
A dissociated trick
Go into therapy—Get in real quick
Let in the clowns.
Was I abused
False memory confused
Hypnosis Suggestion Misused
Litigation Pursues. . . .

    BUG OFF THOSE CLOWNS

THE MULTIPLICITY OF MULTIPLES

In the writing of *Sybil*, Schreiber had made a bid for fame and the kind of immortality that a seminal book can sometimes grant its author. Instead her star faded while—ironically—that of her subject shone ever brighter. In 1980, MPD advocates successfully waged a battle to get the syndrome into the psychiatric bible, the DSM (*Diagnostic and Statistical Manual of Mental Disorders*), as an important disorder.

    It may be helpful to see exactly how the DSM-IV defines the disorder. MPD/DID, the DSM states, is defined by three characteristics: at least two or more distinct personalities existing within an individual with each personality being dominant (in control) at different times. The individual's behavior is determined by the personality that is dominant at any given time. Each of the separate distinct personalities within the individual is complex and integrated with its own behavior patterns, social relationships, and name. The DSM-IV also notes that the patient often suffers from amnesia insofar as he or she has an inability to remember important personal information or certain blocks of time. The diagnostic bible offers a hypothesis about the formation of the disorder that Wilbur and Schreiber adopted—that MPD/DID "is caused by extreme and prolonged trauma in childhood, such as childhood physical and/or sexual abuse." The DSM-IV goes on to say that "according to experts, the original personality of the person is often unaware of the other distinct alternative personalities."

Far from expressing skepticism about *Sybil* or questioning the credibility of its authors, many reputable psychologists were eager to embrace its conclusions. John and Rhonda Johnson, for example, published a book called *We, the Divided Self*, in which they not only affirmed the accuracy of the case as described in *Sybil*, but also claimed that it was in a league with its two famous predecessors, *The Three Faces of Eve* and Morton Prince's *Dissociation of Personality*, cases which they considered of similar credibility (Watkins and Johnson, 1982). To bolster their argument further they larded their book with protocols taken from psychiatric therapeutic interviews. Some advocates of MPD later had occasion to repudiate their earlier views. A retired psychiatrist, Ralph Allison, sent me a letter in which he admitted that after careful review of Sybil's case and others (including Eve's), he'd come to the conclusion that they weren't "bona fide" cases of MPD and that the purported alters were actually "Internalized Imaginary Companions." (See Appendix 4.)

It didn't take long for the number of cases and therapists specializing in the treatment to escalate as well. And the number of personalities that victims claimed grew in a similar fashion.

Indeed, a leading American MPD therapist, Richard Kluft, maintained that he identified over 1000 personalities in one individual. Nor were the newly uncovered personalities (or alters) always necessarily human. Some were identified as cats, dogs, stuffed animals, and, in one case, a lobster. By the late 1980s, MPD had become a staple of daytime TV talk shows. Roseanne famously announced that, because of abuse in her childhood—a claim her parents flatly denied—she now had 21 alters among them Bambi and Piggy. In 1991 a book was published which actually purported to help readers who'd been diagnosed as multiples. The authors urged both patients and their therapists to write about their experiences. These writings could take many forms including poetry. The authors recommended this particular method so that "readers who are diagnosed with MPD themselves may choose to think of these writings as a measuring stick against which they can compare and contrast their own experiences." This exercise, the authors contended, could have an added benefit: "Spouses and friends may benefit from the sense of community found in these pages" (Cohen, 1991).

More recently the disorder has gained a foothold on the Internet where support groups have sprung up on sites with names like Divided Hearts, Shattered Selves, and Crazy People Incorporated. Several recent books have discussed this problem from different points of view.

THE FORGOTTEN TAPES

Every couple of weeks Herb Spiegel, a distinguished psychiatrist, and I get together for lunch. We generally talk about our work and colleagues. But one particular lunch—in May 1997—sticks out in my mind. Spiegel asked me if I would mind taking a look at the proofs of an interview he'd given to a writer for the *New York Review of Books*. The interview focused on Spiegel's association with Sybil, the most famous multiple personality disorder case of all time. This came as a shock to me. At no time in the history of our relationship had Spiegel ever so much as hinted to me that he knew Sybil. "That was because you never asked," Spiegel told me. There was another connection: I knew Flora Schreiber—we had been colleagues at John Jay for years until her death. It was then that I remembered the tapes Schreiber had given me long ago. The tapes held confidential conversations between Sybil and her psychiatrist, Dr. Cornelia Wilbur. But I hadn't listened to them in years, no one had. For that matter, no one knew that they existed. I had even forgotten about them. But I wondered whether they would cast light on a case that had set in motion a cascade of events that would forever change the social fabric of America. Or to put it another way: the tapes, if they were what I thought they were, could prove a bombshell.

The question uppermost in my mind when I walked out of Spiegel's office that day was whether after a quarter of a century I still had the tapes. Although I found that I'd discarded most of them, a thorough search produced two that had somehow survived numerous spring cleanings. Much later I was to find a two-hour tape of a therapeutic session between Sybil and Wilbur as well.

When I began to listen to the first tape, I failed to recognize who was speaking. Was it Wilbur I was hearing? Or was it the mysterious Sybil herself? Suddenly a gravelly voice filled the room. It was unmistakable. I knew at once that it was Flora Schreiber.

CHAPTER 7

FLORA

When I first met Flora I was doing research on language and speech at the New York Psychiatric Institute. In the early Seventies I was invited to assume a full-time teaching position at John Jay College of the City University of New York. It wasn't long after taking up my teaching duties at John Jay that I came into contact with Flora Schreiber who was head of public relations for the school. A clever, talented writer, with a pop book on child development and language under her belt, she inspired admiration, envy, and resentment. As I recall, she could put over the charm but she could be a vicious bitch when she lost her temper. A frequent contributor to *Science Digest* and other magazines, she was an endless self-promoter. In her PR bio, which she made sure to send to anyone who might be of help to her, she claimed that she had been "a friend of every President since [Franklin D. Roosevelt] and . . . most of their families." (A copy of her bio can be found in Appendix 4.)

In 1972, Schreiber approached me with a bag full of cassette tapes. The tapes, she said, were recordings of therapeutic sessions. She was hoping to use them for some research she was pursuing. At the time I was studying the connections between mental illness and on–off speech patterns. The object was to see whether the vocalization of a person measured by computer could be used to assess mental health. She described it as an ideal research project for me. She knew I was also working at the Columbia University New York State Psychiatric Institute and that it had a good reputation and the research journal might publish it. I had no inkling that she was writing the book (*Sybil*) before she came to me. We weren't going to analyze what was said on the tapes Flora gave to me. We were simply going to analyze speech patterns. The experiment never got off the ground. I played the tapes but I told her no, it was impossible to comprehend because of the noise. To the best of my knowledge, she never found any scientific journal to publish the paper. Nor did she ever ask for the tapes back, saying that she'd already transcribed them all.

The publication of *Sybil* marked the height of Schreiber's career. Her next book failed to stir anything like the sensation that its predecessor had. And with a change in administrations at John Jay her influence began to wane. She was pushed back into the department to teach. She died in the late 1980s. That was the last I heard of her. Her death had no impact on me. Flora was a potentially dangerous person in my eyes—hysterics like her are always "potentially dangerous."

AN ANALYST ON PARK AVENUE

We know that Cornelia Wilbur first got in touch with Schreiber in 1962. Soon afterwards she introduced the writer to Sybil. To Schreiber, Sybil seemed constrained and remote, but Schreiber says she attributed her behavior to her illness. What made Schreiber decide to pursue the project was Wilbur's reputation as "an analyst with a large Park Avenue practice." And the therapist was willing to provide a wealth of raw material for Schreiber to draw on—a compilation of case notes taken from no less than 2354 therapeutic sessions that went back almost a decade. Because Sybil was a talented artist (and bright too, with an alleged 174 IQ) Schreiber conceived of the story as a case history that would illuminate "the role of the unconscious mind in creativity."

As I listened to the two tapes a quarter of a century later, I realized that these tapes were not recordings of therapeutic sessions at all as I had assumed. The two tapes I'd saved contained instead a recording of a rambling conversation between Schreiber and Wilbur about the book that would become *Sybil*. How would they construct it? What did they want to establish in the readers' minds? There was Wilbur recalling the therapeutic sessions: "She introduced me to all the personalities.... Uh, you did do that on the [sodium] pentothal?" And there was Wilbur explaining how surprised she was to realize that she might be dealing with several personalities as recounted in a conversation with Schreiber. "So I said hello, and I . . . as I recall it I said hello, Sylvia, and she said, I'm not Sylvia, I'm Peggy, don't you know the difference? That was the first time I realized that she perceived herself differently. And I think I evaded the answer, or said I didn't notice, something like that." Later she admits to Schreiber that she suspected she was dealing with a dual personality. "I said to myself, Oh, my God, I bet she is like the Beauchamp case, more than one person" (Schreiber Archive, Box 37).

From all that I have discovered, I concluded that the three women—Wilbur, Schreiber, and Sybil—are responsible for shaping the modern myth of multiple personality disorder. A psychological oddity, so bizarre and rare that it did not merit much publicity in most textbooks before 1973, multiple personality disorder had acquired a sudden respectability and acceptance. And it wasn't a disorder that was just limited to America. "MPD is being exported from the US as effectively as Diet Coke and the Gap," wrote social critic Elaine Showalter in *The* (London) *Observer*.

THE CRIMINAL ILLUSION OF AN EXPERIMENTAL PRINCIPLE: THE PRIMAL SCENE

Freud may have invented the notion of the primal scene but it was Wilbur's inspiration to appropriate it to account for Sybil's condition. On the tape in my possession the therapist describes to Schreiber just how important she believes "the concept is to the narrative. And this business of the primal scene. And [Sybil] being forced to sleep in the same bedroom with her fucking parents." "They screwed in front of her," Schreiber chimes in, her voice shaking in anger. "She could see because her crib was here, the window was there, and the streetlight was right outside. She could see her father having an erection and putting it in her mother 's vagina . . . Did you know that?"

The construction of the primal scene in the book in particular and the depiction of sex in general was a matter of some concern for the collaborators as we can see from this exchange between the two:

> SCHREIBER: Because you actually you have a lot of sex in the parental objects?
> WILBUR: Too much!
> SCHREIBER: Quite a lot of it from the readers' point of view.
> WILBUR: Yes.
> SCHREIBER: And some of it is pretty sexual, too.
> WILBUR: Yes. Like mother playing horsey with the little kids, and sticking her fingers in the vaginas, and carrying on the other sexual things with the little young girls, etc.
> SCHREIBER: Yes, oh, my, . . . egh. Well, and also the whole primal scene, that is sex. I'm thinking in terms of the sex view in relationship with Sylvia with her father. You are a big girl you can't sit in my lap. There may have been a sexual relationship then.
> WILBUR: Yes, and this business of her not being able to do his feet. Well, you've got that in there. (Schreiber Archive, Box 37)

Taking their cue from Wilbur, her disciples made childhood sexual abuse into the cornerstone of a diagnosis on MPD. Almost all multiples have been female—almost nine out of every ten—and their stories reflect Sybil's influence. Each story follows a typical scenario: A distressed adult woman seeking help for depression or other psychological problems enters therapy in which hypnosis usually plays a part, then seemingly develops an alternative personality, then another and another, all with different characteristics than her own "host" personality. The act of splintering into so many different selves is viewed by MPD therapists as a mechanism to repress the memories of childhood sexual abuse. These therapists assume that the more severe the sexual abuse, the more personalities will be created. About 25 percent of MPD patients will go on to develop memories of satanic rituals, involving large numbers of devil worshippers, child sacrifice, and cannibalism. As many as 50 percent will begin to cut, burn, or mutilate themselves. It is under hypnosis that the therapist is able to finally evoke the painful memories of abuse in order to pave the way for an eventual cure. Ultimately—in theory anyway—all the alters are integrated into one functioning person.

Sybil, it became obvious, just didn't make multiple personality disorder a fashionable illness in North America and abroad. With its emphasis on childhood sexual abuse it also spawned two other related obsessive phenomena: one was the belief that people were being poisoned by buried memories and the other was that only by reawakening those memories through hypnosis was recovery possible. Together, the three phenomena constitute what I term "a trinity of affinity."

THE TRINITY OF AFFINITY

In 1994, MPD was renamed Dissociative Identity Disorder (DID). (Dissociation refers to a disruption in the various parts of mental functioning that constitutes consciousness: forming and holding memories, assimilating sensory impressions, making sense of them, and maintaining a sense of one's identity.) By stressing the dissociation experienced by the person rather than the splitting of personality, the name change in the DSM reflected a groundswell of critical response to the whole idea of multiple personality disorder. Longtime opponents of the MPD movement—for that was what it had become—saw a decline to what they termed "a psychiatric craze." "Ignore the alters!" urged Dr. Paul McHugh of Johns Hopkins Hospital, calling for an end to MPD treatment. "We've just seen the rise and fall of a fad. And call it a fad for that's what it was. The multiples had in effect been producing a demand for therapists who in turn overproduced personalities in their vulnerable patients" (McHugh, 1999). "The problem with dissociation, as with so many other purported unconscious mental processes, is that it cannot be discerned and studied apart from the behaviors it is intended to explain," McHugh wrote in an article in *Commentary*. "What generates and sustains these behaviors is the power of their effect on others, whether doctors or onlookers. But once attention has been transferred from the behavior itself to the imagined mental state of the patient exhibiting it, a diagnosis—dissociation—can be triumphantly involved through reasoning that goes in circles. . . . MPD is, in fact, a form of hysteria—that is, a behavior that mimics physical or psychiatric disorder. . . . It was the 1973 best-selling book (and later TV movie) *Sybil,* describing an abused patient with sixteen personalities, that launched the whole copycat epidemic of MPD. . . . Although the MPD epidemic is now subsiding, the 'disease' itself remains enshrined in the DSM-III and DSM-IV, a textbook case of an alleged disorder whose identification is based entirely on appearance and then sustained as valid by its listing in DSM."

As McHugh points out, a fad can be dangerous. People who sought treatment found to their dismay that the "cures" were in many ways far worse the "disease" they were supposed to have. It appeared that in many instances these MPD specialists were actually making troubled people sicker so that they could continue to treat them. "Therapists influenced by Sybil are 'unconscious con artists,'" in Herbert Spiegel's words, "working at 'memory mills,' diagnosing MPD in patients, and producing 'phony memories'. They are taking highly malleable, suggestible persona, who might have a dissociative disorder and molding them into acting out a thesis that they are putting upon them."

How does this "molding" happen?

Most often it is achieved by the use—rather the abuse—of hypnosis.

Hypnosis is not a one-way street: its success, however you wish to measure it, is based on the degree of interaction and cooperation between the two individuals involved. So obviously trust and motivation—on the part of both participants—is also an essential factor in what the results will be.

WHAT HYPNOSIS IS—AND IS NOT

Hypnosis is widely misunderstood, no doubt in large part because of the myths perpetrated in movies and other popular media. How many times have we watched a young man or woman being put "under" as their eyes follow the metronomic swing of a pocket watch? Hypnosis has often been derided as "not real" because it takes place "in the mind." It doesn't fit the American medical model, which is mechanical and reductionist. Hypnosis, in other words, seems like just so much hocus-pocus, without any physiological basis. But hypnosis can be a valuable therapeutic tool. I know of no better explicator of the phenomenon than my colleague Herbert Spiegel.

First we should make clear what hypnosis entails. According to Spiegel, hypnosis can be defined as "a psychophysiological set characterized by a complex perceptual capacity for attentive, receptive concentration with parallel awareness. That is, the subject can be aware of a perceptual set and, at the same time, feel along side that set" (H. Spiegel, 1981). Hypnosis is also frequently, though not universally, a part of the hypnotic phenomenon. In a paper on the subject of hypnosis and amnesia, David Spiegel points out why disorders of identity, related to dissociation and spontaneous self-hypnotic phenomena, are so important. "We experience ourselves all the time doing things that are automatic and seem involuntary," he writes, "but we interweave experience with sufficient episodic memory that are identified with a unified conception of self. The problem is not the occurrence of identity dissociation, but rather the failure to achieve the usual overriding sense of unity of self" (D. Spiegel, 1998).

Now let's clarify what hypnosis is *not*.

Hypnosis is not sleep, Herbert Spiegel points out in his essay "Hypnosis: Myth and Reality" (Spiegel, 1981). On the contrary, it is the *opposite* of sleep—"a form of intense receptive integrated concentration." As evidence, David Spiegel cites the fact that the EEG patterns typical of sleep are nowhere present in the brain under hypnosis. A person doesn't "concentrate" in a dream state, after all.

Hypnosis is not projected on the patient; in fact, hypnotizability is an innate capacity that we all share to one degree or another; all the therapist is doing when he hypnotizes a subject is tapping into that capacity.

Hypnotizability is often associated with mentally ill people, but nothing could be further from the truth, David Spiegel points out. As it turns out, many individuals who do suffer from severe mental illness, neurological deficits, or severe character disorders are not easily hypnotized at all because they are incapable of concentration.

Another popular misconception is that hypnosis can only occur when the doctor decides on it—when, in effect, he has the patient fix his eyes on the watch—but in fact, hypnosis can often occur spontaneously, especially in challenging situations or under duress.

Many people believe that hypnosis is dangerous (recall the controversy that Mesmer caused) mainly because they are under the impression that subjects can be easily manipulated while they are in a trance. Here again David Spiegel makes an important distinction; while it's true that hypnosis can be used mischievously if it's used by someone with malicious intent (or by someone who doesn't know what he's doing), in itself hypnosis is not dangerous; it is a tool and as such is neutral.

At the same while a therapeutic tool, it is not a therapy per se; "at most it creates a receptive matrix in which a treatment strategy can be used with a high leverage effect" (Spiegel, 1981).

Studies on many MPD/DID cases have found that hypnosis has mixed results. As with "normal" subjects, the efficacy of hypnosis depends to a great degree on the cooperation of the patient. People with MPD/DID can prove quite resistant to hypnosis and a small minority of them require formal induction on each occasion. A few, on the other hand, seem very malleable.

About five percent of the U.S. population as a whole is extremely susceptible to hypnosis. Sybil was among them. We know this because Herbert Spiegel hypnotized her when she came to him for treatment. He was initially introduced to her by Wilbur. "I got a call from her one day. . . . She asked me if I could examine the patient [Sybil] and help her clarify the diagnosis. . . ." At the time Wilbur suspected that Sybil might be schizophrenic. Spiegel agreed.

He didn't think she was schizophrenic, though she was suggestible to an extreme. "I examined Sybil and discovered that she was highly hypnotizable." In fact, she was in a hypnotizable elite, perhaps the top one or two percent. Because of her rare ability Spiegel began to use her in research studies. "She had amnesia that you could command her to have for certain events, she had post-hypnotic sensory motor alterations on command, you could stimulate hallucinations with her, which only the hypnotic virtuosos could achieve." Curiously, though, he had no success in experiments on age regression with her, which is surprising in light of the importance age regression under hypnosis plays in Wilbur's account of how she succeeded in integrating Sybil's personalities.

At this point in Sybil's treatment Spiegel admits that he had no idea that the patient, much less her therapist, believed that she had multiple personalities until one day in the middle of a hypnotic session, Spiegel recounts, Sybil burst out, "'Well, do you want me to be Helen?' And I said, 'What do you mean?' And she said, 'Well, when I'm with Dr. Wilbur she wants me to be Helen.' I said, 'Who's Helen?' 'Well, that's the name Dr. Wilbur gave me for this feeling.'" It turned out that any of her sixteen personalities only appeared after Wilbur began to use hypnosis. Sybil's mother, Spiegel maintains, might have been a schizophrenic, but he discovered no evidence of sexual abuse by her or Sybil's father. In other words, there was probably no primal scene.

Obviously Wilbur took issue with Spiegel's position. In a conversation with Schreiber she noted, "Spiegel, who worked on the case, said he met about seven of the personalities but he refuses to accept the concept of multiplicity, which I feel is a contradiction. But he said he felt she was 'a brilliant hysteric.'"

As I noted above, although hypnosis is neutral, effective or not depending on how it is used, in the wrong hands, it can be badly used or worse, used to exploit the subject. It is unlikely that Wilbur had any malicious intent in treating Sybil but before we go on it might prove worthwhile to note some of the problems that can arise when hypnosis is misused.

For instance, hypnosis can help remove a symptom from a subject without planting another one in its place. However, there are instances, Spiegel cautions, when a new symptom will develop. That can happen if the doctor predicts that a new symptom will occur or if the patient directly or indirectly believes that he is expected to acquire a new symptom. A doctor has to take special precautions with cases of MPD/DID. The prevailing personality must agree under hypnosis not to interfere with the alters. Even if this takes place, stalemates in treatment can still result because of intrusion of alters that the therapist was unaware of. Richard Kluft in his paper, "Varieties of Hypnotic Intervention in the Treatment of Multiple Personality," published in *The American Journal of Clinical Hypnosis*, cites other examples of cases that go terribly awry when the doctor bungles the hypnosis. In one case a therapist focused on a sexually oriented personality in a female patient who resented her marriage and used hypnotic techniques to suppress personalities who expressed anger or disagreed with him which compromised the treatment. In a second case, a therapist tried to use hypnosis to approach an alter who was perceived as a threat to the then-dominant personality; he persisted despite signs of mounting anxiety on the subject's part until she bolted from his office. The third case Kluft cites turned out to be even more of a catastrophe. A therapist was using hypnosis for first time on a patient known to have three personalities; rather than integrate the personalities, the therapist made the problem worse. He tried seven procedures, each of which led to a severe regression with cascades of alters emerging until the patient had become severely agitated and had fragmented into no less than 21 ego states (she was later successfully treated and integrated) (Kluft, 1982).

Therapists have to be especially careful when treating the most suggestible personalities, such as Sybil. Sybil was a Grade 5 personality (using a scale created by Herbert Spiegel). It is estimated that about five to ten percent of the population occupies this extreme end of the scale. Grade 5's characteristically have the capacity to shift immediately and almost imperceptibly from normal consciousness into a deep hypnotic trance. For these individuals memories can seem extremely real even after returning to consciousness; moreover, the subjects often recount these "memories" with as much emotion as they would if the events really happened. At one point Wilbur told Schreiber that she believed that Sybil only knew her personalities as if in a dream; after listening to the other personalities on a tape she would recognize them because "it felt right."

"Hypnotic concentration," David Spiegel states, "is analogous to looking through a telescope lens in a camera." What he means is that while the view is detailed, the field of vision is narrow. The hypnotized person undergoes a process called absorption, which is defined as "a tendency to become fully involved in a perceptual imaginative or ideational experience" (Tellegen, 1981; Tellegen and Atkinson, 1974). The subject's "cognitive resources are fully allocated to the central task, with little in the way of distraction." Any information that is beyond the field of vision simply doesn't register on the consciousness, or, as Spiegel puts it, the information becomes "dissociated from conscious awareness" (Spiegel, 1990). In that sense, hypnosis can be understood as a controlled and structured dissociative episode (Nemiah, 1985; Spiegel and Spiegel, 2004). So, in effect, a dissociated state in which various personalities are manifest (e.g., a state of MPD/DID) can often be accessed in another dissociated state (e.g., hypnosis). Spiegel observes that individuals who are especially prone to absorption tend to be more highly hypnotizable than those subjects who are not engaged so totally in their experiences (Spiegel, editor, 1994).

Therapists who are not aware of just how suggestible these Grade 5's are can create a good deal of mischief by buying into the subject's illogical or contradictory material and even planting suggestions into their memory systems. "[I]t is quite possible to so contaminate the memory of the subject that he confuses the hypnotic implantations with his own knowledge," Herb Spiegel writes. "Then by so fusing them, he cannot tell one from the other."

By the same token, the Grade 5 will believe the suggestions are real, establishing a treacherous bond between therapist and subject based on a system built on quicksand. Herbert Spiegel has referred to this phenomenon as the "honest liar" syndrome. In his view, "such individuals are saying what they genuinely believe to be true, despite the fact that they are responding to implanted memories. These people make good witnesses because they are sincere and believable . . . ."

There is only one trouble, Spiegel adds: "they are entirely wrong." (See H. Spiegel and D. Spiegel, *Trance and Treatment: Clinical Use of Hypnosis*, 2004, p. 414 where the authors refer to the incident and call attention to my disclosure of a therapeutic tape clearly demonstrating Wilbur giving instructions to her patient.)

Suggestibility works especially well with subjects who are eager to please their therapist, more so if they feel they've been neglected by their mother and look upon the therapist as a surrogate. Therapists may reward their patients with praise for elaborating on or dredging up further such memories.

"Phenomena analogous to and bearing dramatic but superficial resemblance to clinical multiple personality can be elicited experimentally or in a clinical situation if one tries to do so or makes technical errors," states Richard Kluft in his paper "Varieties of Hypnotic Intervention in the Treatment of Multiple Personality" (Kluft, Notes 7 and 8). He adds: "Furthermore the phenomena . . . can be elicited by hypnosis and overinterpreted as multiple personality" (Kluft, Note 7).

The patient cannot be viewed as the innocent victim, though, simply soaking up suggestions and ideas that the therapist, unwittingly or not, has implanted. On the contrary, the patient may do everything in her power to sustain the relationship and if that means buying what the therapist is selling, so be it. For instance, in her famous letter to Wilbur denying that she had MPD, Sybil explicitly stated that she was inventing symptoms to beguile Wilbur and keep the therapist interested in her case. (See Appendix 3.)

It is helpful to keep in mind the problems that the misuse of hypnosis can produce as we go along for it might shed some light on how Sybil—a highly hypnotizable hysteric in Herb Spiegel's assessment—was transformed into a multiple by Wilbur.

Several years after Spiegel had treated Sybil, Schreiber and Wilbur sought him out. "They both came to see me to ask if I wanted to be a co-author with them . . . " Spiegel recalled. "They said they would be calling her a 'multiple personality.' I said, 'But she's not a multiple personality.' I think she was a wonderful hysterical patient with role confusion, which is typical of high hysterics . . . I saw her 'personalities' rather as game playing. Schreiber then got in a huff. She said, 'But if we don't call it a multiple personality, we don't have a book . . . .' So I said, 'OK, go ahead, but I don't want to be identified with that.' Both women were very angry" (A. Dufrense, 1997). Even Schreiber must have been assailed by doubts from time to time. Once she asked Wilbur, "Do you think the sophisticated reading public will accept your little fantasy of multiple personalities?"

It was, I think, an interesting choice of words.

THE CRUCIBLE OF THE SIXTIES

In my opinion, the book and film versions of Sybil can, at one level, be understood as a social dream, i.e., symptoms of social distress and psychopathy of everyday life. (I have elaborated on this theme at some length in my book *Manufacturing Social Distress,* Chapter 5, "Dreams That Money Can Buy.") The Sybil case is a quintessential example of how phony facts create phony problems that in turn create phony solutions. Sybil is a triggering mechanism in the natural evolutionary development of reported false memory, child abuse, and the misuse of hypnosis in the treatment of the mentally ill. It's little surprise then that the myth of Sybil began in the tumultuous years of the late sixties when revolution was in the air and the prevailing orthodoxy was under attack from every quarter. Writers like Thomas Szasz questioned the very definition of an illness, dismissing it as a myth. R.D. Laing questioned the nature of insanity. It was society that was sick, he asserted, not the person labeled mentally ill.

Throughout the seventies and eighties increasing numbers of cases of childhood abuse were reported, often many years after the abuse was said to have occurred. Some notorious cases involving allegations of abuse at daycare centers received extraordinary attention in the media, setting in motion court battles that sometimes lasted for years and frequently ended without any convictions. That was because proof in many instances was hard, if not impossible, to come by; in some states up to 60 percent of abuse reports could not be substantiated. One study revealed that investigators dismissed 82 percent of all allegations of abuse by daycare operators.

The accusations based on memories that had purportedly been repressed took on ever more Byzantine aspects. The allegations of childhood abuse now included reports that the incidents had occurred in diabolical rites. Ritual abuse of children was believed to include sexual sadism and pornography, physical torture and highly sophisticated psychological manipulation; vaginal and rectal penetration were supposed to be a common feature of these rites. Moreover, prominent individuals were often reputed to have participated in these rites and then covered up their crimes; it was because of their high-level connections, it was said, that the police and the courts failed to pursue these cases. Survivors, often with the "help" of therapists using hypnosis, had to sort out the truth from inchoate memories, dreams, and associations. Not coincidentally, many of these "survivors" went on to develop MPD/DID. Typical of these cases, only the alters were aware of the abuse that they had experienced at the hands of the cult perpetrating these rituals while the predominant or core personality had repressed the memory and had no way to account for why he was suffering such psychic pain. The trauma was thought to have caused the self to split and induced the amnesia. A vivid account of the phenomena can be found in J. Acocella's book *Creating Hysteria: Women and Multiple Personality Disorder*. She points out that the belief in a "cure" by fusion of the personalities varied depending on the loyalty that therapists could inspire among their patients for their particular positions on the issue. If they believed, so inevitably did their patients (Acocella, 1999).

Don't think that these bizarre accounts were so rare. In one poll, of 2709 members of the American Psychological Association who responded, 2292 reported knowledge of ritual abuse (Gould, 1995). In 1992 alone, groups set up to help "survivors" of childhood abuse received thousands of calls reporting abuse in which rituals figured prominently; Childhelp USA logged 1841 calls pertaining to ritual abuse, Monarch Resources of LA logged 6000, Real Action Survivors tallied nearly 3500, and Justus Unlimited of Colorado 7000. Professional journals tracked the trend. I conducted a survey of citations of *Sybil* in social science journals from 1974 (immediately after publication of *Sybil*) to 2004; the trend was unmistakable: the number of citations remained steady (3 to 5) up until 1980; over the next several years the number rose dramatically, reaching a high of 14. By the 1990s, however, the number of citations of *Sybil* declined appreciably, returning to the levels of the mid-1970s (see accompanying figure).

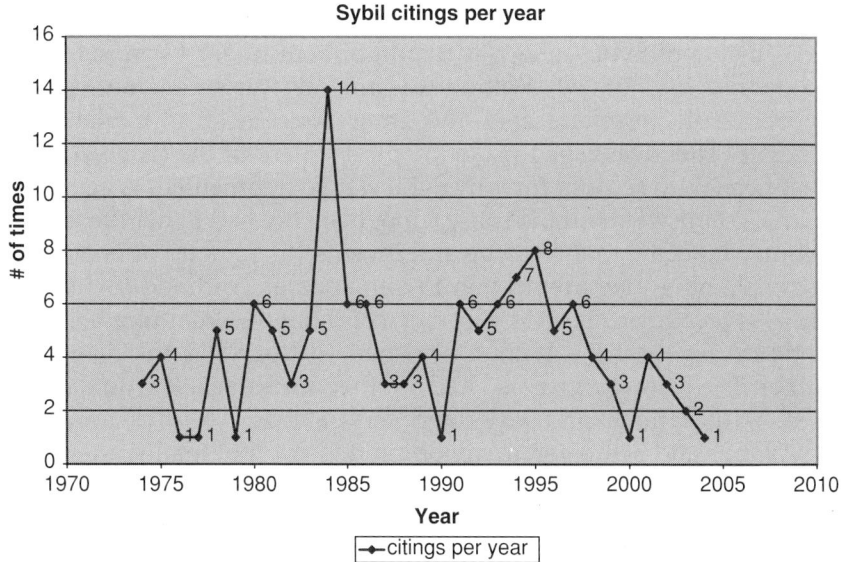

A backlash was predictable; in 1992 a group of people who were accused in some cases and convicted of sexual abuse formed an organization called the False Memory Syndrome Foundation (FMSF). It launched a campaign to expose therapists who it believed were implanting memories and engaging in unethical behavior that had the effect of creating ever greater numbers of "victims," "survivors," and false multiples.

But what was going on in the minds of Schreiber and Wilbur when they were putting the book together that directly or indirectly contributed to so much mischief? Did they believe their story? Did they perpetrate a hoax on the American public or did they actually believe in own tale? Was the answer to be found on the tapes that Schreiber had given to me? I had to listen to those tapes repeatedly because it is almost impossible to digest them at first listening. To put it in context of the history it wasn't a boom, it wasn't a eureka. All the same I knew I had something very important.

In August 1998, I presented my analysis of the tapes at the annual meeting of the American Psychological Association in San Francisco. After beginning my presentation with a brief rundown of the literature relating to MPD and discussion of the current theories about hypnosis, I dropped the bombshell. After having recently listened to the recordings for the very first time, I was shocked to hear how much important information was contained therein that would help us understand the very real story behind Sybil as a multiple personality. As the rapt audience listened to the taped conversations I proceeded to analyze what they were saying. It was Wilbur, I contended, who had labeled Sybil a multiple. The therapist wasn't finding the personalities inside of Sybil—she was planting them under hypnosis. With her patient hypnotized, Wilbur was manufacturing memories and concocting the primal scene—the grand illusion of an explanatory principle. The idea was to make the punishment fit the crime, to give a justification to account for why Sybil was so fragmented. When Sybil became confused about the role each personality had in her life, it was Wilbur who came to the rescue and invented the lineup of personalities, explaining their connection to one another. And once Sybil was made to recognize the cause of her condition—sexual abuse at the hands of her mother—Wilbur then had to teach her to "hate" her mother. The primal scene also had another advantage. It would make the book sensational and sexy—and very salable.

Wilbur and Schreiber, in my opinion, were "not totally unaware" that the story that they told was wrong. Nonetheless, I said I would prefer to believe that there was as much self-deception as deception of others. Once you start making up a story to suit your own needs it can take on a life of its own. Schreiber might have repressed the memory of how the story began and then once it became a success there was no turning back. Schreiber recalled that "Dr. Spiegel, who worked on the case, said he met about seven of the personalities but he refuses to accept the concept of multiplicity, which I feel is a contradiction. But he said he felt she was 'a brilliant hysteric.'"

HIGHLIGHTS AND THE IMPLICATIONS OF THE TAPE RECORDINGS

The tape recordings can be broken down into ten section headings:

1. *Labeling Sybil as a multiple personality.* Initially, Wilbur tells Schreiber, she had no idea Sybil/Sylvia was a multiple. In recounting Peggy's emergence—the first personality to do so—to Schreiber she makes it sound like she was completely caught off guard, even flummoxed: "So I said hello, and I, as I recall it, I said, 'Hello Sylvia,' and she said, 'I'm not Sylvia, I'm Peggy, don't you know the difference?' That was the first time I realized that she perceived herself differently. And I think I evaded the answer, or said I didn't notice, something like that. Then I said . . . 'Tell me something about yourself.' Because I didn't know what I was dealing with."

" But you did suspect . . . ?" Schreiber says.

" I sure as the dickens did."

"But you felt you were dealing with a dual personality."

"I certainly did. A dual personality. I said to myself, Oh, my God, . . . she is like the Beauchamp case . . . more than one person. So I said, tell me about yourself, and she said . . . well, she did tell me about herself. She said that she was not Sylvia. She said that she got her name from her mother calling her Peggy Louisiana and that she liked to do black and white paintings . . . " (Schreiber Archive, Box 37).

In a letter she wrote to Schreiber, Wilbur provides a slightly different version of the same event: "The personalities were named before I got into the case. I discovered this quite by accident and followed up on it. One day Peggy was in the office and I called her Shirley and she said, 'You always call me Shirley.' In surprise I asked her what her name was and she said Peggy Lou. That was when I found out that she was a multiple personality. They were named as they emerged by the personality that emerged" (Wilbur to Schreiber, unpublished letter, July 26, 1965).

And the reason for these personalities, the two women agreed, could be summarized in one word—pain. "When this pain was intolerable Sylvia disappeared and another personality appeared," Schreiber affirms. "It wasn't actually the fact that Peggy remembered, but that Sylvia forgot. The other personalities didn't forget."

Once Wilbur had not only accepted but embraced the notion that Sybil was a multiple she began to dig deeper to find out just how many personalities there were.

Her strategy was to allow all the personalities to be "free to come forth, no matter who uses the body." Wilbur tells Schreiber how she went about this enterprise: "Then she [Sybil] went on, uh, and told me about Peggy Lou and Peggy Ann. And then I said to her . . . I wanted all of them to feel free to come during the appointment hours, no matter who was . . . using the body. I wanted all of them to feel free to come." Wilbur then indicates she will tell Sylvia that she was a multiple personality.

2. *Assigning the multiple personalities their personal characteristics and planting Vicky rather than probing her.* It is clear from Wilbur's own words that she was not exploring Sybil's psyche for the truth but rather planting the truth as she wanted it to be (even if she wasn't aware that that was what she was doing). For example, she explains, "And I said, well, there's a personality who calls herself Peggy. And uh, I said, she is pretty self-assertive . . . she can do things you can't, and she [Sybil] was very, uh, obviously perturbed by this." Wilbur continues: "And I said . . . she wouldn't do anything that you wouldn't approve of. She might do something that you wouldn't think of doing . . . . And, uh, I told her . . . there were at least two others, or three others, two Peggys. And, . . . it was Peggy Lou and Peggy Ann. And I said the other one calls herself Vicky. And she said, oh, I remember that."

3. *Inventing the primal scene, the grand illusion of an explanatory principle, and making the punishment fit the crime in the book.* The Freudian idea of the primal sexual scene and sexual abuse are obviously topics that will make any book both sensational and sexy. In keeping with these themes, Wilbur states, "And this business of the primal scene. And being forced to sleep in the same bedroom with her fucking parents. And I mean they were . . . is a very large thing you see. And this thing you see, that constantly drove Mary to want to have her own house." Flora Schreiber replies, "Connie . . . Did Mary carry the burden of the primal scene? I thought it was Peggy who did."

At this point, Wilbur begins to discuss the story in the first chapter of the book. Here she brings up the details of the primal scene, during which Sybil is only a few years old. Assuming literary license, Schreiber elaborates by remembering for Sybil as she would imagine it to be. Wilbur explains, "They screwed in front of her. She could see because her crib was here, the window was there, and the streetlight was right outside. She could see her father having an erection and putting it in her mother's vagina . . . Did you know that?"

4. *Projecting the creators' guilt about perpetrating a fraud on to others; there is a madness in their method and method in their madness.* The conversation then drifts into the benefits of the enterprise and Wilbur mentions her hope, "I hope to God the book makes money before Florence [Sybil's mother] drops dead."

The question of what kind of therapy was administered then becomes the topic of conversation. Wilbur says that she once heard that Dr. Franz Alexander, a pioneer in psychosomatic medicine, had allowed himself to get personally involved with his patients in order to help them. That was all the precedent she apparently needed. Wilbur stated, "So because I became involved enough . . . in the multiple personalities so that when trouble arose, there wasn't anybody else I had to go to but for her. She had no family. And if anybody was going to keep track of her, I had to. Well, now this, according to the formalist, in psychoanalysis, is stepping outside. But I learnt this trick from a very, very fine source. I learned it from Franz Alexander. And uh, uh, the reason was, because I respected these people a great deal."

When Schreiber asked Wilbur whether she had actually worked with these therapists, Wilbur answered, "No I had not. But I knew a great deal about their work and knew that, uh, they were not beyond experimenting in terms of their relationship with patients."

5. *Manufacturing Sybil's memories.* One must remember that memories, especially in DID cases, can be easily created if one is not very cautious. From the evidence provided by the tapes it is clear that Wilbur showed no such caution. "The first time we got any memories back, was . . . when . . . I gave her pentothal . . . and I said, 'When you were on pentothal you said so and so.' And she said, 'Oh, I hadn't thought about that in years. I've forgotten all about it. . . .' So I decided that I lost too much . . . trying to tell her what she said. So what I did was to tape what she said . . . played the tapes back so she could hear herself say it. Now this was very interesting. She would remember this for a certain period of time and then she would lose some of . . . it . . . Re-forget . . . Now one

of the things that happened with the pentothal was that she liked it a great deal because it relieved her anxiety and the day after she had pentothal, she felt perfectly well . . . And, as a consequence, she became quite . . . involved. And on two or three occasions very demanding, about having pentothal . . . And it worried me because I had the feeling she was getting addicted. At least psychologically. And I didn't want to go from a multiple personality to an addiction."

In one of her letters Sybil admits to her addiction, noting that she would like to give up her medications and only take them when she's depressed. That she was highly overmedicated might have contributed to her false representations in her mind of what had actually occurred; this was likely the case under pentothol and it was doubly true later under hypnosis. Schreiber refers to sodium pentothol as "truth serum," which of course it is not but, for her purposes, it worked well. Under pentothol Sybil almost invariably remained in hiding—she appeared only once—leaving the field to the other personalities. But until she began to fear the development of an addiction Wilbur appeared to use the drug more and more to recover the memories and emotions she felt were still buried deep within Sybil. At one point she assured Schreiber, "We'll have some pentothal sessions as Sylvia and see if we can't get why guilty feelings, etc." Schreiber wants to emphasize the importance of the "truth serum" in her story. "You introduced me to all the personalities . . ." she says to Wilbur. "Uh, you did do that on the pentothal?"

Wilbur replies, "Well, excepting sometimes . . . well, I did do it on the pentothal too. I mean, I would say to whoever was talking to me . . . well who are you? Well, I'm talking for, you know, and they'd name three or four. And I would say, what does Peggy think about this? What does Vicky think about this? And they would say, Well, I don't know. And I would say, can I talk to Vicky . . . I could summon them [all]."

So it seemed that Wilbur was addicted to the drug, too, just in a different way.

After giving up on pentothol Wilbur turned to hypnosis in order to achieve what Schreiber called a way of "unleashing the unconscious."

6. Shaping the rationale for Sybil as an honest liar. During some of the sessions Wilbur is obliged to remind Sybil about her condition: ". . . isn't there some connection between you and these other personalities?" she asks. Then Wilbur goes on to explain to Sybil that she was a multiple personality and there was a connection. To Schreiber she puts it this way: ". . . right after, I explained to her that she was a multiple personality. And I said, I am sure . . . there is a connection between you and these other states. And you need to find that connection . . . to build a bridge between you and these other states." Nonetheless, Sybil becomes confused about her personalities, especially whether they are aware of each other.

7. *Sybil becomes confused about her personalities.* At this point it is important for Schreiber and Wilbur to work out who's who in the lineup of multiple personalities. Wilbur begins the discussion: "She [Sybil] said, 'I can explain it to you but it is very difficult.' She said, 'Here on this side is Sylvia. And here on this side is me, Peggy and, I guess, some others.'" Wilbur goes on to say, "See, I knew about Peggy and Vicky at this point but I didn't know much about the others. And she said that there isn't any connection between us at all . . . Except way underneath . . . And she stuck her hand under her leg like this. Yep. She said, except way underneath. And she said, 'There isn't really a connection, there's just a possibility of a connection. . . .' Well, I've thought about this many, many times. And I think that what she was trying to say, was that if you consider all the altered states of consciousness, say in layers . . . that up here . . . there isn't any real connection between Sylvia and us. But way down deep, there is a connection."

8. *Creating the cause—"The Abuse Excuse."* The conversation between the two women now begins to address the particulars of the sexual abuse. Wilbur explains, "If Sylvia got put upon by somebody they [the other personalities] were just terribly annoyed that Sylvia didn't do something about it." Flora Schreiber comments, "Yeah, but in childhood when mother . . . ah, stuck a . . . you know, ice water up Sylvia's bladder. The rest of them felt it."

Wilbur replies, "Uh, yeah, because they shared the body but they didn't have the emotions." Schreiber responds, "Now Peggy, and Clara, and Ruthie, report cruelties. Several of the personalities report cruelties. . ." Then Wilbur cautions, "But you need to watch it. Are they reporting cruelties that they were experiencing?"

Schreiber replies, "Or are they the Greek chorus for Sylvia?"

9. *Admitting to a false confession; Sybil's amnesia wears off.* It is typical for hysterics, as well as some Dissociative Identity Disorder individuals, to experience an amnesia effect and then for it to wear off, thus making them look as if they are inconsistent in their understanding of what happened to them. Sybil gives us a beautiful illustration of the amnesia effect. For example, Flora Schreiber states, "And there is one thing you mustn't forget . . . is Sylvia's fantastic letter . . . in which Sylvia said it was all a hoax. You know, that she never was a multiple personality. And, her mother was very good to her, and everything. It

was a total denial." Here is an excerpt from that exercise in "total denial": "And you might ask me what about my mother . . . that too falls into the category of happen-stance . . . I cannot explain it except if I have an extra sense that tells me what a catatonic schizophrenia is like . . . or unless THAT is somehow linked with my real trouble . . . the things I told you about her (the extreme things, that is) were not true . . . I did not exactly 'make them up' ahead of time nor plan to say them . . . they just sort of rolled out from somewhere and once I had started and found you were interested, I continued . . . under pentothal I am much more original than otherwise, so I said more . . . it made a good story and it accounts for some of the fake symptoms I displayed." It is telling that in the excerpt of the letter that appears in the book Schreiber omitted several lines. (The full text of this letter can be found in Appendix 3.) For instance, Schreiber leaves out any mention of Sybil's suggestion that she might be schizophrenic or that she might have faked her symptoms so that her case would make a "good story" because she realized that she was intriguing Wilbur. Nor does Schreiber make any reference to Sybil's mention of sodium pentothal. In fact, about all that Schreiber does include is Sybil's defense of her mother and her assertion that her upbringing wasn't anywhere as bad as she had previously claimed (Schreiber, Books, 1989).

10. *Teaching Sybil to hate and then explaining it.* Our last section deals with an irresponsible by-product of what happens when a therapist becomes too emotionally involved in the treatment of a patient. Wilbur and Schreiber have become the surrogate parents for Sybil but in order to claim their new power they must destroy any competition which naturally includes Sybil's real parents. The need to purge the parents—especially Hattie—reveals itself throughout the therapeutic tapes: "you know mother did lots of things to make you angry and frightened, and I know most of them . . . I know she gave you medicines that hurt you, and I know she filled your bladder up with cold water and hurt you, and she used the flashlight and so on and hurt you. I know she stuffed the washcloth in your mouth and cotton in your nose so you couldn't breathe, I know about all those things. What else did she do that made you angry? Sweetie, hmmm? Dear heart? What else did she do? It's all right to talk about it now."

THE REACTION

I had no idea just how much interest this talk had generated, much less the firestorm that I'd set off with my exposure of the tapes.

THE MYTH EXPLODES

Shortly after leaving the conference hall, I called my answering machine. I had 25 messages from almost every imaginable media source. Ted Koppel and a *Dateline* producer were on my machine. When I got to San Diego a few hours later, a crew from the tabloid TV show *Extra* was lurking in ambuscade, waiting to capture my comments on tape. I was astonished at the response to my talk on TV and in papers throughout the country and abroad. "Doubt Cast on 'Sybil' Story" (*Boston Globe*). "Psychologist: Forgotten recordings cast doubt on Sybil" (*Miami Herald*). "16-Person Sybil was bogus tale—expert" (*Hamilton Spectator*). "Multiple Personalities: True disorder or an acting job?" (*Macon Daily*). "Psychiatrist's tale debunked" (*Toronto Star*). And one of my favorites: "17 Persons, one big set-up" (*Detroit Free Press*).

I had my skeptics, too. In a column that appeared in *The Chicago Tribune*, Howard Kleinberg writes, "While Rieber would have us accept that the tapes he possesses document that Sybil's story was infused with suggestions from her psychiatrist—thus creating multiple personalities—what are we to think of Rieber himself?" Then he proceeds to question my account of how I found the tapes: "Could he [Rieber] have been the inspiration for the Disney flick *The Absent-Minded Professor*? Do we accept at face value Rieber's story that he had these tapes in a drawer for 25 years and simply forgot about them?" He makes no judgment—he's content to leave his questions in the air—but concludes, "Everything, everyone is under the spotlight of revisionism and rediscovery.... Nothing should surprise us anymore or make us believe."

Nothing? That strikes me as a bit of an abdication of responsibility.

There were still some mysteries to clear up, though, questions that hadn't been answered by the tapes. I obtained access to some of Schreiber's files at John Jay Library. (There was also a secret file which was subsequently opened to the public but not before some of the papers, apparently too sensitive for outside readers, were removed.) At the bottom of one document I came across a provocative statement scrawled in her own hand. "I am now working on the most extraordinary case ever to hit the psychoanalytic literature," she'd written. Then she'd added: "Who is Sylvia and what is she?" She'd crossed out a name and substituted "Sylvia." "Sylvia" was the name that Schreiber and Wilbur had used in their conversations before—for whatever reason—they'd finally settled on the more poetic "Sybil." It's possible that Wilbur, who was widely read in early psychological literature—recall her preoccupation with Prince's work on dissociation—was inspired to name her famous case after reading Henry James's critical assessment of Nathaniel Hawthorne. The relevant passage occurs in Chapter V: "The most touching element in the novel [*Blithedale Romance*] is the history of the grasp that this barbarous fanatic has laid upon the fastidious and high-tempered Zenobia, who, disliking him and shrinking from him at a hundred points, is drawn into the gulf of his omnivorous egotism. The portion of the story that strikes me as least felicitous is that which deals with Priscilla and with her mysterious relation to Zenobia—with *her mesmeric gifts, her clairvoyance, her identity with the Veiled Lady, her divided subjection to Hollingsworth and Westervelt, and her numerous other graceful but fantastic properties—her Sibylline attributes*, as the author calls them. Hawthorne is rather too fond of Sibylline attributes—a taste of the same order as his disposition, to which I have already alluded, to talk about spheres and sympathies (James, 1879) (italics mine). I cannot prove that Wilbur ever read this essay, much less was inspired to name her patient "Sybil," and yet one cannot deny the tantalizing nature of this text, which brings together so many of the elements associated with the disorder—mesmerism, clairvoyance, divided subjection, and Sibylline attributes. James criticizes Hawthorne's novel because it seems to lose its anchor in real life. "As the action advances, in *The Blithedale Romance*, we get too much out of reality, and cease to feel beneath our feet the firm ground of an appeal to our own vision of the world, our observation" (James, 1879). He could have said the same about *Sybil*. There is no way to be certain how acquainted Schreiber was with Victorian literature, but she might have come across an 1845 novel by Benjamin Disraeli (later British prime minister) that had proven quite a sensation in its day. It was entitled *Sybil, or the Two Nations*. Sybil, it seems, is never allowed to venture out into the world alone.

But what was the name that Schreiber had crossed out in favor of Sybil? I assumed it was the real name of the patient. At that point her identity was still a mystery.

Another mystery was more easily resolved. When I finally got around to rereading *Sybil*, I had been struck by the number of personalities Wilbur had ascribed to her patient. But why sixteen? Why not fourteen or eight or three or three hundred? There was something about the number sixteen that kept gnawing at me. Then it hit me. I knew that Schreiber must have read *The Mask of Sanity* by Hervey Cleckley. (Cleckley had also been a coauthor of *The Three Faces of Eve*.) In *Mask* Cleckley had detailed several distinguishing characteristics of a psychopath. There were, I recalled, sixteen in all. I felt sure I had the answer.

WHO IS SYBIL AND WHAT IS SHE?

From time to time I would run into a historian named Peter Swales who calls himself "an archaeologist of knowledge" and has made a name for himself as a debunker of Freud. More recently he turned his attention to unmasking the identity of Sybil. Reasoning that there must be some connection between "the true facts and a fabrication," as he put it, Swales used the book as a guide. His search finally led him in late 1998 to a small conservative Midwestern town called Dodge Center in Minnesota. Sybil, Swales discovered, was really named Shirley Ardell Mason. But he was too late to meet her. She'd died peacefully at home on February 26, 1998, of breast cancer. She was 75.

Actually what Swales had done was *rediscover* the truth about Sybil's identity. Sybil was revealed as Shirley Mason in August 1975 when the *Minneapolis Star* identified her and named her parents as Martha and Walter Mason, the models for Willard and Henrietta Dorsett. The paper also stated that the book's Willow Corners was actually Dodge Center, a town located 80 miles southeast of the Twin Cities. Schreiber had refused to confirm the report, admitting only that she'd been to Dodge Center (where she'd failed to find those mysterious "woods" where Hattie/Henrietta had allegedly committed so many outrages) (*Minneapolis Star*, August 27, 1975). Even though the news item was picked up by the entertainment weekly *Variety*, the revelation barely made a ripple and disappeared from the collective memory—so much so that when Sybil's identity was again disclosed in 1998 it came as a surprise.

But when and how Sybil's true identity came to light, while an intriguing footnote, are of less significance than the story of Shirley Mason's childhood and adolescence in Dodge Center.

The only child of Mattie and Walter Mason, a hardware-store clerk and carpenter, Mason was raised as a strictly observant Seventh-Day Adventist. Dodge Center residents recall a somewhat withdrawn, slender girl with a talent for painting. While her mother was known to display bizarre behavior, no one in the town knew of any instances of the sexual and physical abuse ascribed to her in the book. In 1941 Mason left for Minnesota State University sixty miles away; in 1945, however, she suffered a breakdown and experienced severe anorexia, which kept her from graduating until 1949. It was in the early fifties that she first met Wilbur in Omaha. After her mother's death, she moved to New York where Wilbur was then practicing. Though the treatment lasted for eleven years the relationship between the two continued. When Wilbur left New York to take a teaching job at the University of Kentucky in Lexington, Mason felt adrift. She never married or had children. The book's success, however, gave her financial freedom, allowing her to move to Lexington to be near Wilbur. Wilbur died in 1992 and Schreiber in 1988. Wilbur left Mason $25,000 and all of her royalties from the book. During her last years Mason spent most of her time taking care of her cats, gardening and painting until arthritis made it too difficult for her to hold a brush. In spite of painful memories of her church in Minnesota, she remained devoted to the Seventh-Day Adventists. "She was happy," a friend recalled. She refused treatment for a recurrence of cancer, feeling that she'd already experienced enough trauma in her life. "She was not afraid of dying," the friend said.

I ran into Swales not long after Mason's identity had been revealed for a second time. (I was not aware of the earlier *Minneapolis Star* report.) The first thing I remember Peter Swales saying to me was that he hoped he was not infringing upon my territory. I quickly responded as follows: "Not to worry Peter, you are interested in who Sybil was. I am interested in who Sybil wasn't." As we fell deeper into conversation, Swales offhandedly mentioned that when Mason first moved to New York in the late fifties she'd lived for a year in a six-story walkup apartment on York Avenue between 78th and 79th Street. I stared at him. "That's uncanny! I know that building," I said, "I was living there the same year she was. We could have passed each other a hundred times."

CONCLUSION

Thus far, with brief and therefore "unable" pen, I have been able to tell the story about how it is possible to manufacture a multiple personality. The conditions surrounding my ability to expose this case were entirely serendipitous. Had it not been for a personal friendship with Flora Schreiber and Herb Spiegel, none of this material would have surfaced. More specifically, the tapes that Schreiber had given me would have never been examined again if not for my subsequent conversations with Dr. Spiegel.

The question of whether or not the Sybil case was an out-and-out fraud, of course depends upon your personal definition of that term. No matter what you wish to call it, it was a conscious misrepresentation of the facts. A fine line between self-deception and the deception of others is an important issue here. Unquestionably, Schreiber and

THE MYTH EXPLODES

Wilbur wanted to make Sybil a multiple personality case no matter what. This is clear when you examine their response to Dr. Spiegel that the publishers wanted a book on multiple personality when Spiegel had already informed them that Sybil was simply a case of hysteria.

From my personal knowledge of Flora Schreiber, I am quite certain that she had convinced herself that the story was true, even though she more than likely knew that it wasn't at the very beginning. (Recall her use of the words "little fantasy.") Once you start making up a story to suit your own needs, it can take on a life of its own. The creators of Sybil, I would suggest, repressed the remembrance of how it began once they'd gotten into the thick of it. By August 1975, there were already four million copies in print and it had been a bestseller for six months and was still selling 40,000 to 50,000 copies a month. Not only money was involved; there were a lot of ardent readers who for their own reasons had embraced the story and considered Sybil a martyr or perhaps a heroine. The authors could hardly have repudiated their own myth without incurring the wrath of their audience which was to grow appreciably once the TV movie was aired.

When it became a financial success, there was no turning back. In the final analysis, Sybil is a phony multiple personality case at best. It is notable for the considerable attention it received and for the pernicious phenomena it helped abet, if not to spawn, but in many ways it was typical. With multiple personality disorders, patients and therapists—and I should add the media and the public—don't know when or where to stop. In their view more is always better.

III

Seminal Cases of Multiplicity
A History

Boston nerve specialist played the detective in relentlessly pursuing the multiple minds which for years befogged the mentality of Miss Beauchamp—He tells in a recently published volume of the pranks and torments practiced by his patient while in one of these subconscious states, which were painful and embarrassing to her when conscious as another personality—Dr. Prince's problem was to find the real self of his patient and to drive away its tormentors which he did by most drastic treatment and with the aid of hypnotism.

Boston Sunday Globe, February 25, 1906

TWO SOULS IN ONE BODY?

A CASE OF DUAL PERSONALITY

BY

HENRY HERBERT GODDARD
Ph. D.

PROFESSOR OF ABNORMAL AND CLINICAL PSYCHOLOGY IN OHIO STATE UNIVERSITY, AND AUTHOR OF "PSYCHOLOGY OF THE NORMAL AND SUBNORMAL," "JUVENILE DELINQUENCY," ETC., WITH ILLUSTRATIONS AND CHARTS

Stranger than fiction is the unusual case of a dual personality, a living "Jekyll and Hyde," in which two identities, one an apparently normal nineteen year old girl, the other a refractory child of four, were alternately in control in the same body. An extraordinary situation was presented in the fact that between Bernice Redich, the adult personality, and "Polly" Redich, the juvenile personality, absolutely no connecting links could be found. Professor Goddard, a foremost authority in the fields of abnormal and clinical psychology, relates in this volume his first investigation of this strange and uncanny phenomenon, the various characteristics of the two opposing personalities, and the processes by which he endeavored to bring about a normal psychological condition. To the professional the book will prove a case-record of unusual interest and value and to the general reader it will provide an even more fascinating insight into a world of modern science where reality surpasses imagination and where the expert technique of the investigator is the source of both surprise and admiration.

8

Fourteen Seminal Cases

From the received views of vulgar opinions, we have shown that old prejudices often leave some footsteps on the individual mind and society. The history of hypnosis and dissociative identity disorder are no exceptions. From the alchemists came the pharmocologists. From the phrenologists came the neuroscientists. And from the mesmerists came the psychotherapists. Nevertheless, one must take care when one assumes Charlotonism—sometimes they are and sometimes they are not. We will now present a narrative of thirteen of the most important case histories of dissociative identity disorder from the eighteenth to the twentieth century with the understanding that more might appear to put their stamp on the twenty-first. Our objective here is not only to provide the facts as we know them to shed light as to how these cases emerged and transformed over time, but also to construct an "interactive table," reprinted at the end of the chapter on pp. 180–181, to illustrate how the various cases are both similar and different in their symptomatolgy as well as the intervention techniques used to address them.

MARY REYNOLDS, 1811

The case of Mary Reynolds seems to be the earliest case of multiple personality ever reported. William James, in his *Principles of Psychology*

(Holt, 1890), gave a rather detailed account of it, with a bow to the original chronicler, a Dr. Weir Mitchell.

This "dull and melancholy young woman," as James described her, lived with her family in the backwoods of Pennsylvania. One morning in 1811, when she was about eighteen, she failed to get up at her usual time. Members of her family went to her room to awaken her but could not do so. Some ten hours later, in the evening, she finally awoke, but in an extraordinary state of mind. Indeed, "state of mind" may not be a very apt phrase to describe her condition, since it was precisely her mind that seemed to be missing, or at least her memory. She did not recognize any of her family or friends, her room, the house, or the surrounding countryside. Her vocabulary was limited to a few elementary words, but they clearly had no meaning for her. Her body in both structure and function was that of an eighteen-year-old woman, but her mind gave every indication of having reverted to infancy. Again it was chiefly her lack of memory that suggested this; some other aspects of her mind, such as her ability to appreciate the beauties of nature, seemed relatively unimpaired.

Apart from her ability to pronounce a few words, it seemed necessary to reintroduce her to the world all over again. In spite of the efforts of her family she was slow to learn. Everyone she knew previously were either strangers or enemies. Gradually, she began to read and write. At the same time her depression began to lift, and she became rather cheerful and confident, no longer showing any sign of being fearful of people. On the contrary, she was suddenly very sociable. Then several weeks later she underwent another protracted sleep and when she awoke she was in a different state. This time she recognized her family. She was quite surprised by her circumstances. She was aware of everything that had happened to her in her primary state, but any experience or acquaintance that she'd encountered in her secondary state was completely lost to her. After several more weeks the same thing happened again, only this time when she awoke she had returned to her secondary state and resumed right where she had left off, acting as if it was just waking up after one night's sleep. These alterations from one state to another continued for the next fifteen or sixteen years. The alterations only ceased when she reached the age of thirty-five or so, leaving her in the second state. There she remained for at least twenty-five years without change. Gradually, though, she began to change; the fun-filled, mischievous, but hysterical, woman, who was fond of jokes and given to absurd beliefs little by little turned into a somber and practical-minded woman. During the last twenty-five years of her life she lived in the same house as the Reverend John D. Reynolds and kept house for him. Mary Reynolds died in January of 1854 at the age of 61. This case stands out for two reasons; the first is that it is probably the earliest referenced case history of dissociative identity disorder and the second is that it involved two of the most important nineteenth century experts in the field: Weir Mitchell and William James.

RACHEL BAKER, 1814

(M. M. SIMPSON AND E. T. CARLSON, 1968, AND JOHN DOUGLAS, 1815)

The case of Rachel Baker, a twenty-year-old woman from Onondago County in upper New York State, was one of the earliest cases to appear in the American medical literature on multiple personality disorder. The case was first written up in the form of an 1814 pamphlet by Charles Mais entitled "The Surprising Case of Rachel Baker, who Prays and Preaches in her Sleep." The pamphlet made her both famous and a subject of considerable speculation. (The case was subsequently considered in a book by Simpson and Carlson, *The Strange Sleep of Rachel Baker*.) What made her case remarkable was that she would appear to fall asleep, and then begin to "preach" fluently. In the fall of 1814, she was brought to New York City so that eminent physicians could study her. A group of five physicians were consulted, led by Samuel Latham Mitchill who had founded the country's first medical journal some years before. Such was her notoriety, however, that people were unwilling to allow the professionals to monopolize her. So her remarkable talents were also demonstrated nightly at local taverns. The attention she stirred in New York caught the attention of Mais who compiled his stenographic reports of her prayers and exhortations for publication, making sure to include an introduction from a medical authority, one Dr. Samuel Mitchill among others.

Rachel Baker's major symptom was her somnambulistic preaching. Her manner of preaching seemed to indicate a capacity for language and articulation that she never demonstrated in her ordinary waking life. Rachel did have some religious training and she certainly had a preoccupation with religion. Simpson and Carlson described her as melancholy or depressed. By the age of seventeen, Rachel was consumed by a belief that she was a sinner in need of redemption. Her first "devotional somnium," or sleep-preaching, was reported to have occurred on November 28, 1811. During her first sleep-preaching, Rachel's pronouncements were self-deprecating and anguished. Later on her sermons took a different turn and she began to speak of a merciful God and described a serene picture of Heaven. In 1813, she began an apprenticeship as a women's cloak-maker. Sometimes Rachel's devotional somnium was interrupted by sickness. Her sleep-preaching was frequently interrupted by illness including recurring headaches and a bout with the measles. The sleeping sermons would begin punctually at 9 pm, Rachel's bedtime, and would last anywhere from 45 minutes to one and a half hours. These preaching episodes would be preceded by an interval marked by heavy breathing and spasmodic bodily movements. After a few minutes Rachel would begin speaking in a "forceful" and clear manner. She would lie still as she spoke and answered questions. Bewildered doctors checked her pulse but found it normal. Most of her other vital signs were little different from those of a normal sleeper. At the end of the sermon, Ms. Baker would once again exhibit spasms similar to those that had preceded her preaching, only more pronounced. She would then lapse into normal sleep. When she woke she would have no memory of the sleep-preaching. Observers were particularly struck by the incongruence of her odd nighttime behavior and the personality and behavior she displayed while awake. The "preacher" seemed to be another personality entirely. There are similarities between Rachel's condition and epilepsy or hysteria, as noted by Dr. Mitchill in his introduction to Mais's pamphlet. Mitchill concluded that Rachel's sleep-preaching was a state of consciousness between waking and sleep. Evidently her case continued to generate interest for she returned to New York on several occasions, although little is known about how long her nocturnal sermons went on for. In the literature, Rachel Baker's case history rivals that of Mary Reynolds in terms of the publicity it aroused and the questions it raised about identity and consciousness. Nevertheless, Rachel's stands out because it was examined and studied by so many prominent physicians and because it was published. In fact, Mais's pamphlet about the sleeping preacher was the first of its kind, initiating a literary subgenre that would ultimately include *The Dissociation of a Personality*, *The Three Faces of Eve*, and, of course, *Sybil*.

MOLLIE FANCHER (Dailey, 1894)

Known as the "Brooklyn Enigma," Mollie Fancher was alleged to have exhibited five distinct personalities. Around the age of fifteen, Fancher developed what her doctor labeled "nervous indigestion." Doctors recommended horseback riding as a treatment. The therapy didn't work as intended; in May 1864 Fancher was thrown off her horse. Her head hit the pavement and several of her ribs were broken. In spite of the blow to her head she appeared to recover. A year later, while climbing down from a streetcar, Fancher once again sustained a bad fall after being thrown violently to the ground and knocked unconscious, and then dragged down the street. Once more she suffered several broken ribs in addition to other injuries serious enough for doctors to think she might not make it through the month. Nonetheless, she pulled through. However, she was bedeviled by a host of physical symptoms including atrophy of her limbs, paralysis, spasms, and series of unexplainable ailments. It was during her difficult recuperation that she experienced her first so-called trance. Over the next few years, her body would periodically be wracked by intense spasms. In February 1868, desperate doctors gave her chloroform to try to control the spasms; the treatment seemed to work. But instead of going into convulsions, she went into a trance during which she apparently carried on a conversation with her mother in heaven. Her suffering wouldn't let up and she was barely capable of eating and so doctors had to resort to forced feeding. Yet when she underwent trance states she could show unnatural strength. She also exhibited a gift for clairvoyance, though it wasn't something she could turn on at will, and it was not always reliable.

The spontaneous trance states that Mollie Fancher experienced over the years typically consisted of spasmodic contractions of the body. Sometimes her eyes would turn up and back, but she always remained sightless. During a nine-year period, she is said to have written some 6500 letters. She also displayed a gift for handicrafts, producing a vast amount of fine embroidery and beautiful waxwork which entailed cutting and coloring of flowers. Predictably, her case attracted the interest of the press which published extensive accounts about her and made her a celebrity. The *Brooklyn Eagle* seems to have been the first newspaper to cover the story in 1866. Over the next several years, various periodicals and newspapers followed suit including the *New York Sun* and *New York Tribune*.

Her case took a new turn when she made the acquaintance of one Mr. George F. Sargent who took an interest in her and visited her many times during the late 1860s. According to his account, it was at this time that the most remarkable features of her case appeared. She began to manifest what Sargent identified as different personalities. Each of these personalities demonstrated distinct facial expressions, inflections in voice, and degrees of intellect. These personalities would usually emerge only for short periods of time. Nonetheless, Sargent maintained that he could request their appearance and they would respond; he identified them by name as Sunbeam, Idol, Rosebud, Pearl, and Ruby. After undergoing these changes, Mollie would return to consciousness but in a weakened state. Sargent seems to have played a major role in the last fifteen years of her life, especially as it relates to the appearance of her personalities.

Sargent's claims were met with considerable skepticism. The famous alienist Dr. George M. Beard was quoted in the *New York Sun* expressing his opinion that Mollie Fancher's extraordinary behavior was more explainable by trickery than anything else, especially her purported powers of clairvoyance. Many friends of Mollie Fancher came to her defense. Beard was unconvinced: "We have not, in our profession, a more honorable or able body of men than some of the Brooklyn physicians that have been directly or indirectly connected with the case of Mollie Fancher," he acknowledged, "and yet the instincts of the majority both the general practitioners and specialists of nervous diseases reject all their testimony relating to claims of clairvoyance, mind-reading, and prophecy."

Mollie spent the last years of her life going in and out of her various states, observed by curiosity-seekers who were interested to see her demonstrate her extraordinary powers for herself. Mollie and Sargent both earned a good deal of money from the book and various promotional events. The significance of Faucher's case rests mostly upon its long life in the public eye, especially in her home of Brooklyn. It also had the effect of stimulating awareness of other cases of multiple personality disorder that emerged at the end of the nineteenth century.

ANSEL BOURNE (Bourne, 1872)

In October 1857, a carpenter by the name of Ansel Bourne left his home in Rhode Island, and set off for a nearby town. He never made it. As he was traveling he was suddenly seized with an idea to attend a religious gathering. His mind kept telling him to go "to the Christian chapel." He then began to feel dizzy, sat down, and apparently lost consciousness. He was taken home in a carriage; after examining him, his doctor reported that he was perfectly insensible. Having had partial amnesia, the doctor concluded, the patient had been touched by the "hand of God." Afterwards Bourne continued to visit the chapel, and became more intensely dependent upon his religious beliefs. Over time he suffered a few more mild attacks, but each time would wake up much more settled and contented with his life. He described the narrative of his personal events that had taken place in 1857.

Bourne then seemed to drop out of history for about thirty years, but the story was recorded and widely recounted. The experience gained him a certain celebrity and prompted him to become a part-time preacher in his community. At the age of sixty-one, he experienced what he referred to as a seizure. This occurred in 1887, when he went to a bank in Providence, Rhode Island, to withdraw some money to pay for a farm which he wished to buy. After finishing the business, he entered a carriage to go to his sister's house, but he never arrived. Nothing was heard of him until March 14th. On that date, a man going by the name of A. J. Brown, who had rented a small shop in Norristown, Pennsylvania, woke up in a frightened state and asked the people in the vicinity what he was doing there. He claimed that his name was not Brown, but Ansel Bourne, and that the last events of his life that he could recall had taken place in Providence, Rhode Island, on January 17th. He had complete amnesia for anything that had happened to him in Norristown. Actually not much had happened; the people who knew him described his life in Norristown as quiet and uneventful. He had struck them as a simple shopkeeper and had never displayed any abnormal behavior that they could discern. He was quiet and regular in his routine. After regaining his original identity, on March 14th, he was taken home and resumed his normal life in Rhode Island. What had happened to Bourne during his unusual Norristown period remained buried for the next three years until the preacher was introduced to William James.

James decided that hypnosis should be tried in order to uncover the facts in this case. While under hypnosis Bourne was able to provide a detailed account of his experiences during the first two weeks of his secondary state. To James his behavior seemed characteristic of an ordinary fugue; Bourne had forgotten his personal identity, assumed a new name, and wandered from place to place. Once his lost memories were recovered, James asked him why he might have done such a thing. He replied that he'd just wanted to get away somewhere and get a rest. This case was one of the first, most important—and most thoroughly investigated—examples of a classical "fugue" type of disorder which had been frequently described in the literature during the nineteenth century. The significance of the case was elevated by the fact that William James used hypnosis to untangle the dynamics and mystery of the patient, but he wasn't the only one to find Bourne of interest as a hypnotic subject. Hodgson also hypnotized Bourne in 1871 and later published an article about the case, ensuring that Bourne's unusual experience would find its place in the annals of dissociation (B. Hodgson, 1892, "A Double Case of Consciousness," *Proceedings of the Society for Psychical Research*).

FELIDA X, 1887 (AZAM, 1892)

What we know about Felida X comes from a summary of the case by Dr. Eugene Etienne Azam which appears in the *Dictionary of Psychological Medicine*. Before Azam plunges into his description of the now-famous Felida X, he makes reference to another case of what was termed "dual consciousness," which was described by Robert Macnish in his very popular 1816 book, *The Philosophy of Sleep*. Macnish's dual consciousness case, Azam contends, was the first to his knowledge that had ever been published.

The earlier case involved a young, well educated woman of a good background who suddenly fell into profound sleep. When she returned to consciousness several days later, she'd forgotten everything she knew and had to learn how to perform even the most mundane tasks like a child. She made very good progress though it took a considerable amount of time. Then, without any apparent cause, she lapsed into a similar sleep state. When she woke again, she found herself in the same position as before, again without any recollection of what had happened to her before going to sleep. For four years she continued to pass from one state to the other. For example, during one state, she possessed all the knowledge which she had acquired during her youth, but during the second state, she only knew what she had learned since the first state had ended.

Once he'd recapitulated Macnish's case, Azam then went on to describe his well-known case of Felida X. When Azam wrote about the case, thirty-two years had already passed since Felida had been under his care. Felida was fifteen years old when she first saw Azam; she was hysterical, suffered from convulsions, and was thought to be insane. Yet she was also industrious, intelligent, and, in Azam's words, had a "serious type of character." Like Macnish's patient, Felida had a tendency to fall into a long, deep sleep by apparently doing nothing more complicated than simply sitting down. These sleep states could last sometimes for two to three months at a time. Typically, when she awoke, she would exhibit a personality that was entirely different from the one she'd had when she went to sleep. The new personality was merry and frivolous, prone to laughter and fond of jokes, whereas the pre-sleep Felida was rather serious and inhibited. Moreover, the new personality suffered none of the illnesses that Felida suffered from. Felida's case was typical in that in her so-called second state she had a complete knowledge of her life and history. She could also recall periods when she'd undergone other unusual states, which were similar to the one which she was experiencing at the time.

By 1858, the so-called second state was lasting one to three hours each day. In the years that followed, the duration of the second state increased and seemed to occur at the same frequency as the periods in which the normal condition prevailed. She was living a dual life. After a while the second state became more dominant so that the normal periods might last for two to three days while the abnormal periods would persist for four to five months. Her life had become insufferable because she had virtually no memory of a major part of her life. But, as Azam noted many years later, she gradually experienced a recovery:

> Now in 1891, Felida is forty-seven years old. Her general health is bad, for she has an ovarian tumor. Her intellectual condition at present is as follows:-For the last nine or ten years the periods of the second condition have diminished in time of duration to lasting a few hours only, and appearing only every twenty-five to thirty days. So that Felida is almost cured, and will be perfectly so at the epoch of the menopause.

Ellenberg has described Felida X as "a one-way amnesic multiple personality," which means that A knows nothing of B, but B knows about both itself and A. Azam coined the term "dual personality" to describe a person like Felida. This case was a particularly important one in France because of several factors. For one thing, it was a case in which the doctor maintained the patient under hypnosis during treatment for such a long period of time. For another, the case influenced Janet and other intellects of the day who made constant reference to it at various conferences during the latter part of the nineteenth century. Positivists, such as Taine and Ribot, made frequent use of the case, too, to discredit the work of the famous philosopher Cousin. Largely forgotten now, the dispute hinged upon what school of thought would obtain the professorship of psychology at the College de France.

MARCELINE (JANET, 1907)

We owe our knowledge of the case of Marceline to an account of Pierre Janet. The parallels between her case and Azam's Felida are striking. Marceline suffered from severe recurrent hysteria. Janet described Marceline as an emaciated bedridden woman, incapable of standing or even urination. Because she couldn't eat or urinate normally, Janet attempted hypnosis in order to see if that would help. She responded well to the hypnosis, regaining her mobility and urinating without difficulty. There was one problem: her miraculous recovery was only possible so long as she was in the hypnotic/trance state. Once she was awakened, she reverted to her previous debilitated condition. Moreover, she couldn't recall anything that had happened during hypnosis. Janet discovered that hypnosis was required periodically if she were to receive any nourishment at all. By chance her parents visited her while she was in the hypnotic state, and under the impression that she was cured, took her home. Things went well for a short period of time, but Marceline experienced a recurrence of the symptoms. Her parents brought her back to Janet for further treatment. In a paper delivered at Harvard, Janet described the progress of her care: "Gentlemen, things continued in this way for fifteen years. Marceline would come to me in order to be put to sleep, enter into her alert state, and then go away happy, with complete activity, sensibility, and memory." She would remain "cured" for several weeks, only to relapse again. Her amnesic episodes recurred so often that they became a problem over the following years. In his summary of the case Janet suggests that Marceline's condition was so similar to Felida's that he proposed calling her an "artificial Felida." That is, she was a case of dual personalities or what we now might call a disordered state of divided consciousness. In the first state she suffered from depression with amnesia while in the second state, which occurred under hypnosis, she had complete recall. Janet thought this case was so important that he constantly made reference to it in most of his publications and it figured prominently in a famous series of lectures that he delivered at Harvard in 1906.

MARY BEAUCHAMP (Prince, 1905)

Mary Beauchamp is one of the three best-known cases of multiple personality in American medical history. (The other two are Eve White and Sybil Dorsett.) We owe the account of Mary's case to Dr. Morton Prince, a Harvard-educated physician who taught at the Tufts College Medical School in addition to pursuing a private practice. Prince was intensely interested in the new developments in psychology, including the use of hypnotism as a therapeutic tool. (He later founded the highly respected *Journal of Abnormal and Social Psychology*.) One of his patients was a hospital nurse who had suffered a "nervous breakdown" as a result of the pressures of work, whom he called Mary Beauchamp. He reported her case in his book *The Dissociation of a Personality*, which we discussed earlier.

Miss Beauchamp was an extremely inhibited person with deep religious feelings and high ethical standards. Both because of her temperament and upbringing she was much too shy to feel at ease talking about her emotional problems even with a close friend. It was Prince's idea to relax her and draw her out by trying hypnosis. Although the hypnosis did not bring about anything like a complete transformation, it did succeed in loosening her inhibitions and making her more open to talk about herself. Indeed, after a few sessions under hypnosis, her health and outlook seemed to be improving.

And then one day Prince was startled to hear her referring to herself in the third person while describing something she'd experienced. "She" did this, Mary said, "She" felt that, and so on. Moreover, he began to notice differences in the way she looked and moved and spoke, as though she were imitating some other person. Who, he asked her, was this "she" she was referring to? The question seemed to confuse her. When she didn't immediately reply, Prince tried to help her out. "It's you," he suggested, "You are this 'she.'" "No, no," she remonstrated, "*She* doesn't know what I know, she doesn't have the same thoughts." "But you have the same body!" Prince pointed out. "Yes," Mary agreed, "but that doesn't make us the same person!"

Finally the doctor conceded the argument. Yet in their next session a few days later, the young woman—again under hypnosis—denied that she'd done what the doctor said. Prince awakened her and put her into a trance again, and this time she clearly recalled the incident. After a few such alternating denials and affirmations, the doctor began to accept that he was dealing with two different personalities.

Prince noticed she rubbed her eyes a great deal while she was under hypnosis. Although he tried to discourage this habit, he attached no particular significance to it, assuming that it was simply a symptom of her nervousness. During a conversation with the other personality, however, he learned that it was she who was doing the eye-rubbing because, she explained, she wanted to "get her eyes open." Alarmed by this information, he redoubled his efforts to discourage the practice, fearing that if the second personality did manage to "get her eyes open," she would thereafter be able to assert her existence more freely and thus aggravate Mary's problems.

In spite of his efforts this is exactly what happened. Not long afterward, at home, Mary became excited over something and the second personality emerged. Without the doctor there to discourage her, she rubbed her eyes until indeed she got them open and from then on the second personality could emerge at will. As time passed, the alter became an ever more assertive and independent personality, privy to all of Mary's thoughts and even able to control her behavior at times. Unlike Mary, she was carefree and mischievous. She even chose her name quite capriciously, inspired by the name of a character in a book she happened to like. From that time on she was known as Sally.

Not surprisingly, Mary Beauchamp hadn't been a completely ordinary child. Although Dr. Prince apparently never learned much about her family or her home life, he did discover that she'd had certain mystical experiences. When Prince learned about the power of these childhood religious associations, he was able to use them whenever his patient was especially troubled or under a lot of stress by summoning up a vision of Jesus Christ or the Virgin Mary. Mary invariably found these visions consoling and even if the problem she was facing couldn't be immediately solved at least she no longer considered it insurmountable.

In addition to religion, she had two great passions in her life—one involving career, the other love. She had always wanted to be a hospital nurse and managed to become one in spite of her emotional instability. She also harbored a passion for a man whom she had known as a child. Much older and more sophisticated than she, he seems to have assumed the proportions of an unattainable but absorbingly desirable god. Even though she had seen very little of him in the ensuing years, she had never forgotten him.

One evening about six years before her first visit to Dr. Prince, Mary was chatting with another nurse in a second-floor sitting room at the hospital. It had been a rough evening for her. An especially severe thunderstorm had been raging outside earlier, so that her nerves were on edge to begin with. Then one of the mental patients had become delirious and rather violent, and this unsettling experience had made her very jumpy. As she rested in the sitting room trying to recover, a face unexpectedly appeared at one of the windows. This alone might have been startling enough to shock her, but the real shock came when she recognized the face in the window as that of her old friend and hero from her younger days.

The shock evidently was profound, even though she soon learned that she hadn't been imagining things; her friend had merely yielded to a prankish impulse. Stopping off on his way to New York, he had come to the hospital, and having noticed a ladder left against the wall (apparently by some workmen at quitting time), had climbed up to the window to look in. The explanation was not enough to calm Mary down. For several days she remained at a high level of agitation, pacing the wards and walking about the hospital grounds, barely getting any sleep or rest. Although her disturbance gradually subsided, she began to grow slowly and steadily more excitable and agitated as time went on. It is small wonder that Dr. Prince, in diagnosing her condition after her first visit, described her as seriously neurasthenic.

Over the next seven years of treatment, the doctor found no reason to substantially modify his initial diagnosis. Sally became increasingly dominant, providing Mary with some surcease from her distress, but Mary had to pay a heavy price in return. Sally thoroughly disliked Mary ("I hated her, Dr. Prince!"), and, since she knew all of Mary's thoughts and feelings and could often control her actions, she had the ability to indulge in malicious, even sadistic tricks that would make Mary miserable. Of the two personalities, however, Dr. Prince considered Sally much healthier. While Mary was better educated—unlike Sally, for instance, she could speak French and write shorthand—she was pathologically "religious," morbidly scrupulous, anxiety-ridden, generally depressed, and not infrequently in pain. In contrast, Sally (who was never in pain) was fun-loving, carefree, irreverent, bright, lively, and saucy—in short, an engaging and cheerful companion. Yet her character was marred by the cruelty she exhibited in her treatment of Mary.

Within a few weeks of Sally's first emergence—incidentally, she dated events as happening before or after the day when she "got her eyes open"—she was able to "come out" for hours and even days at a time. At first she usually would emerge in response to an unconscious distress call from Mary, but it wasn't long before Mary lost even this control over these experiences, which to her of course were simply blackouts. And it was often during these blackouts that Sally would play her rather nasty practical jokes.

One day, for example, she stuffed a box full of spiders and snakes, wrapped the box very tastefully, addressed it to "Miss Beauchamp," and left it on a table. When Mary emerged, she opened the package and reacted just as Sally had hoped. Never mind that the snakes weren't poisonous; Mary was thrown into a panic. To make matters worse, she had to scramble around to retrieve the slithering things that had managed to escape.

On other occasions Sally would hire a hack to take her deep into the countryside. Passing a gate to some remote, thoroughly isolated farm, she would ask to be let out on some pretext, saying, for instance, she could walk the rest of the way. After the hack was out of sight, she would toss away whatever money she had left and wake up Mary, who thus would be forced to walk or hitchhike back to town. These experiences were exhausting and embarrassing, and needless to say, they did nothing to settle her nerves.

Sally had another trick she liked to play that drove Mary crazy. A friend of Mary's had asked her to knit a blanket for her newborn, and Mary had gladly agreed. It turned out to be quite a project, though, taking much longer than Mary could possibly have contemplated, for, whenever Mary had the blanket nearly finished, Sally would take over and unravel it. After going through this Sisyphean experience several times, Mary finally emerged from a blackout one day to discover herself in a great web of tangled yarn. In sweeping whorls and hopeless snarls, the yarn was wound around the chairs, the tables, the bed; Sally had looped the yarn over the pictures on the wall and even wrapped the strands around Mary herself, who was obliged to cut her way out of a woolly chaos.

Sally didn't limit her acts of harassment to Mary's blackouts. At times she would actually take over Mary altogether, leaving Mary still fully conscious but deprived of any power to reassert control, and make her do painful, humiliating things. She would attack Mary's overdeveloped sense of decorum, for example, by making her sit with her feet up on the mantelpiece, in a sprawling position that would be considered gauche even in our more casual times. Despite her great mortification, Mary could do nothing about the situation until Sally would at last relent and allow her to regain her dignity and composure.

Sally also exploited Mary's insistence on always telling the truth. To Mary, telling even a half-truth or a white lie was sinful. So naturally Sally would force her to tell outrageous lies. On one occasion, when a friend asked her who lived in a hovel at the edge of town, Mary heard herself uttering the name of a well-known dowager. Her astonished companion remonstrated with her, pointing out that this seemed unlikely in view of the dowager's great wealth. "Oh," Mary was compelled to reply, "she lost all her money and was reduced to these circumstances." Of course, the dowager was still living quite comfortably in her mansion elsewhere in the town, and Sally was aware that both Mary and the questioner knew it.

On yet another occasion Sally caused Mary to tell a wild story about a new baby in the neighborhood, in which she insisted that the newborn didn't have a bone in its body and was only being kept alive by a special diet of oatmeal. It's not hard to imagine Mary's horror at hearing herself say such things and at seeing the expressions on her listeners' faces.

Such malicious pranks were by no means Sally's only means of making her victim's life miserable. At times she would hide money from Mary, forcing her to beg for a few coins. In the morning Mary would find a nickel or five pennies on a table, usually with a note explaining that this was her spending money for the day and cautioning her against going into debt. Sally even stole her postage stamps. On these occasions, if she wrote a letter, she would have to leave it on the desk; later she would find a stamp affixed to the envelope, but only if Sally approved of the letter's contents. Sally's own correspondence with her was quite voluminous: Mary would constantly find letters awaiting her in the morning, criticizing her character and conduct and regaling her with reports about all of the unkind things that her neighbors had said about her, all of them quite untrue. When she was feeling in an especially creative mood, Sally would include some malicious doggerel.

Mary's greatest handicap in this unequal battle was blacking out while Sally was in control, whereas Sally not only was privy to all of Mary's thoughts and emotions but was capable of independent thought herself. She smoked a cigarette in front of Dr. Prince, something that Mary would never do. In a subsequent interview the doctor remarked to her that after Mary had resumed control that same day, she'd shown signs of tasting the tobacco-smoke residue in her mouth. "Oh, yes," Sally said, "she [Mary] thought you must have given her some quinine but was too timid to ask why."

Sometimes Sally would simply vanish. One day, for instance, Mary inadvertently tore up some paper money instead of a half-written letter. Sally would have stopped her but she failed to put in an appearance. Sally made sure to inform Prince about this incident during the next interview, though. The doctor in turn informed Mary when *she* reappeared. Mary didn't believe him and went to check her coat pocket, but of course, found not the cash she expected but a tattered letter. She still insisted, however, that she couldn't have destroyed the money. Prince sought to convince her of the truth. For this purpose he didn't rely on hypnosis alone. Instead he chose another tool at his disposal—a crystal ball.

Prince often used the crystal-gazing technique, sometimes in conjunction with hypnosis, to reveal a patient's suppressed experiences. (He had employed this technique to "show" Mary wantonly smoking a cigarette, a shocking vision for the proper Miss Beauchamp.) But even Prince couldn't quite control the visions that Mary would perceive in the crystal ball in which case he would have to call upon Sally's help in making the correct interpretation.

In one of these visions, Mary saw herself get out of a sickbed, pace up and down, climb onto a windowsill, and throw out an inkpot. Although she recognized the room, she could neither recall nor explain the incident. But Sally could—and did. Mary, she explained, was quite ill with pneumonia and had dreamed that she was walking along a beach. In a delirious sleepwalking trance, she had climbed up on a rock (the windowsill) and tossed a stone (the inkpot) out into the water. Sally knew all along not only what Mary had done but also why she had done it.

Prince continued to work with his patient through the years. She seemed to have periods of improvement and then of relapse; he could never feel confident that there was any long-term trend in either direction. And then one day, as he was about to hypnotize her, the patient remonstrated that only Dr. Prince should do that. Despite his efforts to identify himself, she kept insisting that he was Will, the old friend who had visited her at the hospital in such unconventional fashion, about whom the doctor knew nothing at this time. The doctor did not press her further to reestablish his identity, but during subsequent interviews she gradually came to accept him and his function. He soon discovered the reason for the confusion; he was no longer dealing with either Mary or Sally, who, of course recognized him, but with a much different personality. This woman, Christine Beauchamp, seemed mentally healthier and more mature than either of the others, and even more knowledgeable, although she could not remember nearly so much of her own early history. Because of her lack of recall, and presumably because of an apprehensive jealousy, Sally called her "The Idiot." (She regularly derided Mary as "The Saint" although, while Mary could inspire contempt, she could not evoke jealousy the way that Christine did.)

Christine proved very adept at losing herself in fantasies; with the doctor's help she was eventually able to reconstruct her past quite fully and accurately. As he worked with her and her condition improved (he never did know just why), he became ever more convinced that she, and not Mary or Sally, was the real person behind the dissociations. Gradually Christine seemed to absorb the other personalities. At first she did so under hypnosis, but later she could do it on her own without any therapeutic intervention. Finally the day came when Dr. Prince felt confident that she was cured, and he discharged her. His feeling was justified by subsequent events: she suffered no further relapses, and eventually married and had a family. And, so far as is known, she lived at least much more happily ever after.

HELENE SMITH, 1900 (FLOURNOY, 1900)

We know about the case of the medium Helene Smith thanks to Theodore Flournoy, a disciple of Wundt, a medical doctor, philosopher, and psychologist. In 1894 he was invited to attend a séance by the medium. Helene Smith, whose real name was Catherine Muller, was an attractive woman who was about thirty when Flournoy met her. She was a devout believer in spiritualism, but unlike many psychics and clairvoyants of her time, refused to accept any money for her mediumistic work, relying instead on her salary as the employee of a Geneva department store. Flournoy was the kind of man who believed that everything was possible and that the weight of evidence must always be in proportion to the strangeness of the fact at hand. So it is not surprising that he agreed to attend this séance. He was so intrigued that he studied Helene Smith for nearly six years and then wrote a book about it called *From India to the Planet Mars*, which enjoyed great popularity. He concluded that Smith's revelations during the séances were figments of her imagination, based on forgotten memories and subconscious desires. Her case was characterized by three personalities which took the form of purported reincarnations: a fifteenth-century princess, Marie Antoinette, and a Martian. As a "Martian," she offered vivid descriptions of its landscapes, inhabitants, and their language.

According to Flournoy, Helene was a well-educated and articulate woman who was frustrated in her social and intellectual aspirations. She reminded Flournoy of a child who was eager for praise. Flournoy theorized that her unconscious repression of memories, which Flournoy called cryptomnesia, might explain her purported clairvoyance and telepathy. He interpreted the seemingly different personalities that Helene Smith manifested during her trance states as arising from primitive or infantile recesses of the mind. He attributed them to unconscious childhood memories of books that she'd read and demonstrated that the Martian language had the same basic grammatical structure as French.

Flournoy presented this case to a group of distinguished psychologists at the Fourth International Congress of Psychology in France. In some way his presentation was a kind of prelude to subsequent presentations to the Congress by such luminaries as William James, Pierre Janet, Theo Ribot, Charles Richet, and many others. Shortly after the presentation, his book appeared and was an immediate success. Not unlike many cases at the end of the twentieth century, Flournoy's *From India to the Planet Mars* was controversial and set off many unfair criticisms of his involvement in this case. Nevertheless, it stands as a hallmark presentation in the history of multiple personality, especially in terms of how well Flournoy used a psychological interpretation of the unconscious to better understand the extraordinary nature of this phenomenon.

THOMAS HANNA, 1905 (SIDIS AND GOODHART, 1905)

Many cases of multiple personality disorder typically are characterized by the occurrence of trauma that then appears to triggers dissociation. The case of Reverend Thomas Hanna fits this pattern. In a case recounted by Boris Sidis and Simon Goodhart in 1905, Hanna suffered a traumatic head injury after falling out of a carriage. When the victim awakened several hours later, another personality called Tom had appeared.

What makes this case unusual is that the predominant personality Thomas not only recalled the accident but was able to provide his doctors with a full account of Tom's experience of the event six months after his recovery. Under similar circumstances, other so-called dominant personalities could never recall what their alters were up to; usually it was the other way around. Thomas's report, verified by journal notes and recollections of doctors, friends, and relatives, forms the core of the case history.

The morning after Thomas—or rather Tom—emerged from his coma, he tried to talk. Although he could still speak, he no longer knew the meaning of the words that poured forth; the best that he could do was to repeat the phrases he heard from the people around him. He failed to understand why the people around him had no idea what he was trying to communicate. But he had a more important problem to cope with—hunger. For Tom, hunger was such a novel sensation that he didn't know what to do to relieve it. Fortunately, someone made sure that he was given breakfast. Although he couldn't identify hunger, he quickly learned how to satisfy it, but only with the help of a good friend. Food became such an overriding preoccupation that it was all his friend could do to keep him from gorging himself. For the next day or two his greatest inconvenience, as Thomas later put it, "was from hunger and the inability to state the need."

It took some time, though, before his friend realized that he was unable to grasp the meaning of the words he was saying. So his friend began to teach him just as she would a small child. She started with the word "apple" while holding an apple in her hand. Once Tom seemed to make the connection between the word and the object, she rewarded him by giving him the apple to eat. The friend, however, didn't realize that the lesson hadn't taken as she'd hoped. Tom understood "apple" only as a synonym for "food," failing to draw any association between the fruit and the word. So any time he became hungry, he naturally asked for "apple." Until his friend diagnosed his syntactical problem, Tom had to subsist on a diet composed exclusively of apples.

Nonetheless, it didn't take long for Tom to relearn the language that his—or rather Thomas's—accident had briefly denied him; once he learned the meaning of a word, he never forgot it. But there were problems. Although concrete nouns and verbs were fairly easy for him to grasp, abstract nouns and verbs, and other parts of speech like prepositions, proved hard for the teacher to illustrate and the learner to absorb. One can imagine the difficulties presented by the deceptively simple word "fast," which acts as four different parts of speech and has a myriad of meanings. The personal pronouns caused considerable confusion as well, since the teacher pointed to Tom while saying "you," which caused him to refer to himself as "you," too. Phrases also could confuse him since he was inclined to think of them as a single word with a distinct meaning. After being told, for instance, that a black hen was a "black hen," without his having seen a hen before, he identified a white hen as a "white black hen" as well. In general, however, the setbacks were minor, and the learning, or relearning, proceeded at a reasonably satisfying pace for all concerned.

Seeking to accelerate his return to normalcy, his doctors decided that he should consult specialists in New York. For Tom the train trip was an astonishment but nothing compared to the thrilling sights and sounds that greeted him once he was walking about the city itself. His faithful brother, who was accompanying him, could hardly keep up with his questions.

The two specialists his doctors had recommended took an intense interest in his case. Initially they concentrated on restoring his memories before the accident but their efforts were in vain. He had almost no recollection whatsoever of life before the accident. Compounding the difficulty, it seemed that in his secondary state he had no idea what it meant to "forget" anything. When any aspect of his past did intrude in his consciousness, Tom dismissed it as a dream.

The doctors decided to tackle the unusual challenge of trying to teach someone what it was like to forget. If it worked, they hoped, he might come closer to recognizing his long-term memory lapses for what they were.

This ingenious scheme worked at least to some degree. Tom was put in a position where he was forced to admit that he'd forgotten some fact or event. This experience, Thomas testified later, made a deep impression on him, but by no means was it deep enough to throw a clear light on his former existence. Tom acknowledged that he might have forgotten some things as Tom, but Tom wasn't prepared to admit that a huge chunk of his life—as Thomas—might have been forgotten. And so the doctors resorted to hypnosis.

Tom's hypnotic dreams were very vivid and filled with extremely detailed scenes from his former life as Thomas. The doctors triggered the dreams by suggesting people, places, and events from his life before the accident. Since the Reverend Thomas Hanna knew Hebrew, the doctors read some Hebrew verses to Tom but needed to recite only a few lines for Tom to complete the rest of the verse. How he could do this, though, he had no idea; he later said that he'd "felt as if they were being spoken by another mind using my tongue."

The doctors continued their attempts to jog his memory for a long time without any visible results, but their efforts must have had some sort of attritional effect. One morning about four, he awoke after a restful night's sleep. But the "he" who awoke was not Tom, but Thomas. He stared at his surroundings in utter bewilderment. The last thing he recalled was riding home in a carriage with his brother. So why then wasn't he in his own bedroom? Springing up from the bed in a panic, he rushed to the other bed and shook its occupant awake. When his roommate turned out to be his brother, he demanded an explanation. His brother guessed what must have happened. Asking Thomas to remain as calm as possible, he called one of the doctors. The two men tried to explain what had happened to him, but Thomas—for that was the person who now seemed to be in charge—was having none of it. Certainly, he said, he of all people would remember the accident they described, and he didn't. Nor was he inclined to accept the possibility that this wasn't April 16th, the day after the accident. And he wasn't inclined to believe that several weeks had passed without his being aware of it. If this were some sort of elaborate practical joke, as he suspected, he really couldn't see the humor in it. It evidently was quite a scene: while the doctor took notes, frantically recording every word that Thomas said, his brother was dancing around the room in jubilant relief. Meanwhile, Thomas was at his wit's ends trying to make out what was really going on.

After some questioning, Thomas finally had to admit that he recalled getting his foot caught in the blanket on the floor of the carriage. This recollection introduced a little uncertainty into his heated protests. Then either his brother or the doctor—the record is silent on which one it was—pointed out that there was a way of demonstrating that this was not the morning of April 16th as Thomas assumed. The two men showed Thomas a watch reading 4:15. If it were April it would still be dark, but he could see clearly that the sun was coming up. The evidence was incontrovertible; at least a month had gone by.

Perhaps this sudden realization was too much for him. He dropped back to sleep. His brother and the doctor waited for about half an hour, and then when he stirred, they woke him again. But now the "him" was Tom, not Thomas.

By now the other doctor had arrived, and for the rest of the day the three men attended Thomas/Tom as he alternated between sleeping and waking and between the two personalities, or states. While in the primary state, Thomas knew nothing about what had happened to Tom in the secondary state and vice versa. In each state he firmly resolved to be helpful to the doctors and to do his best to remember what had happened and yet in the other state he couldn't even remember the resolution.

The doctors were determined to keep him awake at all costs to prevent him from drifting in and out of states and personalities. They spelled each other, hammering away at him with recollections from one state to the other, trying desperately to integrate the two personalities. After several hours of this treatment, Thomas began seeing glimpses of Tom's life. This was all the encouragement the doctors needed to redouble their efforts despite their weariness and their patient's near exhaustion. As evening came on, Tom began to buckle under the pressure. Since he could discern no signs of improvement, he was convinced that the doctors and his brother were merely being obstinate. Yet he continued to cooperate. On the other hand, Thomas was gaining strength even as Tom's was ebbing, making more frequent and forceful appearances. His glimpses of Tom's life became clear, sustained recollections. The two personalities continued to merge. Thomas, by what he later described as "a deliberate, voluntary act," brought them together for good, in both senses of the word.

Thomas struggled to organize his memories in order to get them into the proper sequence for his own sanity and "so as to present a continuous history." Before the year was out, Thomas was a whole man once again and Tom was never seen again.

DORIS FISCHER (W. Prince, 1915)

Sometime in the late 1890s a little girl named Doris Fischer was thrown to the floor by her drunken father during a violent quarrel with her mother. Although she was uninjured, she was never the same. From then on she was moody and unpredictable. Her family never knew what she was going to do next.

Nor, by and large, did she. She had no certainty whether she could control her body or her mind. The reason, it turned out, was because she—that is, Doris—wasn't the only one who had a say in what she did or thought; she shared her body and mind—rather precariously—with a new playmate named Margaret, a child of her own age who somehow mysteriously existed within her. This other self was usually a delightful companion, but her charmingly impish character was marred by a nasty streak of jealousy. Margaret was very possessive and was quick to assert her claim to anything that she considered hers, be it a toy, a doll, a ball. She expected Doris to respect her property rights scrupulously and should Doris fail to comply, Margaret would punish her by scratching her face. It took only a few episodes like this for Doris to learn her lesson. She became extremely cautious about which possessions she used for fear of angering Margaret. Margaret was not the only secondary personality produced as a result of her father's violent behavior, although she was the only one that Doris knew about. Doris talked in her sleep now, a great deal more than she ever had before, though it doesn't seem that anyone ever took the trouble to listen to what she was saying. It wasn't until she was a young adult that the source of these nightly ramblings was another, distinct personality, quite different from either Doris or Margaret. The monologues then became dialogues, for this new personality, who came to be known as Sleeping Margaret, was quite willing to answer the questions that were so eagerly put to her. Unlike Doris and Margaret, she was always conscious, always aware of what the others were doing. Nothing (awake) Margaret was thinking was lost on her and she seemed aware of everything that was going on around her. Despite her name, sleeping was the one thing she did not do.

Sleeping Margaret presented no problem for Doris, since she emerged only when Doris was asleep. Unlike Margaret, Sleeping Margaret was mature and self-controlled, and nothing she ever said was compromising or embarrassing. She never made any effort to take control of any part of Doris's body, manifesting her presence only in facial expressions. On rare occasions she would sit up for a few moments but that was all. If Sleeping Margaret had been the only secondary personality, Doris might well have gone through life without taking notice of her, Sleeping Margaret's, behavior.

Sleeping Margaret was a great help to Dr. Walter F. Prince, who treated Doris during the last forty months of her illness and who reported the case in 1915. Prince was a doctor of divinity to whom Doris was brought for help. He was manifestly a man of uncommon intelligence and understanding, with a similarly bright and sympathetic wife. He was interested in the new discipline of abnormal psychology and had the added advantage of being acquainted with the Christine Beauchamp case as reported by Morton Prince (no relation).

In working with Doris, he and his wife relied on the advice and help of a friend who was a reputable neurologist. They also benefited from the guidance of Sleeping Margaret herself; she seemed genuinely concerned about Doris's condition. Although Sleeping Margaret wasn't privy to Doris's thought processes, but only to Margaret's, nonetheless she was able to learn a great deal from Margaret about what Doris was thinking and was quite willing to divulge what Margaret told her to Dr. Prince. It was Sleeping Margaret who provided him with most of his information on the history of the case, which he could then check against the recollections of Doris's relatives and friends.

While Doris's family was unaware of her dissociated personalities, they were able to shed some light on her problem, recalling that since she was a little girl she behaved like a manic depressive, swinging from one emotional extreme to the other. As Sleeping Margaret later explained it, Doris remained completely submerged for the first three months after that shattering quarrel, yielding the floor (literally, to a great extent) to Margaret. Then, over the next several years, she began to emerge, at first very briefly (often for only a few seconds), but gradually for longer periods and with greater confidence. Once she had learned how to accommodate herself to Margaret's possessiveness, the two seem to have gotten along splendidly most of the time.

When Doris turned seven and was packed off to school for the first time, tensions arose between Margaret and Doris. As far as Doris was concerned, the settled routine of the school day was quite welcome, but for Margaret it was an intolerable bore. A natural mischief-maker, Margaret reveled in the role of class cutup. She frequently absented herself from school for as much as an hour or so, especially on warm days, when the classroom became as stuffy and oppressive as the lessons. Sometimes she returned sopping wet from such forays without offering an explanation. For the first few months, Margaret resented school and complained to Doris about being incarcerated in a classroom, but eventually stopped her grumbling when she realized that there was nothing Doris could do about it. All the same Margaret continued to play the part of the renegade, attending to her schoolwork only when Doris was called on to do some writing or conjugating of verbs, both activities which Margaret enjoyed for some unfathomable reason. In spite of having to appease another personality, Doris somehow managed to do quite well, regularly bringing home report cards with A's and B's. There was one subject, however, in which she was given an F: conduct.

Margaret had become something of a Frankenstein's monster: created to fill a need, she had proved very hard to live with. As she grew older, Doris developed considerable skill in dealing with the embarrassing predicaments in which Margaret often left her. Unlike Margaret, though, Doris was unconscious when submerged, at least in the sense that she never remembered anything that had happened when Margaret was in control. Since Margaret might decide to recede at any time—in the middle of a conversation with some friends, for instance—Doris had to spend a lot of time and effort casting about in uncertain waters, groping for an excuse to explain her behavior. ("I'm sorry, Gladys, but I don't think I understood that last remark," etc.) Although Doris became quite good at dissembling, the effort took a great deal out of her. As a child she had received punishment for things she didn't know she had done; as a young girl she received blank stares, puzzled frowns, sly smiles, and disbelieving snickers for things she didn't know she had said. It was all very trying.

In her first four years of school, Doris blacked out for most of every evening. When she emerged from the amnesia she would find dolls and toys strewn all over the place; while she was absent she would discover that Margaret had done some of her homework and had left several notes for her as well (Margaret's handwriting was quite distinct from Doris's), most of them taking Doris to task for something she had done. But after four years of schooling Margaret's mental development was arrested—she never got much beyond age ten or eleven—while Doris's continued normally. Within a year or so the schoolwork that Doris could do without any trouble proved utterly beyond Margaret's ability. As a result Margaret lost interest completely; since she could no longer offer any help to Doris, Margaret stuck to what she did best—mischief making. When Doris was ready for high school, Margaret was determined to prevent her from going, even keeping Doris from attending her graduation exercises at middle school.

Margaret triumphed. Doris gave up on the idea of higher education and settled for a job instead. Not that Doris was necessarily unhappy; now that she was getting a regular salary she could share some of her wages with her mother, whom she idolized. But Margaret wasn't happy even if she'd managed to scuttle Doris's high school plans and she continued to give Doris trouble. In hindsight it seems clear that Doris was on the verge of further dissociation and that it was simply a matter of time before something would trigger it. That trigger came one day when Doris was seventeen and her mother died.

Her mother's death was sudden and unexpected. One May morning, after Doris had left for work, her mother began to feel unwell. By the time Doris got home her mother was in bed, and very sick. By two the next morning she was dead. Doris managed to hold on long enough to call the doctor and make the necessary arrangements, but then Margaret took over. This time, however, she lasted only a few moments. As Sleeping Margaret described the situation later to

Dr. Prince, the left side of the head was seized by a piercing pain, Margaret abruptly disappeared, and a new personality, who was to be known as Sick Doris, appeared on the scene.

Now it was Margaret's turn to have a nuisance on her hands. Doris herself had completely disappeared and remained absent for two months. As for Sick Doris, she had no memory whatsoever; she was so helpless that she had no idea how to use a glass or a spoon. She had no vocabulary. She could only perform the most basic functions: she could move her arms and legs as though by instinct; she could pick things up, and she could walk. When it came to eating and drinking, however, she had to learn how to do them, imposing an additional burden on poor Margaret, especially. Sick Doris also had trouble dressing and undressing: at first Sick Doris was under the impression that her clothing was an integral part of her body, an impression that made her as militantly possessive as Margaret. For a while she failed to discern the distinction between the animate and inanimate, although movement of any kind fascinated her. Indeed, for the first day or so of her existence Sick Doris had no firm grasp on the distinction between self and other. By and large, she was a brand-new baby residing in a seventeen-year-old body.

Margaret set about educating her without much enthusiasm but with great resolve. Working night and day, Margaret succeeded in equipping Sick Doris with a simple working vocabulary in about a week. Her pupil was a quick study, and the learning process took place at a considerably faster pace than would have been possible with a genuine infant, since it mostly entailed a process of recalling memories lodged in Doris's unconscious. We can reasonably assume that this is what happened because it wasn't long before Sick Doris achieved an adult level of knowledge and competence, which ten-year-old Margaret couldn't possibly have provided. Margaret had given her a helpful start to be sure, but then Sick Doris was able to do well enough on her own and was soon following Doris's old routine without serious mishaps, going to work each day, doing the housework in her off hours, shopping for groceries, preparing the meals, and so on.

Sick Doris, as her name suggests, was not a very attractive person especially compared to the impish Margaret, nor was she as loving as Margaret or as intelligent as Doris. Unlike either of the other personalities, Sick Doris had no sense of humor. In conversation they invited eye contact; she avoided it just as she did all physical contact. She spoke largely in a monotone with something of a rasp. She was withdrawn, nervous, and distant, although she did have friends, possibly because she was in the habit of lavishing gifts on them.

The three personalities had a different view of religion, too. Margaret thought that church and Bible reading were "dumb stuff." Doris, by contrast, regularly went to church and read the Bible, but was hardly a devout or fervent believer; her religious devotion was mainly intellectual in nature, not spiritual. Sick Doris, however, embraced ritual and found far more solace in the spiritual aspects of religion than Margaret or Doris.

While generally competent, Sick Doris was simply never able to fathom some basic tasks such as learning how to set a clock or a watch. Yet in other things her skill was breathtaking; she embroidered, for instance, not only with great artistry but at an almost unbelievable pace. She was so good in fact that when she entered a contest, she finished a complicated piece of embroidery in twelve hours which the judges had expected to take forty-eight. What made this feat even more astonishing was that she managed to do it in one sitting, interrupted only by the occasional cataleptic seizure a few minutes or so in duration, while she sat rigidly in her chair, eyes glazed, needle clutched in her upraised hand. Every time this happened she resumed her work quite unaware of the attack. These exhibitions of her virtuosity happened fairly frequently and usually were capped by a performance that must have been startling to the uninitiated, when Margaret emerged to celebrate completion of some task with an exuberant victory dance.

For the next five years, from age seventeen to twenty-two, Sick Doris was the dominant personality although she was often replaced by Margaret, especially when Sick Doris was tired or distressed over some unpleasantness. Sleeping Margaret was active, too, providing some measure of continuity if not stability. But Doris herself remained almost completely submerged, appearing for only a few minutes at a time. In those five years, Dr. Prince later estimated, she probably was "on deck" for a total of less than 75 hours.

One morning some fifteen months after her mother's death, Margaret fell down some stairs, suffering a severe blow on the head. That night a fifth and final personality emerged—another sleep-talker—whom Margaret dubbed Sleeping Real Doris chiefly because she talked more or less as Doris might have been expected to talk in her sleep. Yet at other times she spoke quite differently, in a distinct and much more unpleasant voice accompanied by facial expressions quite unlike Doris's. Throughout her existence the fifth personality stayed in the shadows, never fully formed, always in a state of some bewilderment. One could hardly blame her.

When at the age of twenty Sick Doris came to Dr. Prince for help in the late autumn of 1910, he accepted her as a troubled but single personality. Even on her first visit, however, her behavior changes were frequent and radical enough for him to suspect that he was dealing with some sort of split or dual personality, and after a few more visits his suspicion deepened into conviction. Her home life, he soon learned, was sufficiently miserable to place a severe strain on a vulnerable personality: her mother's death had left an enduring void, and life with father was very difficult at best. (One of the first times Margaret confronted him she cried out repeatedly, "Daddy, don't hit me!")

Finding Sick Doris pathetic and her condition fascinating, Prince and his wife invited her to visit them whenever she felt the urge, and soon she was doing so quite regularly. After a year he began to keep a diary on the case, which of course he later drew on as the basis for his famous *Journal* article.

Then on Sunday, January 22, 1911, Dr. Prince reported a day of crisis. There were three visits that day. In the morning Sick Doris arrived with a complaint that she had awakened with bleeding scratches on her arms and on her hip. After Prince had provided her with first aid and some badly needed sympathy, she went home.

That afternoon Margaret put in an appearance, obviously in a playful mood. Dr. Prince reacted by asking her whether Margaret wanted to tease him. Oh, yes, she replied in delight. Very well, he countered, but urged her to leave Sick Doris alone. Margaret's attitude changed immediately. Her grin was replaced by a scowl. Her response was firm and monosyllabic. No! She stormed out of the doctor's house fuming.

That evening the Princes' next visitor was Sick Doris, who arrived looking very tired and dispirited. To their efforts at conversation she responded only with grunts and monosyllables; soon she was curled up on a sofa, fast asleep. Then Margaret emerged but in one of her fouler moods and began scratching viciously at the neck and the left hip. Dr. Prince tried to stop her, of course, but Margaret proved too strong and agile for him. Desperately, he decided to try the power of suggestion. In a loud voice that he hoped would have an impact on her, he began making the kind of statements associated with hypnosis—"I am taking away your strength," "You're growing weaker, weaker," and so on. It worked, or something did. Her resistance grew steadily weaker, until finally he was able to say, "your strength is gone," as indeed it was, for her resistance had stopped altogether. Her facial expression had also altered, and when she awoke it was as Sick Doris.

But the real crisis was just beginning. Sick Doris had awakened in a state of extreme lethargy. She could speak only haltingly, with great effort. She also seemed to be drifting into a coma, and the Princes feared that she might be dying. Dr. Prince felt her pulse; it was weak and had dropped to 54. In a few moments she was so quiet that Dr. Prince bent down over her to see whether he could detect any breath.

He was startled to hear her say in almost a disembodied voice that she was in danger but referring to herself in the third person—"She is," not "I am." She implored the doctor to arouse her at once. Fearful that she could prove to be a victim of amateur hypnosis, he began shaking her, gently at first and then roughly, while the voice urged him on to even greater effort. When she failed to respond, the voice demanded that the Princes walk her up and down the length of the room until she was revived. This wasn't easy, for she had gone quite limp, but they managed to drag her around until the voice assured them that she was coming back and soon would be all right.

Her prediction proved to be right, except that for the life of them the Princes couldn't make out *who* was all right. However, they were astute enough to observe that Sick Doris and Margaret were alternately in control. For the initial thirty or forty minutes the alternations (and alterations) were very rapid, averaging perhaps two per minute and were clearly manifested by changes in what the two personalities said, how they said it, and how they looked when they said it. Meanwhile, the body was growing freer of the lassitude that had seized it. She first regained control over her feet and legs, then over her hands and arms, until finally Margaret was able to go on the attack again. Restraining her this time was easier, however, and after a while she dropped into a deep sleep, from which Sick Doris awoke in time to go home and make breakfast for her father. It was five o'clock in the morning.

The following evening Sick Doris returned. She was exhausted and said very little. She told Dr. Prince that the one thing she had asked of God was the very thing that He had refused her: to be released from this life. Had she, asked Dr. Prince, ever prayed for the departure of the voices she heard? The question seemed to give her intense pain. No, she replied. Dr. Prince persisted, recommending that she at least try that approach. The pain only seemed to intensify, her expression changed, and Margaret emerged to angrily remonstrate with him. "Do you fear prayer?" Dr. Prince asked. "Yes," she replied. "Can it weaken you?" "Yes," she repeated. He proceeded to recite a prayer aloud, which had the immediate effect of putting Margaret quietly to sleep. ("She has gone away for now," Sleeping Margaret confided.) After about twenty minutes, Dr. Prince called on her to wake up. She did so, with a beautiful smile that he found totally unfamiliar. After it had disappeared, Sleeping Margaret explained that he had met Real Doris for the first time. She had appeared for only a moment, and now Sick Doris was back. After making sure that she felt well enough, he sent her home.

The doctor didn't want to send her back home, sensing that it would put her health at risk. He still held out hope that she might be cured, but only if she could be freed from her father's influence. Early in March, as he phrased it in his diary, he "wrung from the father a reluctant and entirely heartless consent for his daughter to live for a while with the family, which she was destined never to leave." That family, of course, was the Princes', and the effect of the move was immediate. On the following day Doris herself appeared long enough to be told of the move; she received the news with astonishment and undiluted joy. As time went on she began emerging more often and for longer periods. Sick Doris, by contrast, began to weaken. Her memories began to fade and to merge with Doris's to the point where Margaret complained that she could no longer get through to her.

As Sick Doris grew weaker, the real Doris grew stronger. On March 10th she spent the entire night in the emerged state, for the first time in over seventeen years. By the 16th Sick Doris clearly was losing the power of her five senses, especially taste and smell. She was permitted to do housework but was not allowed to do any sewing because of the likelihood of cataleptic seizures. This restriction must have been a severe blow to her, since sewing was what she lived for. By early April she could no longer remember what her father's house looked like or how to get there; nor could she recall any incidents of the preceding day. She grew ever more childlike and lethargic as her memory waned. By April 10th she no longer recognized Dr. Prince, calling him "Mister" and pleading with him (for she sensed what was happening) not to let her disappear. By the 21st she no longer knew her own name.

In early May, her sense of taste and smell having long since departed, her vision began to go. First she was afflicted with a kind of tunnel vision, and then with a foreshortening of her field of view. By midmonth she could see nothing that was more than about a foot away from her eyes, nor could she recognize her own hand in front of her face. She became increasingly infantile. She could only maintain a horizontal position because her neck could no longer support her head in an upright position. She emerged now more and more rarely. Finally, although it couldn't be clearly labeled as such, there was a last time.

Then it was Margaret's turn. She was already weakened by Sick Doris's deterioration and disappearance. Her tantrums, thus deprived of their principal object, became less frequent and less violent. The Princes embarked on a program of keeping her asleep and otherwise restricting her activities as much as they could without irritating her. As the months passed, signs of deterioration began to appear, hut the process was much slower than it had been for the less energetic Sick Doris. It also took a somewhat different form; she was less lethargic and her cognitive capacity began to diminish. Margaret seemed to speak and behave more like a nine-year-old, then she reverted to an eight-year-old, then a seven-year-old, etc. By September 1912, her speech resembled that of a small child unable to fully pronounce words—"brekit" for "breakfast," for instance. Two months later she developed a German accent and began to use German expressions. (At the age of five she had spent some time in the company of German farmhands.) The name Fischer no longer meant anything to her, and she had no recollection of her parents. Her vision was failing, as were her other senses (except, curiously, her sense of touch, which actually became more acute).

As Margaret's strength ebbed, Doris grew ever stronger. When Margaret lost her sight entirely, for example, Doris reported an enormous improvement in her own vision. But overall progress still was frustratingly slow. It wasn't until September 1913 that Doris was finally able to remain in control for as long as twenty-four hours at a time. In February 1914, she was the dominant personality from the 22nd through most of the 25th for an unprecedented total of almost 71 hours. Doris managed to extend her period of control to weeks, and by May she had proved so thoroughly in command of herself—only Sleeping Margaret emerged occasionally, and that may have been all to the good—that Dr. Prince and his neurologist colleague declared her cured.

NORMA (Goddard, 1927)

In the autumn of 1921 a nineteen-year-old woman named Norma turned up in the offices of one Dr. Goddard. We know about Norma because Goddard found the case so unusual that he wrote it up. She initially complained of having a sleepwalking problem. At first glance there was nothing unusual about the young woman. Norma was the firstborn child of a large family and had an above-average intelligence. But she'd been born frail and frail she would remain for the rest of her life.

From the age of six, Norma said that she had walked in her sleep. At the same time, she suffered from a lack of energy and tiredness. As Norma became weaker and weaker, and as the frequency and duration of her sleepwalking spells increased, she began to develop an elaborate imaginary life. When she suffered a nervous breakdown as a result of the strain, she retreated into her imaginary world, losing contact with reality.

Her physical condition underwent a similar deterioration. She was still experiencing episodes of sleepwalking in high school. One day she fell into a deep sleep, and when she woke up, she had amnesia. She no longer knew where she lived; for that matter she couldn't even recall her own name. So she invented a new name, Polly, who was four years old. This was the first appearance of her secondary personality. From time to time she would switch to her normal personality but when she did she couldn't remember the secondary one. Due to her debilitated immune system, Norma was only able to remain conscious while in her alternate identity. It was at that point that Goddard began Norma's treatment; although he was willing to try hypnotism he didn't feel that it was likely to cure her. It seemed that he was right. As the years passed, she suffered from periodic bouts of serious illness and was incapable of earning a living. A third personality named Louise began to pop up periodically. Louise had no memory of the other two personalities. She seemed to be the closest to what one might describe as a normal personality, and therefore, Goddard decided to develop and encourage Louise to dominate in order to suppress the other two, or at least to integrate them into a better functioning one. He hoped to achieve this integration by relying on the "proper environmental conditions."

His approach failed. Polly and Norma would come back time and time again and hypnosis didn't seem to do anything to discourage or suppress them. Goddard could only conclude that Louise wasn't strong enough of a personality to depend upon, surmising that she, Louise, was handicapped because of her amnesia. Goddard then decided to focus his efforts on Norma instead, a more productive choice out since Norma was the only personality who seemed to be growing stronger. The treatment seemed to succeed, leaving Norma as the predominant personality. As far as we know, she remained so for at least the three years that she consulted Dr. Goddard for follow-up visits.

JOHN CHARLES POULTNEY (Franz, 1933)

Three popular books about cases of MPD appeared in the twentieth century—*Three Faces of Eve*, *Sybil*, and Shepherd Franz's *Persons One and Three*. The latter case, which involves one John Charles Poultney, is less clear-cut than most documented cases because it is based on the chronological record his physician Dr. Franz maintained rather than on any serious investigation of the differentiates between the two personalities—John Poultney and Charles Poulting. Amnesia characterized this case as it does so many others. (The third personality, if there was one, was always inchoate, created by inference to fill in unexplained gaps between the emergence of Poultney and Poulting.)

Dr. Franz may not be entirely to blame. This lack of character distinction may have been due to the nature of the case, for John Poultney's words and deeds, at least the way Franz reported them, were not so different from Charles Poulting's. The two personalities spoke the same language, wrote in the same hand, walked the same way, and were motivated by the same work ethic. Each remembered things from the other's life, often without knowing it. The confused blending of the two personalities distinguishes this case probably more than any other feature.

Yet the man's life could hardly be described as that of a well-integrated personality. The real John Poultney was raised in Ireland, where he was born in 1888. His early history was hardly unusual; he went to school, found work and in 1905 he joined the army, served his hitch with the regulars, and was put on reserve in 1907. After leaving the army he married and had two children. He learned to drive several different makes of automobiles (they were much different from one another in those early, experimental days) and earned a modest living as a chauffeur and truck driver. In 1913, apparently unable to find a steady job, he sailed for the United States to seek his fortune. Failing to find it in New York, he traveled around the United States (Detroit, Cleveland, Chicago, Toledo), reconciling himself to $15-a-week jobs with Studebaker and Sears, Roebuck. When Great Britain declared war on Germany in 1914, he returned to Dublin and his reserve outfit, and was assigned to a transport unit. He was then shipped to a garrison outside London, there to await transportation to France. During this period he was promoted to sergeant. It was now September 1914, and he was destined never to remember anything that happened during the next five or six months.

In February or March 1915, he found himself convalescing in a London hospital without having any idea of how he'd gotten there. He had no conscious memory of anything that had happened in his life up to that moment. He was told that his name was C.J. Poulting; this may have been because of unclear writing on his admission card, but he was so unsure of himself that he accepted the name and kept it. He had been brought back from Belgium with a head wound, having somehow joined a group of Belgian refugees. His uniform and any identification cards or papers that he may have carried had disappeared. Indeed, at first he had been classified as a Belgian, but after conducting a physical examination the authorities determined that he must be an American because of the tattoos of Buffalo Bill and the American flag on his arms (both were souvenirs of Poultney's visit to Toledo). After a few weeks of enduring uncertainty and distress, Poultney was vulnerable to any promise of a restoration of his identity. So he was vulnerable to a recruiting sergeant's suggestion that the army would be more than happy to establish one for him provided he agree to reenlist. Since he'd recuperated from his injury he was fit for duty. The army was good as its word; Poultney was now officially C.J. Poulting of Florida, USA, Private No. M2/967530.

One morning the recruits were lined up and asked a series of questions about their qualifications and previous work experience. At one point those with driving experience were asked to step forward, and Poulting did so at once without thinking. Later that day he was taken to a field crowded with cars of all varieties, where he quickly demonstrated his competence in handling a standard American model. Curiously, he found the European cars alien to him, and he had to learn to drive them, even though he'd spent far more time driving European cars in Ireland than he had for Studebaker during his stay in the USA. It was a vivid demonstration of the unconscious linkage between the two personalities.

As a driver in the British army, he saw action in northern France, in Flanders and at Ypres, where he was gassed and returned to England as a casualty. In December 1915, having recovered enough for reassignment, he was shipped to Africa. During the journey he violated blackout security by lighting a cigarette and was clapped in the brig and sentenced to a long term for his infraction. He was already in a bad way since he'd been experiencing brief dissociations. (It's possible the weak third personality may have emerged during this interval, since neither Poultney nor Poulting could later recall anything that had occurred during the blackouts.) Conditions in the brig were abominable. One morning a guard found him hanging by a hammock rope from a beam in his cell and cut him down in the nick of time. The ships officers released him from his confinement with the understanding that he would not report his mistreatment.

Throughout 1916 he saw a great deal of action in Africa as an ambulance driver but continued to suffer from memory lapses. He and a friend were captured but managed to escape. The two began making their way cross-country by foot in a direction which they hoped would lead them back to their own lines. At night they slept in the open. Each evening Poulting would climb into a tree and tie himself to a branch under the impression that this stratagem might offer some protection against any hungry wild animals—especially leopards, which were prevalent in the area. His companion didn't think it was worth the effort and was content to sleep on the ground. One moonless, pitch-black night Poulting was awakened by the sounds of struggle accompanied by deep growling and muffled cries. The next morning he found the maimed and bloody remains of his friend. He went blank, and the next thing he knew he was in a hospital in Nairobi, awaiting transfer to a convalescent hospital in Voi, about 250 miles away.

On the way to Voi he picked up a small monkey and adopted it as a pet. He became very fond of the creature, keeping it on a leash in his hut. Its chattering sometimes proved annoying, however, and one night he tethered it outside, a few yards away from the hut. In the middle of the night he heard it cry out; when he looked out he saw a leopard tearing it from its leash and carrying it off. This second incident was much more traumatic for him than the first, since it produced intense feelings of guilt because he'd taken such a personal responsibility for the monkey. Curiously, though, the trauma was to prove a blessing although it would take about a dozen years for Poulting to understand why.

Early in 1917, he was shipped back to England with malaria. After a few weeks in the hospital he was sent across the Channel again, this time to work with ammunition supply columns in France and Belgium. Injured in an explosion in Belgium, he was brought back to a hospital in Woolwich, England, where he was given a medical discharge and a small pension. After trying to find a job without success, he joined the Red Cross as a driver. Apparently he was drawn to combat. In Calais, during an air raid, he was injured again, this time while rescuing patients from the flaming ruins of a hospital. For his heroism he received the Croix de Guerre. After his recovery in England, he visited his family in Dublin, although later neither Poulting nor Poultney was able to recall the visit. In April 1918, the British military returned him to the United States (assuming that was where he'd come from to begin with), where he spent the rest of the war as a Liberty Bond speaker at rallies held by the Red Cross, the Knights of Columbus, and the YMCA. He was, after all, a war hero.

The months after the Armistice saw a rapid devaluation of war medals. He embarked on a job hunt that carried him as far west as he could go, and in 1920 he wound up in Los Angeles where he found work washing and greasing automobiles. He continued in the same line of work over the next ten years with varying degrees of success. Sometimes he owned his own business, sometimes he was broke and unemployed. His biggest problem, he said later, was that as soon as he had accumulated some money he would be seized by an urge to travel and would forsake everything to go on a trip. Although he didn't remember them all later, he made three trips to Florida, four to Panama, and at least one to New York and to Cuba, among other destinations. Before leaving on his fourth trip to Panama he suffered a blackout, regaining consciousness only when he was debarking a ship at the canal along with several other passengers. He was surprised to find himself in Panama but was delighted to hear that during the voyage he'd been the life of the party. The ship's officers suspected that he might not be who he said he was, but were too sympathetic to his plight to conduct an extensive identity check. Instead they arranged with the port authorities for his return to Los Angeles on the next ship. (This may have been his only return trip that did not include a hassle with the immigration officials.) It was in this peripatetic fashion that Poulting spent the Roaring Twenties.

On a December morning in 1929, he was picked up by the police in Los Angeles as he was wandering aimlessly and rather unsteadily down a deserted street. Reversing the usual procedure, he asked them what his name was, and then what the date was. They were able to identify him by some newspaper clippings and the discharge papers he was carrying. As his confusion gradually cleared, he began acting more normally, but as Charles Poulting, still could not give them any biographical details earlier than 1915. Somehow the American Legion became interested in his predicament (doubtless some of the police officers were members) and asked Dr. Franz, who was in the Department of Psychology at the University of California at Los Angeles, to interview him in an attempt to extract further information that might help to identify him.

Soon the newspapers got into the act. As a result of the publicity he was besieged by curiosity seekers. That was to be expected. What was more surprising was how many people began to claim him as their long-lost father, son, or brother. No claimant was more persistent than a Mrs. Herrman and her daughter Mrs. Dandy. They had become firmly convinced that he was the elder Hermann's husband Charles Stuart Herrman, who had left home in 1913 and hadn't been heard from since 1914. They insisted on taking him home. Poulting came to regret his decision. He soon wearied of the attention they lavished on him and he was unable to summon any enthusiasm for their devotion to Seventh-Day Adventism. And so in mid-February 1930, he left them.

Six days later the San Francisco police found him wandering about in a dazed condition. He now carried cards in his wallet with the names of a Los Angeles police official, a Hollywood doctor, and Dr. Franz. Since he had a home to go to, that was where he went. But he found it just as stifling as before because after a week or so he again left, this time for good, and moved into a friend's apartment.

He also discontinued his daily visits to Dr. Franz, who had been accumulating a good deal of information on the 1915–1930 portion of his life but nothing on his earlier years. On March 4, 1930, the Los Angeles police phoned the doctor to tell him that they had found Poulting again wandering the streets in a daze. He didn't know who he was or where he was, and he resolutely refused to accept the ridiculous suggestion that he could be in Los Angeles, California. After he had been brought to Dr. Franz's office, he mumbled complaints about the police driving on the wrong side of the street; he asked what had happened to his uniform and made vague references to an imminent departure with his regiment. He recognized neither Dr. Franz nor his friend the police official. Dr. Franz asked him to write his name on a piece of paper, eagerly anticipating the result. The patient then proceeded to write "19463 Sgt. John Charles J. Poultney." And then he crossed out the "J." Poultney was back, but evidently Poulting still had a toehold.

Poultney had to be shown several recent newspapers and his own aging reflection in a mirror before he grasped that he was indeed in California in the year 1930. As he warmed up to the gently solicitous Dr. Franz, he began to talk quite freely. For the first time the doctor was able to learn all the details about the other half of his patient. Poultney remembered his life up to 1915 clearly, but nothing thereafter. In an effort to help merge the two memory sets while Poultney was still susceptible to suggestion, the doctor showed his patient a large map of Africa and asked if he recognized any of the place names. The ex-sergeant pored over the map, looking at names that had been familiar to Poulting with great interest but without betraying any sign of recognition until he came across the town of Voi. "Voi!" he cried excitedly. "I was there—I had a monkey!" That seemed to break the dam. Poulting's memories flooded his mind too rapidly for him to describe them. Alarmed that the memories were putting the patient under excessive strain, Dr. Franz ended the interview and told his patient to get some rest.

The next day Dr. Franz showed Poultney a brief autobiography that Pouling had written on the occasion of his first interview. Of course, Poultney was fascinated to have his new memories confirmed in this way; the experience of reacquainting himself with his alternate personality on the page also helped further the process of integration. During the next twelve months the process continued, with only occasional relapses. (When he went to see the movie *All Quiet on the Western Front*, for instance, he shouted in panic during a battle scene and "took cover" in the orchestra pit. Thereafter he avoided war movies.)

Meanwhile, Dr. Franz made discreet inquiries to his patient's relatives in Ireland. Contact was reestablished with his family and eventually Poultney began to correspond with his wife and other family members. He gradually came around to the idea that he should rejoin his family, which he did in July 1931. The last Dr. Franz heard from him was a thank-you note. It seemed that Poultney had adjusted to his new life as a well-integrated personality.

BRIDEY MURPHY (Bernstein, 1956)

Bridey Murphy's case, one of the most controversial of all the cases of multiple personality disorder, was unusual because it was, strictly speaking, not a case history of a living individual. It's more accurate to describe the case in terms of a "channeled" narrative of an individual's past life procured through the medium of hypnosis. The public was introduced to Bridey Murphy by means of a best-selling book in the 1950s written by the purported "channel," Morey Bernstein, a businessman from Pueblo, Colorado. Although he had no professional credentials, Bernstein nonetheless hypnotized a housewife named Virginia Tighe, whom he knew from Pueblo. Under hypnosis, she began to talk in an Irish dialect. She exhibited an entirely different personality than the woman Bernstein was familiar with. She claimed to have been reincarnated. Bernstein saw the dramatic possibilities in such a tale and wrote it up. The story was serialized in a local Denver newspaper before it was turned into a book entitled *The Search for Bridey Murphy*. Readers seized on the account which launched a fad in which other individuals claimed that they, too, had been reincarnated. Bernstein was in great demand and gave many lectures and appeared frequently on network radio and television. Not everyone was so credulous, however. Howard Gardner (1957), the great debunker of popular myths that try to pass for truth, summarizes the "evidence" conjured up by reporters of the Chicago *American*. The essence of their report was summarized by Gardner:

> With the help of Rev. Wally White, pastor of the Chicago Gospel Tabernacle where Virginia attended Sunday School, it did not take them long to locate Mrs. Anthony Corkell. Now a widow with seven children,

she was living in the old frame house where she had lived when Virginia was in her teens. For five years Virginia lived in a basement apartment across the street. Mrs. Corkell's Irish background had fascinated the little girl. One of her friends recalled that Virginia even had a "mad crush" on John, one of the Corkell boys. Another Corkell boy was named Kevin, the name of one of the imaginary Bridey's friends. Note also the similarity of Corkell and Cork, the city where Bridey was supposed to have lived. And what was Mrs. Corkell's maiden name? Bridie (with an "ie") Murphy! (Gardner, 1957)

Although obviously not a multiple like other cases chronicled in these pages are, Virginia Tighe/Bridey Murphy still must be considered a dual personality of a kind; in this case, like the others, two different personalities inhabit the same body at two different times. Which is true of all multiples: they are the same . . . only different.

EVE WHITE/CHRIS COSTNER (THIGPEN AND CLERKLEY, 1957)

One of the best-known and extensively documented and spectacular cases of multiple personality was the one recounted by Corbett H. Thigpen and Hervey M. Cleckley in their *The Three Faces of Eve*. The two psychiatrists originally reported the case in the *Journal of Abnormal and Social Psychology* in 1954 which was expanded into a book. It was later made into a popular movie.

The authors referred to their patient by the pseudonym Eve White to protect her identity. About twenty years later, however, in a book *I'm Eve* (Doubleday, 1977) the author Chris Costner Sizemore (who wrote the book with her cousin Elen Sam Pittillo) revealed herself as the famous Eve.

Chris began dissociating when she was a child. At the age of two, she saw the body of a drowned man hauled from a creek near her home. The shaken girl noticed a homely, skinny little girl standing on the small bridge that spanned the creek. Unlike Chris, who was terrified by the traumatic experience, the other little girl was taking in the scene with surprising equanimity. This preternaturally calm little girl would soon become incorporated into Chris's life—Chris Black as opposed to Chris White.

It wasn't long before a struggle had broken out between the inhibited good little girl Chris White and the unruly Chris Black. Sometimes the former would find herself being punished for something she knew nothing about perpetrated by the latter. At other times she could see the girl and would watch while Chris Black engaged in some forbidden act, yet it would be Chris who got the spanking. Her tearful protests that the other girl was the culprit merely earned her a reputation for lying.

Unlike other cases of MPD, in which childhood abuse figured prominently, Chris was raised in a loving home. However, her privileged status as the only child was threatened when she was six and her mother gave birth to twins. While Chris White struggled to be a good sister, Chris Black was not so accommodating. On one occasion the alternate personality expressed this resentment by poking her fingers in their eyes and biting their feet as they lay asleep. Hearing their wails of pain and terror, their mother rushed into the room to find Chris standing over them and staring at their wounds. Chris had seen the other girl do this terrible thing, but her professions of innocence were useless. It was her own bottom that got the spanking.

Not long afterward, her grandmother died. She and a cousin were playing under the porch of the funeral home when they came across the remains of a small blue cup that had belonged to her grandmother. It reminded her of the time when her alter ego had broken it and then slipped off while Chris suffered the punishment.

As she was mulling over this injustice, she heard someone call to come and say goodbye to Grandma. Standing beside the open coffin, she was lifted by an aunt and instructed to kiss the stiff, pallid face. She screamed and struggled in her aunt's arms until her mother finally rescued her. At the cemetery, still trembling, she watched as the coffin was lowered into the grave. The image of the cold, dark hole might have overcome her if she hadn't been braced by the sight of Chris Black standing nearby, watching the proceedings quite impassively. The incident would become deeply embedded in her unconsciousness.

For the next several months Chris was plagued with nightmares involving her grandmother.

School proved to be a sharp disappointment, entailing much more purposeless sitting than engaging in the kind of creative activity that she had been anticipating. Since she was left-handed, she was forced to learn writing with her right hand. But she became a competent reader and she even composed a little poetry. Meanwhile her alter, wanting nothing whatsoever to do with school, often emerged to wreak havoc, pilfering crayons and other supplies from fellow students, which only earned Chris a reputation as a thief as well as a liar.

The conflict between the personalities was too much to deal with and still pay attention in class. She dropped out of high school. Meanwhile other personalities came and went, perhaps a dozen of them in all, but none proved as durable as the girl she had seen first on the bridge.

Life seemed intent on providing Chris with traumatic experiences, including a brutal sexual assault some months after she quit school. Unable to hold a job because of her alter's capricious behavior, she married, almost in desperation, and soon became pregnant. In January 1948, her daughter Taft—nicknamed Taffy—was born. It was an extremely difficult birth; yet the baby was normal and healthy, and Chris was delighted with her.

But her husband was not so delighted with Chris, whom he found moody and unpredictable. One Saturday evening, pregnant again, the two fell into an argument after he refused her pleas not to go out. During the quarrel he accidentally struck her in the face. Not realizing the force of the blow, he stormed out of the house. Eve collapsed and had a miscarriage. She lay where she fell, dazed and bleeding, until her parents stopped by to visit the following afternoon.

From that point on, she was plagued with headaches and blackouts. She began hearing voices; one especially persistent voice castigated her husband and urged her to take violent measures against him. On two occasions, to protect Taffy from severe punishment, she threatened her husband with his own gun. As time went on, the voice seemed to be assuming more of a life of its own so that Chris would emerge from a blackout to find herself in some unaccountable predicament.

Recognizing that something was wrong, her parents took her to a doctor, who urgently recommended a visit to a psychiatric clinic. This was how she ended up meeting Dr. Thigpen.

During one of her early sessions with him, Chris complained of hearing a woman's voice. The doctor was alarmed; "auditory hallucinations" were usually were associated with psychosis. Yet Chris's response to the voice was typical of someone who was mentally balanced. She was by no means sure that the voice really existed, for instance, and she was terribly worried that her hearing it might mean that she could be losing her mind. Then one day while the doctor was trying to reassure her that she wasn't going crazy, the sober Chris White suddenly went into a kind of catatonic state for a moment before Chris Black emerged. "Hi there, Doc!" she exclaimed.

For several months thereafter the doctor carried on conversations alternately with the diffident Chris White (who knew little or nothing about Chris Black) and the boisterous Chris Black (who knew everything about Chris White, and incidentally didn't like her much). To talk with Chris Black, he would hypnotize Chris White and "call out" Chris Black; to reverse the process he would simply ask Chris Black, whom he could never hypnotize, to bring Chris White back. The necessity for hypnosis diminished as time passed, and before long the transformations, either way, required only simple requests. As the conversations continued, Chris White's health seemed to improve: her anxiety abated somewhat, and the headaches that had plagued her became less frequent and intense. Before long, however, she suffered a relapse, and even the irrepressible Chris Black began showing signs of uncertainty and uneasiness. By now the doctor had become so intimately acquainted with them both that he was all the more astonished when they unexpectedly receded and a third personality emerged.

The new personality introduced herself—a little tentatively—as Jane. She had emerged without any knowledge of either Chris, surprising the doctor as well. Jane seemed unaware of her own past (if she had any), indeed, she was oblivious of anything that had ever happened in history. (The doctor later learned, for instance, that she didn't know who George Washington was and seemed unfamiliar with the passage of the seasons.) Yet, unlike the newly reborn Thomas Hanna, she spoke English well (better than either Chris) and seemed wise beyond her years. Like Thomas Hanna, too, she was a quick study, and over the next several months she gradually became the dominant personality.

Her intervention came none too soon. Before Jane's arrival, the frolicsome Chris Black had grown quite literally irrepressible. Sometimes she would come out in the afternoon, change her clothes (she had squirreled a few sexy outfits Chris White knew nothing about) and then would spend the evenings carousing at a local nightspot. Taffy was left at home to fend for herself. On one of these occasions Chris's husband arrived home to find that the child had fallen and hurt her leg. When Chris Black showed up several hours later in her flashy cocktail dress and with the smell of liquor on her breath, he nearly went berserk. The next morning, of course, Chris White remembered nothing about the episode, but her husband's impassioned account of it, combined with her own awareness of a blackout, caused her considerable unease.

Promoting her peace of mind was hardly very high on Chris Black's list of priorities. On one of her more spectacular shopping sprees, for example, she spent most of a day at several downtown stores, selecting a budget-busting supply of fancy lingerie, shoes and evening gowns as well as an expensive coat. Once she came home she would stow away her outrageous outfits in a closet and then let Chris White try to explain their presence when her husband came home and found them.

Chris White was astounded and shocked to find herself in possession of clothes that she couldn't imagine herself wearing. But her husband could hardly be blamed for rejecting the notion that the new contents of the closet had somehow convened there under their own power. She agreed that the circumstantial evidence was undeniable (as usual, she was vaguely aware of a blackout period), and she promised fervently to do everything she could to return the booty and have the charges canceled.

Her efforts to do so were only partly successful. As a result, Chris Black was spared the humiliation of having to wear those colorless, drab, mousy, and very respectable skirts and blouses to which Chris White was so demurely addicted. A girl with any spirit, after all, can't go around looking like the town librarian.

Chris Black's appearances would take her alter ego by complete surprise. She could leave Chris White window-shopping for fifteen minutes or so—Chris White was always looking for clothes for Taffy, a mission which held no interest for her alternative personality—and hang out at a local drugstore with the assurance that Chris White would never know about it.

The strategy didn't always work out quite so smoothly. One time Chris White unexpectedly discovered herself talking with a strange soldier on a downtown street. She reacted with dismay when the soldier propositioned her. She didn't even have the words to rebuff him. Even so she made clear that she had no wish to accompany him. The puzzled soldier couldn't comprehend why only minutes before she'd been so eager and flirtatious, but ultimately gave up and went away.

Chris Black later told her doctor that after striking up an acquaintance with the soldier and agreeing on a date for the evening she began to have misgivings when he insisted on getting together right at that moment. Since he didn't seem to take no for an answer, Chris Black in her desperation to be rid of him resorted to an extreme measure: she summoned Chris White. Once again Chris White played the role of the patsy.

Chris Black wasn't content simply to cause embarrassment. One weekend, emerging while Chris White was cleaning window blinds, she launched into an abusive argument with her husband, frightening Taffy to tears. Thoroughly annoyed, she called the child a brat and began coiling the window-blind cord tightly about her throat. When the husband came to the rescue, she retreated, leaving to poor Chris White the impossible task of explaining what had possessed her to try to kill her daughter.

There was one occasion, however, when Chris Black did prove to be of some value. In a fit of deep despondency one day, Chris White tried to slash her wrists. That was too much for Chris Black, who emerged to stop her and then sent a note to the doctor reporting the incident.

FOURTEEN SEMINAL CASES

It wasn't long after the suicide attempt that Jane appeared, but Jane proved no instant cure-all. She and Chris White had to resign from several jobs because of Chris Black's incorrigible penchant for goofing up and goofing off. Eventually the personnel manager of a large department store told her that she would probably never be hired by any firm in town because every potential employer knew about her reputation which was attributed to a "strange illness."

Not surprisingly, her marriage deteriorated beyond repair. Chris filed for divorce. Jane concurred in this decision, and of course Chris Black was delighted.

Although all three personalities were in accord, the legal formalities were another matter. Through an arrangement that the doctor had made with an extraordinarily unflappable attorney, all three personalities signed the divorce papers.

Some weeks later Jane met Don Sizemore at a party. She was standing alone when a young man asked her to dance. She informed him that she didn't dance well and suggested that he ask someone else. But he persisted, he wanted to dance with her.

They danced. They talked. They spent the evening together. They began dating. Things grew quite serious, and Jane told him about her peculiar problem. It made no difference, he said. They fell in love.

This relationship continued to deepen, but Jane's condition took an alarming turn. She began having headaches and nightmares. Then one day, while playing catch with Taffy in the grandparents' front yard, she had to crawl under the porch to retrieve the ball. She was suddenly seized by the feeling that she had done this before. There was something dreamlike in the situation, as though, like Alice in Wonderland, she had eaten a biscuit that had made her tall. After she found the ball the feeling subsided.

But she didn't forget about it. In her next session with Dr. Thigpen all three personalities seemed on edge. Even Chris Black was uneasy; indeed, she used the word "scared" at one point and asked the doctor rather pathetically if "we" would ever get well. Once Jane had described her experience under the porch, the doctor asked to talk to Chris White. Jane grew rigid, her eyes widened in fright. She began to whimper, begging him not to make her do it. Then she screamed.

Dr. Thigpen rushed from his office to alert his colleague Dr. Cleckley.[1] When the two men returned a moment later, the patient was calmer but disoriented. Yet despite her confusion, and theirs, both

---

[1] Although Cleckley is credited as coauthor of *Three Faces of Eve*, I was informed by a psychiatrist who knew Cleckley that only Thigpen was actually involved in the treatment of Chris Sizemore.

men sensed immediately that they were dealing with a fourth personality whom they had never met. After she had grown calm enough to respond, they asked her who she was. She didn't know, she replied.

She exhibited none of Chris White's painful diffidence, none of Chris Black's impish exuberance. Although she most closely resembled Jane, she remembered past events not as part of her own separate past but rather from the perspective of what had happened to the three other personalities. Gradually, as she grew still calmer and the interview progressed, she recognized that somehow she did have an identity of her own. When the doctor asked to speak with Chris White, she realized that Chris White was gone, and so was Chris Black. Had Chris Costner finally come into her own?

The answer would come soon enough.

Although Don was a considerate and loving husband, the permanence she had long sought eluded her; because of Don's work, they were always on the move and so home was a trailer. It was comfortable enough and perfectly respectable, but Chris tended to associate "trailers" with a kind of rootless existence that she abhorred. This may have aggravated her chronic insecurity. Whatever the reason, she was soon having problems again—and she was giving them.

The first serious indication that she wasn't well came during an argument with a woman who lived in the next trailer. The woman called her a liar. That got to Chris; she lost her temper and punched the woman in the face, then she jumped on her, bit her on the legs, grabbed her hair, and pounded her head. When Don came home from work he managed to calm his wife down. She was embarrassed and contrite, but not so much over what she had done but rather because she considered her behavior unladylike.

Prudently, the Sizemores moved to another trailer court.

At their new location things seemed to take a turn for the better. After volunteering to help out at Taffy's school, Chris performed so well that the principal asked her to become a regular substitute teacher. That was the good news. But before she could get the job she would need to produce her college transcripts. The bad news was that Furman University, to which she'd written requesting a transcript of her credits, responded that no record existed of her ever having attended any classes there. She hadn't been there of course, but a close cousin Elen had, and Chris had simply indulged in some wishful identification. That ended her substitute teaching career.

Almost anything could imperil her precarious stability. One day she became so provoked by a television program that Taffy was watching that she threw a butcher knife in the general direction of the

TV set (which she came nowhere close to hitting), and then sank to the floor in a dead faint. When she came to, she was lying on a couch, with Don bending solicitously over her, but she couldn't see him. She had gone blind, and she stayed blind until the next morning when Don was driving her to an eye doctor. The ophthalmologist prescribed a pair of low-power reading glasses. Astonishingly, she would still suffer temporary spells of blindness now and then, but whenever this happened all she needed to do was put on the glasses and her vision would be restored.

Don, Chris, and Taffy were destined to live through such troublesome incidents for the next twenty years, a harrowing period marked by headaches, sleeplessness, fainting spells, blackouts, suicide attempts, and perhaps as many as a dozen different personalities. One of them was a woman who went blind under stress; although she was loving and kind, and able to enjoy sex, she nevertheless suffered from anxiety and excessive dependency on others. There were also the competent but too protective woman who obsessively collected bells, the woman who collected turtle figurines, the woman who collected playing cards, the elderly woman who wore only purple, and the two impish girls, one with an uncontrollable passion for strawberries, the other with a similar passion for banana splits. And there was the anxious, prissy woman who believed herself an unmarried virgin and refused to sleep with Don.

Throughout all of this turmoil the family somehow held together through a combination of patience and solicitude. As she grew older, Taffy was especially helpful and supportive. So was cousin Elen, whose work with Chris in writing *I'm Eve* may have offered better therapy than any professional. The physician and psychiatrist who treated Chris in her middle years also deserve a good deal of credit; both refused to deal with any other personalities, treating Chris simply as a single patient.

By 1977, the manuscript had been completed and sent to the publisher, and Chris Costner Sizemore had emerged from the struggle a seemingly free and stable personality. Whatever her remaining uncertainties, she now felt more hopeful and confident than she had ever been before.

Distinctive Features of 16 DID Cases Flow Chart

	Reynolds	Baker	Fancher	Bourne	Felida	Beauchamp
Hypnosis						
Spontaneous	X	X	X	X	X	X
Doctor Induced				X		X
Age Regression	X					
Trauma Type						
General			X			
Nonsexual Abuse						
Sexual Abuse						
Empirical Factors						
Fugue State	X	X		X	X	X
3+ Identities			X			
Sensory Conversion	X		X			
Motor Conversion		X				
Organic Epilepsy						
Pseudo Epilepsy	X	X		X	X	
Placebo Effect						
Religious Enthusiasm	X	X	X	X		X
Somnambulism						X
Therapeutic Intervention						
Cure				X		X
Demographics						
Gender	FEMALE	FEMALE	FEMALE	MALE	FEMALE	FEMALE
Age	18	17	15	31	15	
Social Class	LOW	LOW/MID	MID/HIGH	MID		MID
Education	NO	NO		YES		YES
Family Involvement	YES	YES	YES	YES	YES	

Key to interpretation: This chart is meant to help readers compare distinctive features that link the cases discussed in the preceding chapter, as well as the case of Sybil, discussed at length in Chapters 5–7, and the case of Irene, discussed in Chapter 1. As one can see, many of the cases have a great many elements in common. Hypnosis, whether spontaneous or induced, figures in nearly all of them—14 out of 16. The next most common feature is the fugue state, which was reported in 11 out of the 16 cases. It's possible that Marceline, too, underwent a fugue state, but this cannot be determined for certain because the author did not have access to the original French version of the case history. (As I noted earlier, my use of fugue state is colloquial; fugues are a process and tend

	Marceline	Smith	Hanna	Fischer	Norma	Poultney	Murphy	White	Dorsett	Irene
		X			X	X				X
	X		X	X			X	X	X	X
							X			
					X					X
			X			X		X	X	
			X					X	X	
		X	X	X		X		X	X	X
								X	X	
	X		X	X				X		X
	X		X	X						
			X							
		X		X			X		X	
		X			X					X
	X		X	X		X			X	X
	FEMALE	FEMALE	MALE	FEMALE	FEMALE	MALE	FEMALE	FEMALE	FEMALE	FEMALE
	TEEN			4 TO 5	TEEN					20
	MID		MID/UP	LOW/MID	MID	MID	LOW/MID			LOW
		YES	YES		YES	YES	NO	YES	YES	YES
		YES	YES	YES				YES	YES	YES

to be episodic. The classic fugue is represented by Ansel Bourne; other cases here are indicated as having had a fugue state if they have suffered from a loss of memory of self, whether for a brief time or for months.) Most of the patients whose cases are described come from lower or lower middle class families. Family involvement was also documented in nine of the cases. It is difficult to make any generalization about the educational level of the patients because of the marked differences in educational standards in the late nineteenth century and those of the latter part of the twentieth. The observant reader will also note that most of these cases spanning a little over a century are characterized by sexual abuse and not least, it should be noted that of the 16 cases, the vast majority of them (11) are female.

Robert Raphael (Pace University, New York)

9

Bifurcation of Self

Retrospective and Prospective

> *If they were on the line, they may have even met.*
> *He wants to meet a lot of women.*
> *She has multiple personalities.*
> Advertisement on the side of a New York City bus
> *Digita City NY*

Our investigation of MPD/DID has proceeded along several paths, some running parallel, some converging, and some that simply peter out. Whatever path we've pursued, though, certain themes recur. For one thing, MPD/DID cannot be considered a subject of examination for psychology alone because it is both a product—whether intentionally or unconsciously manufactured (or both)—and a reflection of the society and epoch from which it arose. We need to ask why interest in this phenomenon reached an apogee at two distinct periods in history—at the end of the nineteenth century and at the end of the twentieth. Each period was characterized by a shift in outlook, in which new psychological and medical techniques were seen as a means of finally unraveling the riddle of the self, organically, psychologically, and philosophically. Inevitably, though, these techniques were either abused or misunderstood, and almost always, their promise exaggerated. Any discussion about MPD/DID in *fin de siècle* Europe, for instance, cannot ignore the influence of spiritualism; any discussion of MPD/DID in the later part of the twentieth century cannot ignore the upheavals of the sixties. As R.D. Hinshelwood puts it: "Posing as a medical issue, [DID] is one married to contemporary concerns about personal identity" (Hinshelwood, 2000, p. 213).

Another underlying theme is childhood abuse which in most cases is viewed as a major contributing factor to the development of MPD/DID (Hinshelwood, 2000). However, as we've seen in Sybil's case, establishing the facts of the childhood abuse is hard enough, especially with documentation of said abuse being so questionable, and that it is harder still to prove that this abuse, if it did occur, was responsible for the disorder.

Not all investigators, however, have been so enthralled by the notion that childhood trauma can account for cases of multiples. In a paper written for The *Canadian Journal of Psychiatry*, August Piper and Harold Merskey observe that the evidence in support of this contention is sorely lacking. "However, even if every DID patient were demonstrated to have suffered such trauma, that association, standing alone, would fail to prove that the trauma caused the disorder," they state, adding, "If trauma indeed causes DID, then surely these insults should have been more than sufficient to generate numerous cases of the disorder" (Piper and Merskey, 2004). They point out that so many factors have been advanced to explain the disorder in addition to childhood trauma—including "domestic violence; undergoing a medical procedure; and experiencing famine, rape, war trauma, earthquakes, fires, floods, or the death of a primary caretaker"—that we should be seeing hundreds of thousands of these cases. According to one therapist, even an "overly sensitive" individual could develop DID if, for instance, the individual was "rejected in early childhood because '[her] parents wanted a boy and got a girl'" (Bliss, 1986). Any substantiation that children are at risk for DID, they say, generally relies on self-reporting, whose obviously subjective nature makes it suspect on its face. "If childhood maltreatment were in fact a major cause of DID, and if the increase in DID cases in the 1980s were genuine, then the incidence of traumatic events endured by North American children during that time should also have risen sharply." But there are no data to document such an increase, they note, notwithstanding the curious trend seen in the 1980s and 1990s in which patients began to tell their therapists "about previously unheard-of phenomena" including alters of races or sexes different from the host; alters of different species and alters of demons, angels, and God. But the authors confess that they are at a loss to explain these phenomena. "Why did the perhaps half-plausible 19th-century concept so floridly metamorphose into the totally implausible 20th-century concept?" they ask. Then they throw up their hands: "We know of no convincing reason. In the end, positing scores, hundreds, and even thousands of alters defies common sense . . . " (Piper and Merskey, 2004).

On the other hand, Piper and Mersky discount the existence of DID entirely, insisting that its symptoms "cannot be distinguished from other psychiatric disorders or from malingering." They argue that if anything, the disorder—whatever its nature or origin—is worsened by the treatment. "Hallucinations, increasing discomfort, and severe dysphoria often cause patients to be in states of chronic crisis for long periods of time after DID treatment begins," they note, adding that there is increasing risk of suicide attempts by patients. They also cite a study in which MPD patients "improved dramatically" when their conditions were rediagnosed and treated in more conventional ways. They suggest that therapists who diagnose DID are largely at fault and that the problem is a confusion about the symptoms. "Finally, in the dissociative disorder literature," they write, "conditions that resemble DID are often simply redefined as DID" (Piper and Merskey, 2004.) They believe that in many cases these patients might actually be psychotic or suffer from bipolar disorders. However, this approach, which in effect defines away the disorder by contending that it is simply a matter of misdiagnoses, is another example of throwing the baby out with the bathwater. What they're really saying is that they don't need to find a solution to a problem if there is no problem, or perhaps that, while there may be a problem, it isn't a problem of dissociation but one involving psychosis or a more easily classified, and treatable, mood disorder.

Actually, attempts to classify MPD/DID as a mood disorder go back at least to the early 1900s. In an article for the *Journal of Psychical Research*, one Dr. Albert Wilson, in discussing the case of a female patient named Shand, proposed that in people diagnosed with the disorder, certain moods might predominate and be identified as distinct personalities, each with his or her own name, such as anger or fear. Thus, there would be a Fear alter and an Anger alter. The prevalence of one mood at any given time, he argued, could be accounted for by the constriction of blood flow to one or other part of the brain (Wilson, 1904).

As I have tried to show throughout these pages, any discussion about MPD/DID is a risky enterprise; notwithstanding the formulation of the DSM-IV, no consensus has ever been reached as to what the term means or indeed, what kind of psychological, physical, or social states it applies to. "A . . . tendency seems to be growing, in which multiple personality is a common root cause of an increasing array of diagnoses. Mollen (1996), for instance, makes one such inclusive claim that 'dissociation is about detachment from an unbearable situation' (p. 4). He includes everything from the hidden observation in hypnosis (Hilgard 1977) and the observing ego of Frenichel (1938) to the major amnesia and multiple autonomous personalities, and some hallucinatory states close to schizophrenia. Gathering such a wide range of phenomena under one sweep is making a very large claim to explain a very large panorama of psychopathology" (Hinshelwood, 2002).

A very large claim indeed.

The description "altered personality" can be applied to any number of cases labeled multiple personality. "It could be used, for instance, for any mentally disordered individual who had also been observed in a previous healthier state" (Sutliffe, 1972). That suggests that under some circumstances even manic depression or schizophrenia might be labeled as MPD. The difficulty inherent in attempting to classify and diagnose such an elusive disorder is also found in the vocabulary commonly employed to describe the condition. "Splitting" is often used as a synonym for "repression"—mistakenly as I've shown (see Chapter 5)—but meanings attached to the two words are so different as to risk making apples out of oranges and vice versa. "The current use of, and the later development in, these terms, from many origins, have created a fruitful potential for confusion," Hinshelwood states in his essay, "The Di-vidual Person," adding with possibly unintentional satire: "That potential has been fulfilled" (Hinshelwood, 1999).

But the confusion doesn't end there. What are we to make of the use of the word "alter," or "fragmenting," or "division," or "emergence" or, for that matter, "state"? What does "conscious" or "unconscious" mean when they are bandied about so indiscriminately to describe a bewildering variety of cases and conditions which, when all is said and done (though one doubts that all is ever said and done), have little or nothing in common? And why stop there when the disorder itself is so resistant to being defined, diagnosed, or classified? Hinshelwood characterizes the dilemma this way: "So many people have come back to the phenomenon in their own way. What exactly is it? Do all those terms mean the same thing, in different people's languages, or are there important differences? Are there ways in which an individual is divisible? And, if so, do we need a catalogue to find our way?" (Hinshelwood, 1999).

In the absence of a catalogue, perhaps a roadmap might help so long as one doesn't make the mistake of confusing the map for the terrain it's intended to represent. At the conclusion of his historical survey about MPD/DID, Hinshelwood seems to be groping for an explanation. He is convinced that the culture plays an important role in the development of the disorder. "The two phases of interest, in the late decades of both the nineteenth and twentieth centuries, indicate a definite socio-historical factor," he writes at one point but then concedes that there being no easily definable condition of multiple personality (since it might stem from several factors, depending on the individual case), he simply recommends that each case "must be explored to a depth beyond consciousness," which is not much of a guide at all. Perhaps we don't need a catalogue so much as a roadmap.

In addition, he implicates both sexuality (a familiar scapegoat to be sure) and "the politics of psychotherapy" in the creation and popularity of the disorder, the former because "there are undercurrents of unconscious messages between patients and professionals imbued with unacknowledged sexuality," the latter because of "current political pressures within scientific, pharmacological psychiatry, psychotherapy feels beleaguered," which, he maintains, encourages therapists to search out and in effect promote such an unusual disorder as DID so as to enhance their own importance. In Hinshelwood's view then, MPD/DID is effectively part of a make work program—creating work for its own sake rather than for any productive purpose. Nor does Hinshelwood understand the role the dissociation plays in the disorder. He also overlooks the importance of hypnosis either in the treatment of MPD/DID or in actually creating it. He doesn't seem to recognize that people who are most often identified as having MPD/DID are almost invariably highly suggestible hysterics.

Like Piper and Merskey, Hinshelwood seems baffled and frustrated; unable to account for the disorder or for why its occurrence surges in one era and not in another, he is left to hurl explanations at a target whose shape he can barely make out in hope that one will stick.

Whatever it was in the Zeitgeist that was responsible for the fascination with the disorder, there can be no doubt that a number of psychologists were quick to jump on the bandwagon. And some of them, not being content to confine their "expertise" on MPD/DID to their offices, were eager to offer their services in the courtroom. Psychologist Paul Dell, for instance, became involved in a 1987 homicide case in which he claimed that the defendant, Tom Bonney, was afflicted with MPD and it was because he had the disorder that he shot his daughter 27 times. Dell was one of those who tended to find MPD wherever he looked for it. Like other therapists who had a vested interest in MPD/DID, he believed that it was caused primarily by childhood abuse. He hypnotized Bonney in an effort to bring the other personalities to the surface and warned them when they did emerge that if they didn't cooperate, Bonney would probably be found guilty and sentenced to death, a powerful inducement to present Dell with what he was hoping to find.

In a stinging refutation of Dell's views that appeared in the *Journal of Trauma and Dissociation*, David Spiegel took Dell to task, asserting that his argument was flawed because it "threw out the baby with the bathwater" (Spiegel, 2001). He went on to point out that the current DSM-IV-TR of the APA consistently defined the disorder based on more than 150 years of rigorous clinical observation and research. He referred to Janet (1889), Prince (1907), and Hilgard (1977), reminding Dell that "when knocking down statues, save the pedestals, they come in handy." He also makes note that current nosolgy, while less than perfect, continues to be refined and has stood the test of time (Spiegel, 2001). In other words, MPD is not a disorder that lends itself to just any constellation of symptoms or syndromes that a psychologist might choose on the basis of his own (flexible) criteria.

Michael Weissberg takes a position similar to Spiegel's, which he describes in his discussion of Breuer's treatment of Anna O. He illustrates the capricious nature of psychological theory and psychiatric diagnosis, pointing out that the dialectic of the analyst as a neutral observer versus the analyst as an influential participant in therapy, continues to be the focus of controversy. MPD, he argues, is a diagnosis which became just as fashionable in twentieth-century America as hysteria was in nineteenth century Europe. He also stresses the importance of the patient's cultural milieu in evaluating his condition (Weissberg, 1993).

Louis Oppenheimer takes another tack in trying to understand the disorder, using a little word play in the process. He contends that it's only by drawing on the fields of neuroscience, biology, physics, and philosophy that it's possible to understand the self and how it is organized in the organism. His argument is based on the assumption that dissociative identity disorder is actually an *associative* disorder. "It is a result of deficient integrative and associative processes in the self-system for the use of different ego-centers instead of one" (Oppenheimer, 2000). He further argues that this problem may only manifest itself with individuals showing high cognitive complexity of organization of self, and maintains that the very complexity of the neurological system may affect the associative disorders. He uses this theoretical approach, based on connectionist modeling of neural networks, to explain such phenomena as child abuse and other forms of trauma. By using this approach he suggests that it is possible to place the id in "social cognitive and neuroscience developmental theory," thereby making the diagnosis of DID more accurate. What Oppenheimer doesn't realize is that he is "beating a dead horse." Although he is correct in assuming a process type of theory, which includes biological as well as social factors, he fails to understand that any theory of dissociative disorder must necessarily include some form of association. Dissociation and association are states that fall along a continuum; whenever you have dissociation you must have its opposite, and vice versa. In his attempt to construct a meta-theory he seems to have ignored this obvious relationship (or should I say association?) and pushes the neural network theory as the principal factor without taking into account the role played by factors that are equally, if not more, important (Oppenheimer, 2000).

If, as I believe, MPD/DID is a taxonomist's nightmare, a ghost without a machine in which to reside, its allure—for some elements of academia, the psychological community, and consumers of mass culture—is difficult to deny. There does appear, even after its fashion has faded, a vested interest in keeping the myth surrounding MPD/DID alive. In what might be seen as a quixotic attempt to impose scientific standards on unpredictable human behavior, some psychologists have tried to nail down the disorder by establishing criteria by which to measure and compare cases, using symptoms as their guide. Charles Osgood and his colleagues, for instance, developed a blind analysis of multiples, which, they asserted, "proved to be surprisingly accurate—even to the extent of correctly predicting that the apparently healthy resolution of the case . . . " (Osgood et al., 1976). They invented a scale which classified personalities on the basis of three determinant factors: Evaluation, Potency, and Activity, while cautioning that "there is no guarantee that it will in fact appear in the usual form in any particular individual" (Osgood et al., 1976). In one example, they described one personality in terms of a "potency flavor" (deep, valuable, strong), a second personality as having "an activity and sensory flavor" (valuable, clean, and hot) and a third personality with a combination of flavors—valuable, tasty, hot, and strong.

In another attempt to quantify cases of DID, investigators employed what they called the Dissociative Experiences Scale (DES) to conduct a meta-analysis of over 100 studies on dissociation intended to test some of the theoretical assumptions underlying the scale and ascertain its validity. The authors expressed a degree of satisfaction with the results. The authors noted that the results seemed to rule out the possibility that the disorder could have arisen because of autohypnosis.

Just as the search for a unifying theory to explain the universe has kept cosmologists in business for years, so, too, has the quest for a similarly all-encompassing theory engaged psychologists, hypnotists, therapists, academics, and writers. One theory holds that MPD might be a condition which may actually not be so uncommon, after all; at one point Freud, for instance, hypothesized that such a disorder might arise when different identifications take turn in seizing consciousness (Freud, 1923). He is referring to conflicts between the ego and the id and is further elaborating on the point we discussed earlier in Chapter 4. Here, in the only instance in which he specifically mentions multiple personality, he is making use of the term as a replacement for the word "dissociation," which he was still using in 1907. As I noted, Freud carefully avoided the word because of his wish to distance himself from Janet.

I have remarked that dissociation occurs across a scale ranging from experiences that are pathological on the one end and normal on the other. Indeed, creative inspiration frequently occurs in a dissociated state of mind without which artists and scientists would seldom enjoy their "eureka" moments. But some theorists seem to have gone off the deep end by trying to collapse the continuum so that the disorder is seen as a kind of simulation or an acting-out rather than as an expression of a mentally aberrant condition, whatever its nature or cause.

> All the world's a stage,
> And all the men and women merely players;
> They have their exits and their entrances,
> And one man in his time plays many parts,

Shakespeare's famous lines from *As You Like It* capture an experience that any of us can identify with; we all play different roles depending on the circumstances—as a child, as a sibling, as a parent, as a friend, or as a colleague. But that kind of role playing is a far cry from the manifestation of different personalities that are seen in cases of MPD/DID. Nonetheless, that is the position taken by J.P. Sutcliffe, Jean Jones, and others who contend that all behavior—including multiple personality—can be classified according to the dichotomy: simulated or not simulated. By "simulated" Sutcliffe and Jones mean "pretend to have or feel," "feign," "put on," or "act like." In this light, MPD can be seen as an "escape" "from the anxieties of the strong super-ego repressive personality." By contrast, the alternating personality is typically "easy-going, relaxed, gay and irresponsible" (Sutcliffe, 1972) Because people's behavior, attitudes, interests, tastes, and values can change over time or even in different situations, the author says, "Some ordinary everyday learned behaviors could be called 'automatic'" (Sutcliffe, 1972). That is true so far as it goes; daydreaming is "automatic." But then he makes a leap that leaves logic behind: "It is

BIFURCATION OF SELF

probable then that the difference between the behavior of multiple personalities and normals has been exaggerated. The multiple personality behaviors are not exclusive to a very few dramatically aberrant people, rather do they indicate criterion which normal people might be examined for 'strength of identity'" (Sutcliffe, 1972). That many individuals are emotionally or mentally unstable, or possess only a fragile sense of identity, does not lead to the development of symptoms typical of the kind of cases that we have discussed in this book. The very rarity of these cases, marked by amnesia, fugue states, the emergence of personalities under hypnosis, etc., argues that on the contrary, multiple personality behaviors are limited to a very few "dramatically aberrant" people.

Other psychologists have considered MPD as a kind of simulated behavior, of a different nature—as a sign of malingering, an elaborate ruse some individuals resort to in order to shirk responsibilities or escape punishment. On the other hand, MPD might be a mental disorder sui generis, characterized by various personalities or alters whose existence is generally unknown to the primary personality. Other theories advance the notion that MPD might be "a symptom in a range of primary pathologies" (Hinshelwood, 2002) or, similarly, it can be understood only by viewing it as a multidimensional problem, influenced by social, historical, psychological, and biological factors. But if MPD/DID is so amorphous that it can manifest any number of pathologies, then it's hard to know how it can be definitively identified, let alone treated. Nor do these theories address the issue as to why these cases increase in frequency only at one time but not at another. There is a whiff of capitulation about such arguments, a tacit admission that the authorities on the subject have thrown in the towel. They know that there's a problem but they can't agree what the problem is, how serious it is, or how often it occurs, much less what can be done about it.

However daunting the task of defining MPD may be, it hasn't stopped psychologists from taking a stab at it with mixed, but generally unsatisfactory, results.

One theory, for example, advances the idea that this infantile state survives because of a "failure of the normal integrative process . . . " (Hinshelwood, 2002) On the other hand, the fragmentation may occur later in life often as a response to trauma; in this view, alternative consciousnesses function as a defensive mechanism. There are attempts, too, to attribute the development of MPD/DID to social or cultural conditions or even political currents within the psychiatric community itself. By the same token, medical, forensic, or other social processes may "inadvertently encourage" the formation of nonintegrated personalities

(Hinshelwood, 2002). Letting the culture or society take the rap for MPD—"a disorder conceived in the modern world, a disorderliness deriving from the inadequate conception of the 'individual' to which modernity clings..." (Hinshelwood, 2002)—lets the individual or the therapist off the hook. It makes multiples into martyrs. Sybil is a good example and the thousands of cases of MPD/DID, repressed memories, and alleged incidents of childhood abuse that she inspired can be viewed as a damning indictment of society as a whole.

But where does that leave the therapist when presented with a possible case of MPD/DID? If the problem, as conceived by all these theorists, resists easy classification or diagnosis, the solutions proposed seem even further out of reach. If we are "truly to understand the nature of MPD/DID," as Hinshelwood argues, we'll have to jettison "a whole cultural set of baggage that is deeply invested in the notion of the undivided individual." At the same time he allows that "the 'dividual'... was a non-issue until modernity" (Hinshelwood, 2002). So if it was a "non-issue" until the late nineteenth century, are we to think that the disorder existed previously but just had escaped attention, or was it—more likely—a product of the times, which puts us right back at the starting gate, little more illuminated than when we began?

But perhaps we've been looking the wrong way through the telescope; instead of focusing on the subject—MPD/DID—we might find it more profitable to turn our attention to the observer, namely, the theorist. Investigators of the phenomenon, having formed their theories, often on the basis of very few observations, have a stake in proving them, and so each succeeding case they examine invariably offers them further corroborative evidence. Inconvenient observations to the contrary are ignored or explained away. Janet, for instance, saw MPD as "an elaborate development of autonomatism" (Janet, 1891)—as opposed to having only a physiological explanation—and so he naturally ascribed alterations of states to psychological causes rather than physical ones (Sutcliffe, 1972). Prince was guided by a search for the "real, original, or normal self." And so naturally he was going to look at each case as a vehicle through which he could plumb the depths to uncover the true self. This strategy, however, obviously runs the risk of mistaken diagnosis. And it has an additional difficulty, insofar as lumping different types of cases into the same category, to support a particular theory, any attempt "to arrive at a definitive meaning for multiple personality" becomes "impossible" (Sutcliffe, 1972). There we are, back at the starting gate.

Indeed, as Sutcliffe observes in a paper entitled "Personal Identity, Multiple Personality, and Hypnosis," "Modern clinicians might be expected to be more sophisticated [than their predecessors]. . . . However, in the fuller records supplied by them, one finds more explicit evidence of reinforcement of incipient multiple personality behavior, as well as implicit suggestions leading to such behaviors" (Sutcliffe, 1972). He notes that Thigpen and Cleckley, who owe their prominence to *Three Faces of Eve*, "betrayed a breathless excitement at the prospect of handling a case similar to Prince's [Thigpen and Cleckley, 1957]" (Sutcliffe, 1972). Therapists may claim to be objective and unbiased but they cannot conceal their fascination for a case that may bring them fame and allow them the opportunity to substantiate a theory that had everything going for it but an actual human being to demonstrate its credibility.

Just as therapists and hypnotists (and the media, too) can be assigned a great deal of responsibility for putting MPD/DID on the map, they cannot take all the blame. A receptive public is required as well. Other mental illnesses may enjoy a vogue—ADHD, bipolar disorder, chronic depression—but MPD/DID has garnered attention out of all proportion to its actual incidence. (One presumes that the handful of cases recorded in the literature prior to the publication of *Sybil* as more indicative of its occurrence in the general population.) On the other hand, it is hardly a surprise why MPD/DID has such a hold on the imagination since it goes to the heart of a perennially vexing question as to what constitutes identity, a subject that philosophers and psychologists have been wrestling with for millennia. Multiples challenge our sense of self just as a disorder such as Alzheimer's does, only in the former case the self appears to be divided and multiplied whereas in the latter it seems terrifyingly absent. But no one doubts the reality of Alzheimer's; MPD/DID is sexier and in some sense more enticing as it offers the freedom to be other than what we are (or believe ourselves to be). America, after all, is known as a country where people are free to reinvent themselves. (These days it isn't necessary to reinvent yourself; with identity theft so rampant, other people can do it for you.) Certainly MPD/DID plays into that impulse to break free of one's history and circumstances, to "light out for the territory," even if the nature of the territory has changed.

Perhaps the question we should be asking is not why MPD/DID resonates with so many people, most of whom will never know anyone who has, or claims to have, the disorder (unlike the case with, say, depression or Alzheimer's), but why the disorder became so fashionable in the latter part of the nineteenth century and again in a decade and a half ago?

Certainly, one could argue that in the waning years of the 1800s, the investigation of the human mind—and by extension the nature of the self—assumed a greater urgency with the development of tools and techniques that allowed researchers greater access to the psyche. There were many more weapons in psychologists' arsenals—hypnosis, free association and with Freud's concept of repression, a possible explanation for repression—so it should come as little surprise that psychologists would want to use them. But one must also recall that this was also an era in which spiritualism also held out the assurance of an afterlife. Now it appeared as if it was possible to communicate with one's dead aunt as freely as one's own—or someone else's—unconsciousness.

The development of the myth of MPD/DID, which is related to but nonetheless a separate issue from its psychological or medical significance, however, invites us to look further. Merely identifying factors that appear to contribute to a trend is an exhausting, possibly fruitless enterprise. (We would be remiss if we neglected the Industrial Revolution, the Theory of Evolution, and Social Darwinism, which obviously impinged greatly upon the minds of nineteenth-century Europeans.) What is of more pertinence, I think, is the rapidity of change, the sense on the part of many millions of people that things were getting out of control, that after decades, if not centuries, of relative stability (or stagnation), the pace of events had picked up to such a degree that they would alter the world so as to make it virtually unrecognizable within the span of a generation. With the prospect of profound change—scientific, political, economic, and environmental—comes the threat of a loss of a sense of personal identity. A collective fascination—indeed, infatuation—with MPD/DID is a symptom of social distress. Is it any wonder that when no one can agree on what it means to be an American or a European, so many people begin to see themselves exclusively in ethnic, cultural, or religious terms? As one example, consider how many people in the United States conflate Christian fundamentalist values with American values. The late sixties, which nurtured the myth, also saw the rise of feminism and gay rights, calling into question society's attachment to the conventions of sexual identity. The boundaries are being pushed further—for good or for ill, depending on your view—by demands to legalize same-sex marriage and confer legal rights on people identifying themselves as transgender.

If our sense of identity is being challenged on all sides now, forcing people to throw up ever more elaborate barriers in an attempt to keep them intact, we can only wonder how we as a culture and society will react to the changes that are inexorably bearing down on us.

Science fiction can serve as an early warning. In the 1956 *Forbidden Planet*, an American astronaut receives a "brain boost" from an alien machine that boosts his mental powers. Characters in *The Matrix* trilogy download knowledge into their brains whereas in *Eternal Sunshine of the Spotless Mind,* more a love story than sci-fi, the protagonist has memories of a painful love affair erased from his mind. The nature of identity is given a bizarre twist in Dennis Potter's *Cold Lazarus*, a television drama in which a man's head is kept alive against his—or its—will. (For a further exploration of this theme as it's exemplified in the popular TV series *Star Trek*, especially in terms of the differences between Spock—machine-man—and his, or its, human counterpart Kirk, see my *Psychopaths in Everyday Life: Social Distress in the Age of Misinformation*.)

Real-life science is catching up. Some writers foresee a posthuman era when it will be impossible to distinguish between man and machine. Of course, a question of identity does not arise when a person replaces a leg or an arm or a hip with a prosthetic device. But even if we so far lack the wherewithal to download the *Encyclopedia Britannica* into our brains (assuming we would want to), scientists do have the capacity to tinker with and change our brains by means of neural implants, genetic engineering, mood-altering and memory-enhancing drugs. Ray Kurzweil, inventor of the first computer systems that could read aloud to the blind, has predicted the merging of humans and computers, even calling for replacing the DNA with more reliable software. "Some people just think messing with the brain is unnatural because the brain is the seat of who we are," bioethicist Arthur Caplan has said. "To change it is to change our identity."

Whatever form the disorder takes next, whatever type of myth is propounded to explain it, and whatever the specific circumstances that produce it, of one thing we can be certain: multiples will always be with us, serving as a perpetual reminder of the duality of human existence. Only by understanding the bifurcation of the self will we be able to catch the conscience—and consciousness—of the king.

Let the play begin.

REFERENCES

Introduction

Froeschels, E. January (1949). A peculiar intermediary state between waking and Sleeping. *American Journal of Psychotherapy*, 2(1), 19–25.

Rieber, R. (1997). *Manufacturing Social Distress: Psychopathy in Everyday Life*. New York: Plenum.

Rieber, R. (2004). *Psychopaths in Everyday Life: Social Distress in the Age of Misinformation*. New York: Psyche-Logo Press.

Chapter 1

Abercrombie, J. (1832). *Inquiries Concerning the Intellectual Powers and the Investigation of Truth*. New York: J. and J. Harper.

Binet, A. (1890). *On Double Consciousness: Experimental Psychological Studies*. Chicago: Open Court.

Binet, A. (1896). *Alterations of Personality*. New York: D. Appleton.

Bleuler, E. (1924). *Textbook of Psychiatry*. New York: Macmillan.

Boerhaave, H. (1745). *Academical Lectures on the Theory of Physic: Being a Genuine Translation of His Institutes*. London: W. Innys.

Boor, M. & Coons, P. (1983). Bibliography of a comprehensive literature pertaining to multiple personality. *Psychological Reports, 53,* 295–310.

Bourne, A. (1877). *Wonderful Works of God: A Natural Case of Ansel Bourne (Written with His Doctors)*. Fall River, MA: Robertson.

Benjamin Rush's Lecture on the Mind. Philadelphia: American Philosophical Society, pp. 489–493.
Crabtree, A. (2003). 'Automatism' and the Emergence of Dynamic Psychiatry. *History of Behavioral Science. 19*(1): 51–80.
Diamond, et. al (1963). *Inhibition and Choice*. New York: Harper.
Finger, S. Gehr, S.E., and West, A.L. (2001). Dual Personality and the Brain: The Case Studies of Louis C. Bruce in the 1890s. *History of Psychiatry, 12*(5): 9–71.
Forbes, W. (1860). *On Obscure Diseases of the Brain and Disorders of the Mind*. London: J. Churchill.
Hodgson (1891–92). *Proceedings of the Society for Psychical Research, 7,* 1891–1892, p. 284–58.
Jackson, J.H. (1958). *Selected Writings*, ed. J. Taylor. New York: Basic Books.
Janet, P. (1907). *The Major Symptoms of Hysteria*. New York: Macmillan.
Kames, H.H. (1751). *Essays on the Principles of Morality and Natural Religion in Two Parts*. Edinburgh: R. Fleming.
Kenny, M, (1986). *Passion of Ansel Bourne*. Washington: Smithsonian.
Kihlstrom, J.F. (1987). First-Ranked Symptoms as Diagnostic Clue to Multiple Personality disorder. *American Journal of Psychiatry, 144*(3): 293–298.
MacNish, R. (1835). *The Philosophy of Sleep*. Glasgow: W.R. McPhun.
Mayo, H. (1837). *History of Physiology*. London: John Murray.
Mitchel, S.L. (1816). A Double Consciousness or a Duality of a Person in the Same Individual. *Medical Repository, 3*: 185–186.
Prince, Morton. (1898). A Contribution to the Study of Hysteria and Hypnosis; Being Some experiments on Two Cases of Hysteria and Physiologico-Anatomical Theory of the Nature of These neuroses. *Proceedings of the Society for Psychical Researh, Part 34*: 79–97.
Rieber, R.W. (1999). Hypnosis, False Memory, and multiple Personality: A Trinity of Affinity. *History of Psychiatry, 10*: 1–11.
Rieber, R.W. & Salzinger, S. (1998). *Psychology: Theoretical-Historical Perspectives* (2nd ed.). Washington, DC: American Psychological Association Press.
Rush, B. (1812). Medical Inquiries upon the Diseases of the Mind. Philadelphia: Kimber and Richardson,
Sidis, B. (1898). *The Psychology of Suggestion: A Research into the Subconscious Nature of Man on Society*. New York: D. Appleton.
Sidis, B. (1902). *Psychopathological Researches: Studies in Mental Dissociation*. New York: Stechart.
Sidis, B., and Goodhart, S.P. (1904). *Multiple Personality: An Experimental Investigation into the Nature of Human Individuality*. New York: D. Appleton, p. 448.
Sidis, B. (1922). *Nervous Ills: Their Cause and Cure*. Boston: Badger.
Simpson, M. & Carlson, T. (1968). The strange sleep of Rachel Baker. *The Academy Bookman, 21* (1): 3
Taylor, W.S., & Martin, M.F. (1944). Multiple Personality. *Psychology Abnormal and Social, 39*: 281–300.
Van Gieson, I. & Sidis, B. (1898). Neuron Energy. *Archives of Neurology and Psychopathology, 1*(1): 1–24.
Wigan, A.L. (1844). *New View of Insanity: Duality of Mind Ruled by Structures, Functions and Diseases of the Brain and by the Phenomena of Mental Derangement and Shown to Be Essential to Moral Responsibility*. London: Longman, Brown, Green, and Longmans.
Wundt, W. (1874). *Grundzuge der psysiologischen psychologie*. Leipzig: Engelmann.

Chapter 2

Ackerknecht E.H., Vallois H.V., Francois, and Gall J (1955): *Memoirs Du Museum National d'Historie Naturelle,* Serie A, Tome X, Small Fac. Paris (English Translation, Madison WI 1956).
Baldwin, J.M. (1901). *Fragments*. New York: Scribner.
Crabtree A. (1993). *From Mesmer to Freud*, New Haven: Yale University Press.
Cullen W. (1769). *Synopsis Nosologiae Nethodicae*, Edinborough: Bell and Creech.
Damasio AR. (1994). *Descarte's Error*: New York, Grosset Putnam.
Gall, F.J. (1811). *Des disposition innees* (On innate dispositions) Paris: 1811 p. 4–7. Translated by Solomon Diamond from his *Roots of Psychology*.
Gall, F.J. (1835). *Critical Review of Some Anatomical-Physiological Works with an Exploration of a New Philosophy of the Morals, Qualities and Intellectual Faculties*. Trans. Winslow Lewis. Boston: Marsh, Capen, and Lyon.
Elliotson J (1982). *John Elliotson on Mesmerism*, F. Kaplan, ed. New York: DaCapo, p. 677–678.
Finger S. (2000). *Minds Behind the Brain*. New York: Oxford University Press.
Flourens M.J.P. (1846). *Phrenology Examined*. Philadelphia: Hogan and Thompson.
Fodor J. (1983). *The Modularity of Mind*. Cambridge, MA: MIT Press.
Forster T.I.M. (1815). Sketch for the new anatomy and physiology of the brain and nervous system of Drs. Gall and Spurzheim, considering as comprehending a complete system of phrenology. *The Pamphleteer respectfully Dedicated to Both Houses of Parliament* 5: 219–243.
Gall F.J., Spurzheim J. (1810–1819). *Anatomie et physiologie du system nerveux en general. Et du cerveau en particulier* (4 vols.) Paris: F. Schoell.
Gall F.J. (1811). *Des disposition innees*. Paris: Schoell.
Gall F.J. (1822–1826). *Sur les fonctions du cerveau* (6 vols.) (English Translation 1835. *On the Functions of the Brain and Each of its Parts*: Boston: Marsh, Cappan, and Lyon.) Paris, Balliere, Vol. 6, pp. 274–275, 288, 292.
Galvani (1791). *D' eviribus Electricitatis inmotu Musculari Commentarius. D'Bononiensi Scientiarium at et Artium Instituto atque Academia Comentarii* 7: 363–418. Reprinted as *Commentary on the Effects of Electricity on Muscular Motion*, Trans. M.G. Foley (1953): Norwalk, CT, Burndy Library, pp. 9–41.
Haller A. (1767). *Primae Lineae Physiologiae . . .* ad Editionem Tertio, Edinborough.
Herbart J.F. (1891). *A Textbook in Psychology*, New York, Appleton.
Hollander B. (1920). *In Search of the Soul and the Mechanism of Thought, Emotion and Conduct*, London, Kegan, Paul, and Trench Trubner co.
Lavater J.C. (1804). *Essays on Physiognomy: for the promotion of the knowledge and the love of mankind*, London, Symonds.
Morgani G.B. (1761). *De Sedibus, Etcausis Morborum Per Anatomen Indagatas Libri Quinque*, Venice, Remondini.
Sauvage F.D. (1768). *Nosologia Methodica . . .* Amsterdam, de Tournes.
Spinoza B.D. (1910). *Ethic*, H., Frowde, ed. London, Oxford University Press.
Warren, H.C. (1934). The *Dictionary of Psychology*. Boston: Houghton Mifflin.

Chapter 3

Buranelli, Vincent (1975). *The Wizard from Vienna: Franz Anton Mesmer*. New York: Coward, McCann & Geoghegan.

Dillain, G. (1925). *A.M. Charcot 1825–1893: His Life, His Work*. Trans. Parce Bailey. New York: Paul Hoeber.
Hall, G. S. (1881). *Aspects of German Culture*. Boston: J.R. Osgood.
Spiegel, H. (1981). Hypnosis: *Myth and Reality. Psychiatric Annals 11*(?0): 336–341.

Chapter 4

Ellenberger, H. (1970). *The Discovery of the Unconscious: The History and Evolution of Dynamic Psychiatry*. New York: Basic Books.
Strachey, James, ed.. (1907). *The Standard Edition of the Complete Works of Sigmund Freud* 24 vol., London: The Hogarth Press and the Institute of Psychoanalysis; Vol. 3, pp. 191–221.
Herman, J. (1992). *Trauma and Recovery*. New York: Harper-Collins.
Hull, C. (2000). *Hypnosis and Suggestibility: An Enlightened Approach*. Norwalk, UK: Crown House.
Rieber, R. and Salzinger, K., eds. (1995). *Psychology: Theoretical Historical Perspectives*. Washington: American Psychological Association, p. 363.
Spiegel, D. (1988). Dissociation and Hypnotizability in Postraumatic Stress Disorder. *American Journal of Psychiatry*, p. 304.
Wilson, G. (1914). *G. Stanley Hall: A Study*. New York: G.E. Stechart.
Wolberg, L. (1945). *Hypnoanalysis*. New York: Grune and Stratton.

Chapter 5

Sinason, V., ed. (2002). *Attachment, Trauma and Multiplicity*. New York: Taylor & Francis.
Schrieber, F. (1973). *Sybil*. New York: Regnery.
Wilbur, C. July 26, 1965. Unpublished letter to F. Schrieber.

Chapter 6

Connelly, S. (1999). *The End of Sybilization. New York Daily News*, p. 000.
Dunne, P. (1977). *Sybil* [Television movie]. New York: Lorimar Pictures. Schreiber.
LeBlanc. A. (1993). Patient as Model of the Therapist: Morton Prince and the Case of BCA, Unpublished paper, pp. 2, 6–7.
Marks, O., (1970). Morton Prince and the Dissociation of a Personality. *Journal of the Behavioral Sciences*. 6(2): 120–130.
Schrieber, F. (1973). *Sybil*. New York: Regnery.
Sinason, V., ed. (2000). *Attachment, Trauma and Multiplicity*. New York: Taylor & Francis, p. 250.

Chapter 7

Acocella, J. (1999). *Creating Hysteria: Women and Multiple Personality Disorder*. San Francisco: Josey-Bass.
Cohen, B.M., Barnes, M.-M., and Rankin, A. B. eds. 1991. *Multiple Personality Disorder from the Inside Out*. Towson, MD.: Sidran Press.
Dufrense, A. (1997). *Freud Under Analysis: History, Theory, Practice: Essays in* Honor of Paul Rozen. North Vern, NJ: Jason Aronson.

Kluft, R. (1982). Varieties of Hypnotic Intervention in the Treatment of Multiple Personality. *The American Journal of Clinical Hypnosis*. 24(4): 238.
James, H. (1879). *Nathaniel Hawthorne*. New York: Harper & Row.
McHugh, P. (1999). Has Psychiatry Lost Its Way? *Commentary*. 108(5): 32–38.
Book Sends Shock Through Dodge Center. *Minneapolis Star*. August 27, 1975.
Schrieber, F. (1989). *Sybil*. New York: Warner Books, p. 374.
Spiegel, D., ed. (1994). *Dissociation: Culture, Mind and Body*. Washington, DC: American Psychiatric Press.
Spiegel, D. Jan (1998). Hypnosis and implicit memory: Automatic processing of explicit content." *American Journal of Clinical Hypnosis*, 40(3): 236–237.
Spiegel, H. (1981). Hypnosis: Myth and reality. *Psychiatric Annals*. 11(9): 336–341.
Spiegel, H., and Spiegel, D. (2004). *Trance and Hypnosis: The Clinical Use of Hypnosis*. 2nd ed. Washington, DC: American Psychiatric Association.
Veith, Ilza. (1965). *Hysteria: The History of a Disease*. Chicago: University of Chicago Press.
Watkins, J. and Johnson, R.J. (1982). *We, the Divided Self*. New York: Irvington Publishers.
Wilbur, C. (July 26, 1965). Unpublished letter to F. Schrieber.

Chapter 8

Azam, E. (1892). *Dictionary of Psychological Medicine*. London: J. & A. Churchill.
Bourne, A. (1872). *Wonderful Works of God: A Natural Case of Ansel Bourne (Written with His Doctors)*. Fall River, MA: Robertson.
Dailey, A. (1894). Mollie Fancher: The *Brooklyn Enigma*. Brooklyn, NY: Eagle Printing.
Douglas, J. (1815). *Devotional Somnism . . . Uttered by Rachel Baker*. New York: Van Winkle & Wiley.
Flourey, T. (1900). *From India to Planet Mars: A Study of a Case of Somnambolism*. New York: Harper & Brothers.
Franz, S. (1933). *Persons, One and Three*. New York: McGraw-Hill.
Gardner, Howard. (1957). *Facts and Fallacies in the Name of Science*. New York: Dover.
Goddard, H.H. (1927). *Two Souls in One Body*. New York: Dodd Mead.
Goodhurt, S. (1905). *Multiple Personality*. New York: Appleton & Co.
Strachey, James, ed.. (1923). *The Standard Edition of the Complete Works of Sigmund Freud*, 24 vol., London: The Hogarth Press and the Institute of Psychoanalysis, 9.
Hodgson (1891-92). *Proceedings of the Society for Psychical Research*, 7: 284–288.
James. W. (1890). *Principles of Psychology*. New York: Henry Holt.
Janet, P. (1907). *The Major Symptoms of Hysteria*. New York: Macmillan.
Bernstein, M. (1989). *The Search for Bridey Murphy*. New York: Doubleday.
Prince, M. (1969). *The Dissociation of a Personality: A Biographical Study in Abnormal Psychology* Westport, CT: Greenwood Press.
Prince, W. (1915). *Proceedings of the American Society for Psychical Research*.
Simpson, M.M., & Carlson, E.T. (1968). The strange sleep of Rachel Baker. *The Academy Bookman* 21(1): 13.
Thigpen, C., and Cleckley, H. (1957). *The Three Faces of Eve*. New York: McGraw-Hill.

Chapter 9

Bliss E.L. (1986). *Multiple Personality, Allied Disorders, and Hypnosis*. New York: Oxford University Press.

Dell, P. (2001). Why the Diagnostic Criteria for Dissociative Identity Disorder Should be Changed. *Journal of Trauma and Dissociation*, 2(1): 7–31.
Strachey, James, ed. (1907). *The Standard Edition of the Complete Works of Sigmund Freud*, 24 vol., London: The Hogarth Press and the Institute of Psychoanalysis.
Hinshelwood, R.D. (2002). *The Di-Vidual: on Identity and Identification. Attachment, Trauma and Multiplicity*. V. Sinason, ed. New York: Taylor & Francis, pp, 212–223.
Oppenheimer, Louis. (2002). Self or Selves? Dissociative Identity Disorder and Complexity of Self-System. *Journal of Theory and Psychology*, 12(1): 97–128.
Osgood, Charles, Jeans Robert, Luria, Zolla, and Smith, Sara. (1976) The Three Faces of Evelyn: A Case Report. *Journal of Abnormal Psychology*, 85(3): p. 256.
Piper, A., and Merskey, H. (2004). The Persistence of Folly: A Critical Examination of Dissociative Identity Disorder. Part I. The Excesses of an Improbable Concept. *The Canadian Journal of Psychiatry*. 49: 592–600.
Piper, A. and Merskey, H. (2005). The Persistence of Folly: Critical Examination of Dissociative Identity Disorder. Part II. The Defence and Decline of Multiple Personality or Dissociative Identity Disorder. *Canadian Journal of Psychiatry*. 49:678–683.
Rieber, R. (2004). *Psychopaths in Everyday Life: Social Distress in the Age of Misinformation*. New York: Psyche-Logo Press.
Spiegel, David. (2001). Deconstructing the Dissociative Disorders: For whom the dell tolls. *Journal of Trauma and Dissociation*, 2(1): 51–57.
Sutcliffe, J.P. and Jones, Jean. (1972). Personal Identity, Multiple Personality, and Hypnosis. *The International Journal of Clinical and Experimental Hypnosis*, 10(4): 242–243, 246, 257.
Thigpen, C. and Cleckley, H. (1957). *The Three Faces of Eve*. New York: McGraw-Hill.
Weissberg, Michael. (1993). Multiple personality disorder and iatrogenesis: A cautionary tale of Anna O. *The International Journal of Clinical and Experimental Hypnosis*, (10)1: 15–31.
Wilson, A. (1904). *Journal of the Society of Psychical Research*.

Appendices

In the pages that follow you will find transcripts of three tape recordings, never before published in their entirety. Appendix 1 consists of three transcripts. The first and second tapes are recordings of conversations between Flora Schreiber and Cornelia Wilbur. The third tape is one of the thousands Wilbur recorded of a therapeutic session with Sybil herself. The tapes are now on deposit with the library at John Jay College, City University of New York, and at the Archives of the History of Psychology at the University of Akron, Ohio. They are available for anyone interested in conducting research on the subject of MPD/DID in general or Sybil's case in particular.

The first two transcripts, both dated April 4, 1971, are taken from recordings of discussions between Schreiber and Wilbur in which they talk about how they will go about writing the book. Side A of the first tape is inscribed "Peggy (illegible)" and Side B is inscribed "Sybil and others." Side A of the second tape is labeled "Early findings" and Side B "Peggy (illegible)." These tapes were found in Scotch Tape cassette boxes C-60. The third tape of the therapeutic session is labeled "Analysis Sybil" on the A side and "S-Analysis" on the B side. This tape was found in a Hitachi cassette box C-60. All notations are in Schreiber's hand.

Please note that because of the poor quality of the tapes there were some unavoidable gaps in these transcripts. The most important portions of the tapes, however, have been recovered and are presented here for the first time. Approximately 60 percent of the contents of the therapeutic tape has been reproduced; interested readers who are able to access the archives in New York or Ohio will have the opportunity to find out what else remains to be discovered.

In Appendix 2, I have included a brief excerpt from the TV movie *Sybil* in which the (fictional) Wilbur reveals to the (fictional) Sybil that she has multiple personalities who have been communicating with her for months, unbeknownst to the primary personality. The reader can compare Hollywood's version of Sybil with an excerpt from a therapeutic tape in which Wilbur insists that Sybil is manifesting the personality of an 11-year-old personality, an assertion that the patient vigorously denies.

Appendix 3 contains a biography of Schreiber meant for publicity purposes as well as the results of an IQ test on Sybil, which clearly indicate that her intelligence was in the normal range contrary to assertions made in the book by Schreiber that, Sybil had a high IQ. In Appendix 4, is a reproduction of the letter written to me by a onetime advocate of MPD, a retired psychiatrist named Ralph Allison, who subsequently had cause to revisit his earlier position.

1

Three Tape Excerpts

Pg. 45, Tape 1
Labeling Sybil a multiple personality: all personalities are free to come no matter who uses the body.

DR. CORNELIA WILBUR

13:08:39:05 Then she went on, uh, and told me abut Peggy Lou and Peggy Ann. And then I said to her, um... that um, I wanted all of them to feel free, to come, during the appointment hours, no matter who was um, using the body.

13:09:07:24 I wanted all of them to feel free to come. And I told Vicky that I would like to tell Sylvia that she was a multiple personality.

Pg. 47, Tape 1
Giving MP's their personality characteristics and planting Vicky rather than probing her.

DR. CORNELIA WILBUR

13:11:28:15 And I said, well, there's a personality who calls herself Peggy. And uh, I said, she is pretty self-assertive. And, um... she... um, can... says that she can do

13:11:50:11	things you can't, and she was very, uh, obviously perturbed by this.
And I said, uh ... she wouldn't do anything that you wouldn't approve of. She might do something that you wouldn't think of doing ... until she couldn't.

FLORA SCHREIBER

You were really probing her ... Vicky.

DR. CORNELIA WILBUR

13:12:03:21	Yeah, but—
13:12:20:13	but it was not something she would disapprove of. And uh, I told her that uh, ... there were at least two others, or three others. I said, there seems to be one, there seems to be two Peggys. And, uh she said, well sometimes my mother called me Peggy, and mostly she called me Peggy Louisiana.
13:12:47:13	But sometimes she'd call me Peggy Ann. And I said, well, that it was Peggy Lou and Peggy Ann. And I said the other one calls herself Vicky. And she said, oh, I remember that. She said, when I was a little girl, I used to dream that I came from Europe and my name Vicky—

Pg. 10-14, Tape 1
Inventing the primal scene. The grand illusion of an explanatory principle.

DR. CORNELIA WILBUR

12:35:54:12	... And this business of primal scene. And being forced to sleep in the same bedroom with her fucking parents.
12:36:16:01	And I mean they were. Uh—[OVERLAPPING VOICES] ... is a very large thing, you see. And this is the thing you see, that constantly drove Mary to want to have her own house.

FLORA SCHREIBER

12:36:29:23	Connie ... Did Mary carry the burden of the primal scene? I thought it was Peggy who did.

Pg. 31, Tape 1
Making the punishment fit the crime in the book.

FLORA SCHREIBER

12:55:06:13 —Now you know, Gladys thought that my sketches, my old profiles and personalities ought to the book just as such. Well, I don't quite, I think it would be much better to integrate that in the book than to place them in the book.

DR. CORNELIA WILBUR

12:55:19:23 Oh yes. Oh yes. Oh yes. I agree. Absolutely . . . it has to be—

FLORA SCHREIBER

12:55:19:23 It has to be worked out as the personalities emerge.

FLORA SCHREIBER

12:55:26:23 That's right.

FLORA SCHREIBER

12:55:27:13 And tell their own story.

DR. CORNELIA WILBUR

That's right. Yeah, that's right.

FLORA SCHREIBER

12:55:28:27 Now, Peggy has to tell the story of the first chapter, in terms of what she, when she went to Philadelphia, and when she did, that whole thing from her point of view.

DR. CORNELIA WILBUR

12:55:39:23 Yeah. Now, um . . . I was trying to think about scenes. There is, of course, the various sexual ones. There's the primal scene. There's, um, mother is taking her around. Uh, yeah and her Peeping Tom activities.

12:55:58:13 And going and gossiping, with women who had just had babies. And so on.

FLORA SCHREIBER

12:56:03:20 Yeah. And the girls in the woods.

DR. CORNELIA WILBUR

12:56:56:05:12 Then there's the girls in the woods by the river episodes.

FLORA SCHREIBER
12:56:10:25 How old is Sylvia at that point?

DR. CORNELIA WILBUR
I told you that in the letter. What did it say?

FLORA SCHREIBER
Oh well, I'll have to refer to the letter. I don't know.

Pg. 8, Tape 2

DR. CORNELIA WILBUR
03:06:27:06 So, to a child, their behavior made absolutely not a drop of sense.

FLORA SCHREIBER
03:06:38:21 They left her in that bedroom. They screwed in front of her. She could see, because her crib was here, the window was there, and the streetlight was right outside.
03:06:47:01 She could see her father having an erection and putting it in her mother's vagina . . . Did you know that?

FLORA SCHREIBER
Yeah.

DR. CORNELIA WILBUR
03:06:55:22 And so they do this, you know, several nights a week.

FLORA SCHREIBER
And then. And then . . . preach the Puritanical crap.

DR. CORNELIA WILBUR
03:07:04:23 Yeah. And then daddy tells her, when she's four and still sleeping in that room with them screwing in front, . . . several nights a week, that she's too big to put salve on his feet.
03:07:18:18 Now if that isn't contradicting himself, I never heard it. And I think it ought to go in.

FLORA SCHREIBER
Oh definitely. That's the hypocrisy feud. That is just an absolute dichotomy between sermonizing and performance. Between practice and performance.

Projection of their own guilt of being a fraud to others.

DR. CORNELIA WILBUR

03:07:39:11   Yeah.

FLORA SCHREIBER

And he was a terrible fraud in that respect.

DR. CORNELIA WILBUR

Yeah.

FLORA SCHREIBER

03:07:35:20   And of course the way he had kept mother from going to a doctor and kept mother from appearing in public when she had a baby, and when she was pregnant. The whole thing is so out of line with his own sexual behavior.

DR. CORNELIA WILBUR

03:07:59:27   Yeah . . . that's—

Pg. 11, Tape 2

FLORA SCHREIBER

03:09:16:12   —I told him so. I think it's crap.

DR. CORNELIA WILBUR

03:09:10:06   No, she isn't going to make anything except out of what . . . [KNOCK ON THE DOOR] . . . There's your man . . . about what she earns and, if anything, this book.
03:09:30:21   And of course . . . [OVERLAP]

FLORA SCHREIBER

Well that has nothing to do with it.

DR. CORNELIA WILBUR

Well, since we are putting things on tape, I'll finish what I have to say about the book.
03:09:38:05   Uh, you know, I've done some praying that the book, for heavens sake, will make money. Because there is nothing I would like better to see than . . . Sylvia—
03:09:49:11   I hope to god the book makes money before Florence drops dead. Because I would like to see Sylvia . . . just,

	you know, ... land based. Ah, Florence would be absolutely furious if Sylvia turns out to have a lot of money out of this and is very successful.
03:10:09:15	Because she'll realize then that if she had played ball with Sylvia, that she might have shared everything. You know.
03:10:22:19	And what she's done is cut herself off. Because—

Pg. 34, Tape 2
There is both madness in their method and method in their madness.

DR. CORNELIA WILBUR

03:31:29:10	Yeah. Um. What I started to say was that I didn't do a formal psychoanalysis. It is a little difficult, do a formal psychoanalysis with the analyst sitting in the chair at the head of the couch, out of the range of vision of the patient, when the patient is sitting huddled on the other end of the couch, peering at you. [LAUGHTER]
03:31:40:28	Uh, you know. And uh, or when the patient comes in, and looks at you and says uh, you know, that their name is different than the person you are seeing.
03:32:04:02	And uh, wanders around the room, uh, and so forth. It's a little difficult.
	—So I became involved enough ... in the multiple personalities so that when trouble arose, I, there wasn't anybody else to go to bat for her.
03:32:18:05	She had no family. And if anybody was going to keep track of her, I had to. Well, now this, according to the formalist, in psychoanalysis, is stepping outside.
03:32:35:10	But I learnt this trick from a very, very fine source. I learned it from Franz Alexander. And if you remember, I said that she should go to Adelaid McFadden Johnson, who was a student of Franz Alexander in Chicago, thinking that, in all probability, she wouldn't be able to get to Franz Alexander, and not be able to afford his fees.
03:32:54:00	And uh, uh, the reason was, because I respected these people a great deal.

FLORA SCHREIBER

03:33:10:06	Had you worked with them?

DR. CORNELIA WILBUR

No I had not. But I knew a great deal about their work and knew that, uh, they were not beyond experimenting in terms of their relationship with patients. Uh, I remember very clearly one uh, case which was subsequently written up, where the young female analyst wasn't getting anywhere with the patient.

03:33:25:23 And she came out of the building, and saw the patient on the sidewalk. And said, uh, if you are going my way, I'll give you a lift. And the girl said she was—

03:33:44:07 going downtown. And the young analyst said, well, I am too.

Pg. 43, Tape 2

DR. CORNELIA WILBUR

03:45:05:02 There are only two techniques that I know of. [OVERLAP] . . . .

FLORA SCHREIBER

_____mnemonics?

DR. CORNELIA WILBUR

Huh?

FLORA SCHREIBER

Mnemonics?

Manufacturing Sybil's memories.

DR. CORNELIA WILBUR

03:45:14:02 No. Um . . .
03:45:15:29 The first time we got any memories back, was . . . when . . . I gave her pentothal. And_____. And then, uh, because what happened was this. I had given her the pentothal and I said, when you were on pentothal you said so and so. And she said, oh I hadn't thought about that in years. I've forgotten all about it.
03:45:48:22 And so she talked about it and I said, you also talked about so and so, and so and so. _____. So I decided that I lost too much . . . trying to tell her what she said. So

what I did was tape what she said. And then I played the tapes back so she could hear herself say it. Now this was very interesting. She would remember this for a certain period of time and then she would lose some of _____ it ... Re-forget.

FLORA SCHREIBER

Re-forget?

DR. CORNELIA WILBUR

03:59:21:25 And she couldn't figure _____ to say I hate her. So what she did was to write this letter. And it was after she wrote this letter that she came through with I hate her, I hate her, I hate her.

FLORA SCHREIBER

Now this is not directly related to this but, did the personalities carry the memories that preceded their individual emergences?

DR. CORNELIA WILBUR

03:59:56:24 I don't understand the question.

FLORA SCHREIBER

Uh, did Vicky remember what happened before she arrived at St. Mary's hospital?

DR. CORNELIA WILBUR

04:00:10:25 Uh, yes, I asked her about that. And uh, she said, well, she said before I came out, I was always there.

FLORA SCHREIBER

04:00:25:19 Now you have said that if the doctors were treating white coat, the denial of rescue hadn't triggered uh, the first emergence of Peggy and Vicky, uh, something else would have.

DR. CORNELIA WILBUR

Yeah. [OVERLAP]

FLORA SCHREIBER

At that point, it was already inevitable that she would become a multiple personality.

DR. CORNELIA WILBUR

Yeah. Yeah ... Yeah.

FLORA SCHREIBER

Now you do believe that this is environmentally induced. There is no genetic basis for it.

DR. CORNELIA WILBUR

04:00:52:00 Absolutely.

FLORA SCHREIBER

And that if her early childhood had been totally different. Shte4 had the loving, kind, sweet, dear mother, and all the rest of it. There if hadn't been a fanatical grandfather—
04:01:06:27 And there hadn't been a over naïve religion, etc., etc., etc., she never would become a multiple personality.

DR. CORNELIA WILBUR

That's right ... That's right. Now if you want to carry genetics, uh, to their ultimate limit. Uh, I would say there are people who are more susceptible, to stress, than other people.
04:01:28:10 And say, but, you know you look at this case and you say, how much stress can any human being _____? I'm sure that this girl was a very solid kind of [COUGH]_____. And that she would have remembered all [COUGH] _____ if she hadn't been put through stress—
04:01:46:06 that was just incredible. There isn't any doubt that she was a battered child. She had bruises. She had a fractured _____ cartilage. She was almost killed on two or three occasions. She was scared out of nightmares.

FLORA SCHREIBER

04:02:01:18 What were the incidences in which she was almost killed? The wheat bin.

DR. CORNELIA WILBUR

The wheat bin.

FLORA SCHREIBER

Head over the gas stove.

DR. CORNELIA WILBUR

The head over the gas stove. And the, the episode of the fractured cartilage because it made it difficult for her to breathe . . .

TAPE ENDS

[MORTON PRINCE ADDITIONS]
Pg. 51, Tape 1

DR. CORNELIA WILBUR

13:15:21:09 You know. And, um, so uh, when she told me her name was Peggy, I thought, uh-huh . . . we've got a dual personality here. This is very interesting. Now what do I do? Well I guess maybe, just like everybody else, you know, you go on and you work and see what makes this happen. And why it is.

13:15:47:15 Uh, it might be a good idea if you got Martin Prince's book and looked it over again. And see what he thought about it.

DR. CORNELIA WILBUR

13:15:56:25 Did you say that to yourself?

FLORA SCHREIBER

Yeah. And uh, ...

Pg. 53, Tape 1

DR. CORNELIA WILBUR

13:17:53:13 —Um, . . . I don't know. I had never treated a multiple personality before. And I didn't know where I was going.

13:18:16:12 But um, . . . I assumed that because a multiple personality is really an hysterical state. And uh, because these things, uh, are definitely treatable, that we would go somewhere.

13:18:41:05 But actually almost all of my thinking at the beginning was in terms of questions. I need to know this. I need to know that. I need to know the other thing in order to be able to explain this to her. And to help her to pull it together.

THREE TAPE EXCERPTS

FLORA SCHREIBER

13:19:00:16 Now her reaction to being told she was a multiple personality was not too explosive was it?

DR. CORNELIA WILBUR

13:19:06:16 No. As a matter of fact, she was relieved.

FLORA SCHREIBER

13:19:10:00 That's what Louise told me.

DR. CORNELIA WILBUR

13:19:12:19 She was relieved because this put a name on it. And this also assured her that she was not the only one that this had ever happened to. And that she had a bona fide condition.

13:19:30:21 You see. She was no longer in the limbo of, I wonder if what I've got is a strange and unusual thing that can't be treated . . . you see.
She had had that worry . . . you know, that maybe she couldn't be helped.

FLORA SCHREIBER

13:19:52:09 And she had read Martin Prince's book about the faintest trace of recognition.

DR. CORNELIA WILBUR

13:19:56:25 Yeah.

FLORA SCHREIBER

And she had seen *Three Faces of Eve*.

DR. CORNELIA WILBUR

13:20:01:13 Uh, uh. No, it hadn't been written anyway until '57.

FLORA SCHREIBER

Uh-huh.

DR. CORNELIA WILBUR

13:20:07:23 And, uh, so I explained to her, and I explained to her that this was another form of the same thing I discussed with her, the business of fugue states. That fugue states were fairly simple alterations of consciousness.

13:20:25:10   Altered states of consciousness. Whereas a multiple personality is the same thing only much more complicated and a whole person, emerged, rather than just an altered state of consciousness.

Tape 2

DR. CORNELIA WILBUR

03:00:05:18   Yeah, that's great. Our time is running out.

FLORA SCHRIEBER

No.

DR. CORNELIA WILBUR

And we don't have much time to get.

FLORA SCHREIBER

03:00:16:07   I've been using some [inaudible]. Even if the time came up. You talk about sexual abstinence.

DR. CORNELIA WILBUR

Excuse me, do you think of the men you date yesterday?

FLORA SCHREIBER

03:00:25:09   Not really.

DR. CORNELIA WILBUR

Uh, when uh, _____about the, told us about the, sex stories and . . . [OVERLAP].

FLORA SCHREIBER

03:00:37:09   Uh, it was uh, Marky, _____, Jerney, Vicki, and Mark.

DR. CORNELIA WILBUR

This is ran too . . . I like to order two main, you have a men _____, thank you so much. Uh.

FLORA SCHREIBER

03:00:58:15   Uh, and uh, there is no uh, you know, there is a sexual feeling involved, and in these uh, relationships, that with sexual activity. Uh, and you, when sexual feelings which

	allows the world, switches on reason, but hasn't the toll of it.
03:01:24:15	And she's just walking down the toll and walking fast, and _____ walking is a, she was moving and she was toward it, and then hits it, and then corrected it. Uh, _____ it was also moving. [COUGHS] and uh, so we can reach the goal, she had fade away.
03:01:47:09	Or stop, or something like that. And it was, orientation, of course, was that, the from you know, up to each other. And then they cross each other, and they re-cross, and something was there, and since . . . that they _____ our orientation. They, as a person, teach you maintain your _____.
03:02:16:01	Uh, to that as honors, or reach out on emergency to stop at this point. I mean, is this kind, kind of beams? Sometimes it would be evolved all the way to, the person thinking it stopped showing the ___ at this place.
03:02:34:20	When they stay first together. And then, uh, they they . . . [OVERLAP].

DR. CORNELIA WILBUR

So, who is, who is the satin? Who is the—

FLORA SCHREIBER

03:02:42:04	It was all this salute. How do you think you should, you should get dressed. But usually, it, it should as a _____ itself. Uh, I _____. Never can see.

DR. CORNELIA WILBUR

03:03:01:15	If you present the lay managing_____?

FLORA SCHREIBER

	With new sessions, that he is not. Uh, he's _____ she actually need. But the that the relationship are the kind of the feelings that in a way, you look at the body the size of the___.
03:03:23:20	Because she made a point in fact he is so written gracefully that the body is not. And uh . . .

DR. CORNELIA WILBUR

Do you tell anybody that she and Bobby had been invited places, and _____ kids.

03:03:41:19   You might have known that all the _____.

FLORA SCHREIBER

Yes, this is by foot.

DR. CORNELIA WILBUR

And this should _____ you said, that when uh, that in uh, I don't know, first basically.

03:03:56:05   You don't know that as a young woman. She's very interested in getting out.

FLORA SCHREIBER

[LAUGHTER] Yeah. She was.

DR. CORNELIA WILBUR

That, you know, you don't get the . . .

FLORA SCHREIBER

03:04:11:13   She would have liked to have got here. And she didn't did. And this is how she develop such things in her mind.

DR. CORNELIA WILBUR

03:04:19:16   That's empty. Hmmm. _____ pain of the containment as that I see it accepting fully of the _____ and now is the one at loww. And uh, and that of course is [OVERLAP] the irony.

FLORA SCHREIBER

03:04:36:04   I think, that uh, in sure your own _____ . Her father, treated her in a way particularly hurt. That with, the, you tend to stimulate her sexual feelings toward him.

DR. CORNELIA WILBUR

03:04:52:17   And yet, he was very keen to the sexual feelings, early, and tried to uh, oppress her, keep her from doing simple things like sitting on his lap, when Judy's four.

FLORA SCHREIBER

03:05:04:19   He made too much of it.

DR. CORNELIA WILBUR

That's right.

THREE TAPE EXCERPTS

FLORA SCHREIBER

03:05:07:23 He wouldn't let her, uh, put socks on his feet.

DR. CORNELIA WILBUR

Yeah.

FLORA SCHREIBER

03:05:19:13 He wouldn't let her sit on his lap. And so on and so forth. So it suggested that she was also satin. And that he was denying her this, because it, disturbed him, and also it has disturbed her. And I thought she needed this. I think she is aware of the fact that he thinks it would be something sexual.

03:05:32:24 And that, did stimulate her ideas, and her own feeling. That the blonde young man has denied her of a father.

DR. CORNELIA WILBUR

Because of what? Because of the energy? Or . . . ?

FLORA SCHREIBER

03:05:48:29 Because he didn't look like daddy.

DR. CORNELIA WILBUR

And she really did it as going treatment today.

FLORA SCHREIBER

Yeah.

DR. CORNELIA WILBUR

03:05:58:25 Pick it up_____.

FLORA SCHREIBER

Uh-huh . . .

DR. CORNELIA WILBUR

03:06:04:07 Is this daddy, did uh, as we've said, is the way he is that is the stimulation, or the way he treated her, cold. And the kind of almost _____ noncomprehension on her part, at first as to why, she's treated like this. You know why he did do.

FLORA SCHREIBER

03:06:24:07 Yeah.

DR. CORNELIA WILBUR

As he did that.

FLORA SCHREIBER

03:06:27:06 Yeah, but he's making me _____.

DR. CORNELIA WILBUR

OK.

FLORA SCHREIBER

So, if they, to a child, their behavior may absolutely no a drop of sense. They left her in that bedroom. They screwed in.

03:06:38:21 The front of her. She could see, because her friend crib was here, the window was there, and the streetlight was right outside.

03:06:47:01 She could see her father having an erection and putting it in her mother's vagina. Did you know that?

DR. CORNELIA WILBUR

Yeah.

FLORA SCHREIBER

03:06:55:22 And, so they do this, you know, several nights a week.

DR. CORNELIA WILBUR

And then, _____?

DR. CORNELIA WILBUR

And. Then preach the Puritanical crap.

FLORA SCHREIBER

03:07:04:23 Yeah, and then, daddy tells her when she's four, and still sleeping in that room with them screwing in front . . . several nights a week, that she's too big to put salve on his feet.

03:07:18:18 So, if that isn't contradicting himself, I never heard it, and, I think that ought to go in.

DR. CORNELIA WILBUR

Oh, definitely. That's the hypocrisy fuel. That is just an absolute dichotomy between sermonizing, and performance between practice and performance.

THREE TAPE EXCERPTS 223

FLORA SCHREIBER

03:07:39:11 Hmmm.

DR. CORNELIA WILBUR

And he, he was a terrible fraud, in that those things.

FLORA SCHREIBER

Uh-huh.

DR. CORNELIA WILBUR

03:07:46:20 And of course the way he had kept mother from going to a doctor and kept mother from appearing in public when she had a baby, and when she was pregnant, the whole thing, is so out of line with his own sexual behavior.

FLORA SCHREIBER

03:07:59:27 Yeah . . . That's absolutely right. What, you know, I, I, sometimes really, feel really sick. 'Cause I would like to have ask him, what in your sense of father is going to say to you?

03:08:20:27 That she died of fit, in the middle of the night, inside the_____.

DR. CORNELIA WILBUR

Maybe she's glad to _____ either. Could be.

FLORA SCHREIBER

03:08:39:10 But of course you know, they completely . . . [OVERLAP].

DR. CORNELIA WILBUR

Get to it, and, and attempting to care about this for your own being a father, when Andy deprives her of what I'm here in.

FLORA SCHREIBER

03:08:50:12 Yes.

DR. CORNELIA WILBUR

And, this should rise _____ pass what I'm sure you can do it. You don't, if you don't need _____. And it probably didn't get around of thinking of thank you.

03:09:02:20   And she saw at the house and uh, what was it . . .

FLORA SCHREIBER

____ ?

DR. CORNELIA WILBUR

03:09:10:06   In the ____. You're real as of her general ____.

FLORA SCHREIBER

That is just so much crap.

DR. CORNELIA WILBUR

03:09:16:21   I'm sure, I told him so. I think it's crap.

FLORA SCHREIBER

No, she isn't going to make anything except out of what [knock on door] there's your man . . . about what____. She earns, and if any thing, she earns the book.

03:09:30:21   And of course . . . [OVERLAP]

DR. CORNELIA WILBUR

Well, that has nothing to do with it.

FLORA SCHREIBER

Well, since we are putting things on tape I'll finish what I have to say about the book.

DR. CORNELIA WILBUR

03:09:38:05   Uh-huh . . .

FLORA SCHREIBER

Uh, you know, I've done some praying that the book, for heavens sake, will make money. Because there is nothing I would like better to see than . . . Sylvia . . . I hope to god the book makes money before Florence drops dead. I, heard some things in the bookstore that they'll___ murdered. Because I didn't ____ now, that one ____ to see.

03:09:49:11   Waiting, and ____. And hope to god, that the book makes money before the first stop then. Because I would like to see Sylvia, just you know, land based. Oh, Florence would be absolutely furious if Sylvia turns out to have a lot of money out of this and is very successful.

THREE TAPE EXCERPTS   225

03:10:09:15   Because she'll realize then that if she had played ball with Sylvia. That she might have shared everything. You know.

03:10:22:19   And what she's done is cut herself off. Because this is what she thinks. And I bet you some of us _____ liquid for mom and Sylvia bought that hut.

03:10:36:09   Now, she won't go forward, and send ___ the money from me. That she's used, _____ at interest. _____you're a fool to buy a house. Rent yourself an apartment, evict yourself into some kind of financial state.

03:10:53:11   Florence said, hmm, _____ Sylvia can buy the house from [COUGHS] then, she let herself down, and let herself she was painting one of these murdering _____.

03:11:10:22   Uh, later, in bus tour around the country and she stopped mine, and said, Sylvia, uh, Sylvia showed her the high. And she said, oh, I can't understand a word why the guy is about.

DR. CORNELIA WILBUR

03:11:23:25   [LAUGHTER] Yeah.

FLORA SCHREIBER

And I'd like to see that them bitching for then. Regardless of how much Sylvia had, I would like to see him hired, _____because _____.

03:11:40:06   Not because of the unit damn thing _____. [OVERLAP]

DR. CORNELIA WILBUR

It sounded like vengeance.

FLORA SCHREIBER

03:11:45:29   Yeah, I think that woman ought to _____.

DR. CORNELIA WILBUR

I wonder if he this woman _____. Whether she has it first.

FLORA SCHREIBER

Uh . . .

DR. CORNELIA WILBUR

03:12:02:02   Are you certain?

FLORA SCHREIBER

Burt? I researched her, but I'm not at all certain.

FLORA SCHREIBER

03:12:06:26 Well, I think she is not in a book. It, you know, she is, you know, she ___ herself long, long, long time. And she did, uh, everything she possibly could.

03:12:24:21 So it, here, you know, the uh, Sylvia's relationship with her father. And uh, she really didn't understand it. You know, uh, well, I don't think she wanted you to accept the fact that the idiot was___.

03:12:45:05 And one lousy father.

DR. CORNELIA WILBUR

Yeah, she is, does belong in that time extinction when he's ... I suppose she does but not too strongly.

03:12:56:15 A vicious life state, yes? In these structured ___ parent. First happened with a real ___ shake up. With a very powerful force exert the great executive, and the great legal, and so on.

03:13:11:29 This is a tremendous figure, that, that ___ escape.

FLORA SCHREIBER

She relented.

DR. CORNELIA WILBUR

03:13:19:08 Hmmm.

FLORA SCHREIBER

She was first in ___ to 16, when she had a miserable life. So, you know, because of this from last year. I sometimes think actually are greater.

DR. CORNELIA WILBUR

03:13:37:11 Well, I think he's it. Actually, didn't he say this in confident? What you've said. He couldn't have been a mover and shaker. A powerful man.

03:13:45:26 In a, in the, armor world. And then allows him in those___ but then usually, usually ___. So that's perfect about him.

03:14:04:20 Now, Florence, redone in the book.

FLORA SCHREIBER

____ do about Corian [PH] and her. You think?

DR. CORNELIA WILBUR

03:14:13:06 Uh-huh . . .

FLORA SCHREIBER

Well, she doesn't know if he's been there.

DR. CORNELIA WILBUR

Oh, no, I don't think she's ____ figure, the just the ____ to make a real deal with her.

FLORA SCHREIBER

03:14:28:11 You know, well, I just see, a puritan book, not eternal, not eternally together. I think. Uh, another ____ in the long fate. [CLEARS THROAT]

DR. CORNELIA WILBUR

03:14:47:27 Well, she, logic, logically knows, she's not supposed to know this book is about Sylvia.

FLORA SCHREIBER

Yeah, I know.

DR. CORNELIA WILBUR

03:14:55:15 So Sylvia should make money on the book. It has to come from some other source. She can't know where it comes from.

FLORA SCHREIBER

Well, I told Sylvia the other day that the only way she could make money was to save some and invest it and take capital gains. And so, I've been acquainting her with this idea so if, uh, Florence asks her where the hell she got her money, she can say well now mother taught me how to invest my money and make capital gains and I've been making capital gain and now I am wealthy, have a maid, and I'm going to Europe this summer and I'm going back to get my PhD and to hell with you sister.

03:15:10:23 I am a really vindictive woman . . .

DR. CORNELIA WILBUR

03:15:42:02 Well, so am I, Connie, I can't stand this, no sweetness in life. If somebody gives you a sock on the nose, you give them a sock in the . . .

03:15:49:16 I do believe in an eye for an eye, and a tooth for a tooth, in human relations. You know, love thy brother is a lot of horseshit.

FLORA SCHREIBER

Well I, you know, I, wonder if, if, [OVERLAP]

FLORA SCHREIBER

One of the songs that adore is Roddy McDowall's song in Camelot. It isn't the meek, the meek don't inherit the earth they inherit the dirt.

DR. CORNELIA WILBUR

03:16:12:26 Quit true except it is a lousy ride . . . But it is a true [OVERLAP]

FLORA SCHREIBER

Yeah.

FLORA SCHREIBER

03:16:18:10 And Lerner did a good job of it.

DR. CORNELIA WILBUR

And like I said, if not the earth, that's what he says, its not the earth the meek inherit, it's the dirt.

FLORA SCHREIBER

You talk of Sylvia's sexual dreams.

FLORA SCHREIBER

03:16:35:07 You talked of the nice blonde boy. Was there any other sexual dreams?

FLORA SCHREIBER

Uh, well, there are other dreams that were certainly sexual in content.

03:16:46:03 You know the person who looks most like this blonde boy, was Dick?

DR. CORNELIA WILBUR

She knew they can _____?

FLORA SCHREIBER

Yeah.

DR. CORNELIA WILBUR

03:16:55:04 Oh the dream preceded it?

FLORA SCHREIBER

Uh-huh ... Perceived it, but that certainly lived like that.

DR. CORNELIA WILBUR

03:17:00:26 What is her rule of thumb?

FLORA SCHREIBER

Well, I, it's very distinctly in the dark. And very slight, not terribly taught. But I'm _____.

DR. CORNELIA WILBUR

03:17:08:26 Yes, when she came from the house and says, what are you talking about? Was the other day. _____ locate him and all that kind of thing? And, and when she gets this letter from Peggy, tears it open ...

FLORA SCHREIBER

03:17:21:25 Yeah, yeah. I was there, that's important, I think that a lot of that was resistance, to rule _____. And it showed the resistance by her refusing bluntly to tell her about Vicky.

03:17:39:16 And that got to be whole _____. I explained to her that she would be _____ if you try to avoid relationship. You try to avoid relationship, I said, this, you know, you call this resistance.

03:17:56:22 And from that on. She said, I know I'm involved in the _____ on earth. And she said, don't say it, and, it was a personal joke, you know, I told her that. I'm _____ about we're saying that she was attractive for _____.

DR. CORNELIA WILBUR

03:18:13:17 Uh-huh ...

FLORA SCHREIBER

Wasn't proved. And she just spills out. You know, I said, I was trying to tell Sorra that you know, about _____, I said she made one.

03:18:26:05   They were so much alike in children. And she just broke up. That [OVERLAP]

DR. CORNELIA WILBUR

Go back to Mankato [PH]

FLORA SCHREIBER

03:18:36:00   Well, less the, less the, they are all right. Now even _____. And she just got the, you see, the multiple personalities we're all really regressive.

03:18:51:09   In other words, they were young.

DR. CORNELIA WILBUR

Passed parts of me?

FLORA SCHREIBER

03:19:00:24   Yeah, and uh, they uh, they all went to (Mankato?) here, but
but they didn't really grow up.

FLORA SCHREIBER

Now, what happened to her in that camp that was important. We . . . she got educated and that was awfully important for her. And her damn father nearly let her starve to death by not paying attention to the calendar and sending any money.

DR. CORNELIA WILBUR

And didn't go to her commencement until Mrs. Christianson or or somebody else, uh . . .

FLORA SCHREIBER

03:19:27:29   Wasn't a Christianson_____.

DR. CORNELIA WILBUR

Somebody. Well, I mean, someone, uh Mrs. Conkley said he should. Yeah.

FLORA SCHREIBER

03:19:31:12 Uh, at Mankato she made a lot of friends and ah, she blacked out. And she, even though nobody knew that she was a multiple personality, she was always getting up and leaving class or running away from the dorm and the school nurse covered up for her. Or she said she was not coming to a party and then turned up she had gone to bed, Peggy had gone to the party. Peggy had done a takeoff on one of the professors had been the life of the party they talked to Sylvia.

03:19:50:17 She was really quiet. And we _____. And the, she were missed coming up there.

DR. CORNELIA WILBUR

Oh, she said, she was very _____. Was not coming to _____. And turned out she had gone to bed, thinking had done parting. Thinking he had done _____.

03:20:09:07 It had been likely the _____. And they talked to somebody about it the next day. Sylvia and . . . ?

FLORA SCHREIBER

Yeah, but she didn't always _____. And married to a _____. You know, now this exhibits just how she lived.

03:20:32:15 And _____ just beautiful. She's done firing, she's done killing. She's ran off across country. And that's what we've been looking for. Was a coverup for _____. She married right on and she lost her_____.

03:20:52:22 Uh, the girls that saw _____ said she was all right. And this is mostly happened to her, by her father's furor. She needs to suppress it.

DR. CORNELIA WILBUR

03:21:10:06 And how smuggled these Christian made a homosexuals _____ of her?

FLORA SCHREIBER

Uh, which, which . . .

DR. CORNELIA WILBUR

03:21:15:23 There is a big sting on _____ in stretch of what's going on.

FLORA SCHREIBER

Yeah.

DR. CORNELIA WILBUR

03:21:21:05 She tried to perceive what, she _____.

FLORA SCHREIBER

No.

DR. CORNELIA WILBUR

Now, that's very dramatic. But I don't know how relevant . . . I want to see.

FLORA SCHREIBER

03:21:31:15 I don't think it's particularly relevant. I think _____ now. Uh. Then she, uh, escorted them, uh, onto the fringe via the . . .

DR. CORNELIA WILBUR

She act to uh . . .

FLORA SCHREIBER

03:22:03:07 That she didn't hurt

DR. CORNELIA WILBUR

I know I lead you that.

FLORA SCHREIBER

03:22:15:08 Yeah. The father, had now, left her, _____ out to Alaska. To help build a _____ and a walking _____. Because she was so odd. She wore gold instead silver and it has never done. She walk on the fringes.

DR. CORNELIA WILBUR

03:22:31:02 Now remain Kado a mother at, one time. I said, one of those things that France joined on the ceiling, and Sylvia said she didn't know. And she didn't know. But uh, but it would later would be, that, uh, Peggy had been trying around . . .

FLORA SCHREIBER

03:22:52:01 But they, much knew the things by the _____ of the furniture. Until she knows what's going on. Her, her

	father said she, said to me. She's walking on the furniture.
03:23:04:23	Why does she wan't to do that? Sylvia never did that. Why does she walk on the furniture? It was completely beridded by his rule. Which Peggy showed. He uh, he called ____ us to the library.
03:23:23:09	And he got out of the car, run the ____ completely. This is really a deep one.

DR. CORNELIA WILBUR

Why did he do that? She, he took her to the library.

FLORA SCHREIBER

03:23:34:22	And she's over an hour. He took her in the car, and ____. And she wanted to go to the library. And so they went to the library. And got a book. And she got back in his car.
03:23:44:14	And he said that he want to stop there. And he stopped and started, and came back ____ oh, yeah. Apparently, and he said that just before it's happened, she talked to him. Not like Sylvia.
03:24:00:10	I guess it was many others who said she just got out of the car and walked off. And she didn't come back for several hours, and it was frightening him. He, he told me it was really, the reason why they lock her in the house.
03:24:13:28	But she's ____ and the pain is worse.

DR. CORNELIA WILBUR

Let's return to the parents and influence of the other personalities. OK, will admit, that day, when you dropped Sylvia in the library. Uh.

03:24:32:08	He met Mike, in the coffee bookshop. He met obviously Peggy, which two are ____. Now, Mary and the, menstruation, episode interest me. Mary was the first one who menstruated.
03:24:57:10	Now, when Sylvia menstruated for the first time. And Sylvia welcomed the surprise?

FLORA SCHREIBER

	It wasn't uh, it wasn't very menstruated. It was ____
03:25:11:19	Sylvia menstruated twice. And mother didn't know a full month. The third time, mother found out. And she

03:25:37:26	said, well, oh, so it's come. Huh? What? Don't you hurt? What? Don't hurt? I always hurt. You hurt today?

DR. CORNELIA WILBUR

Yeah, but who menstruated the third time? Sylvia or Mary?

FLORA SCHREIBER

03:25:48:04 Well, it was Sylvia who started to menstruate. And it was Mary who persist.

DR. CORNELIA WILBUR

But was it Mary to whom Patty was talking at that moment?

FLORA SCHREIBER

03:25:59:19 No, it's Sylvia that Pat is talking to. And Sylvia bear the _____ that she couldn't stand it. She didn't have the nerve.

DR. CORNELIA WILBUR

Because Sylvia . . .

FLORA SCHREIBER

03:26:08:29 Because

DR. CORNELIA WILBUR

03:26:20:15 Because Mary tells the story of being in school, menstruating, rushing out. And she went to the doctor. And she didn't recognize it. She couldn't find it. Because daddy had broke it while Peggy was there.

FLORA SCHREIBER

Now, you see. What's happened, was Peggy, [PAUSE] before that part of it.

DR. CORNELIA WILBUR

03:26:45:21 That same day.

FLORA SCHREIBER

But it occurs to me, it occurs to me that both happened _____. Well, in the first place. Peggy was there instead of their mother. Watched the _____.

THREE TAPE EXCERPTS   235

03:27:03:19   And uh, uh, you know, this is before, the murder. The
               person doing it is supposed to stop. So afterwards, after
               school. _____ . Now Brenda died in April.
03:27:28:00   And she went _____ she's upset. Anyway. [CLEARS
               THROAT] and she was in these _____ on the _____. And
               she was out two weeks. Now she was murdered. She
               has _____.
03:28:06:18   And Sylvia, she was in the house. Sylvia, Mary, and
               Peggy. All no one talked.

                           DR. CORNELIA WILBUR
               This is, after that.

                           FLORA SCHREIBER
03:28:22:22   After. Now I didn't know that Mary menstruated in
               school. When she came home. But firstly Sylvia is very
               different. It teased her mother, the fact that she was
               menstruating.
03:28:35:10   And I bet you that Mary had before, and _____. She
               couldn't find the bathroom, that daddy brought it that
               Bob _____. But Sylvia always used that _____. And
               what she would do in place of that was she reveal to
               her mother.
03:28:56:09   That she was menstruating because mommy never
               asked Sylvia how come she didn't even know she was
               menstruating. And she said, she know, but her mother
               _____. And she was in the ladies room.

                           DR. CORNELIA WILBUR
03:29:10:03   Was it Mary who wanted that? Cause it was clearly
               there. I mean, explanation was obvious.

                           FLORA SCHREIBER
03:29:17:27   So that she ran to the bathroom. And she had her feet
               soaked. And then mother came in and said, why
               aren't you hurt? Why aren't you... carried on like a
               manic.
03:29:29:25   And said, I always and always hurt. And that suggested
               that _____ frightened, and not hurt, and doesn't know
               what's going on. And so she did a terrible thing. That
               the first menstruation she _____.

DR. CORNELIA WILBUR

03:29:55:15 Now, the third, in third or fourth grade, is not an exclusive thing because Vicky was first of being there. The third or fourth grade. And talked of everything being cold, and blue the way she described.

FLORA SCHREIBER

03:30:11:01 Yeah, except that Vicky knows up here. Now you must remember that to everything Vicky is they, she was present, but she did not function. The only person that function those two years is Peggy.

DR. CORNELIA WILBUR

03:30:26:20 All right, now.

FLORA SCHREIBER

Vicky had to be there, because Vicky knew everything that went on, and experience that too.

03:30:37:06 Because she is total continuum, she knows everything about everybody. Sometimes Peggy didn't pay attention of, there are so many things. So she didn't know

03:30:54:11 And vice versa. Vicky knew everything. Everything. And this is one thing that is characteristic of multiple personalities. I have never seen that. It's always one personality that knows everything that's going on.

03:31:29:10 Uh . . .

DR. CORNELIA WILBUR

I want . . . Are you on?

FLORA SCHREIBER

Yeah. Uh, what I started saying was that I do a formal psychoanalysis, it is a little difficult to do a formal psychoanalysis with the analyst sitting in the chair at the head of the couch out of the range of vision of the patient when the patient is sitting huddled on the other end of the couch

03:31:40:28 Peering at you. Uh, you know. And, or when the patient comes in and looks at you, and says you know, that this name is different than the person you are seeing

03:32:04:02 and uh, wanders around the room and so forth. It's a little difficult. It's real difficult. So I didn't point as _____.

	I see so I became involved enough in the multiple personality so when trouble arose, I, there was nobody else to go to but for her—no family.
03:32:18:05	So there's been a couple identities. I had to be there for her, she had no family. And if anybody was going to keep track of her, I had too. Now this, according to the formula in psychoanalysis is stepping outside.
03:32:35:10	But I learned this trick from a very very fine source. I learned it from Franz Alexander. And if you remember I said that she should go to Ben Johnson? Uh, who was a student of Franz Alexander in Chicago. Thinking that in all probability, she wouldn't be able to get to Franz Alexander—and not be able to afford the fees.
03:32:54:00	____ And uh, uh, the reason was because I, respected these people a great deal.

DR. CORNELIA WILBUR

03:33:10:06 Did you work with them?

FLORA SCHREIBER

No, I have not. But I knew a great deal about their work and knew that, uh, that they were not beyond experimenting in terms of their relationships with patients. Uh, I remember very clearly one case, which was subsequently written up, where the young female analyst wasn't getting anywhere with the patient.

03:33:25:23 And she came out of the building, and saw the patient on the sidewalk. And said uh, you are going my way, I'll give you a lift. And the girl said she was going.

03:33:44:07 And the young analyst said I am too. They'll arrange to have her name there. So I went downtown. So they thought____ and uh, and they are talked about nothing. And then, it, reporter was on the way.

03:34:02:21 But the next time, there is some ____. Oh she said ____. But he said, you know what? Honey, ____ at all. Next time, that she wasn't. So when she saw the patient, the patient uh, told her. Now, doctor, I can tell you, what I know.

03:34:31:17 Cause it's not going to ____. Because I didn't see it, that there are some real relationships ____. But you learn yesterday, that ____downtown. And this is ____ now I can tell. During the basic ____.

03:34:53:19	Learn the fact, because _____. Uh, so we, uh, helped her. That I did do anything, and I did. I did it because it for her. It was _____ for me. And she ____ because she _____ because a lot of things are just going to pile up and _____ should be dealt immediately.
03:35:26:19	And definitely _____. She end up in _____. She _____ and she cried. _____ that she would _____ . And said that she have to throw their effort into this. So I called them immediately. And I talked to Sylvia. But obviously Sylvia wasn't, was _____.
03:36:01:22	And _____ said that I popped the _____. Sylvia there. And she said it's so cold there, and it's very _____. And I can't go there, to _____ it's true because she's never going to talk to them. And she didn't know if we knew how they are going to _____.
03:36:25:23	Because she didn't. I know somebody, somebody can always _____. So, I said, I would go down, and go _____ one time ____. And we went down the subway and direct _____ the train.
03:36:55:03	And we lounged at a _____ again. I came back, walk in the front, of ____ station. Entirely of _____. Sylvia? _____ wall. _____ tell me, tell me. And she turned around, and cried. And oh my god. What came over _____?
03:37:24:28	I was so bad to see. _____. I was _____. Find a taxi and take it. And it got to the corner of _____ Street. And by Broad. And we _____. Up to the door. _____ it got into the toll. _____ toll.
03:37:56:17	And _____. And about, she had like and liked . . .

DR. CORNELIA WILBUR

Is this during the same program _____?

FLORA SCHREIBER

03:38:15:10	Uh, well, it was Sylvia.

DR. CORNELIA WILBUR

What jail is it, _____ ?

FLORA SCHREIBER

It was through . . . _____

THREE TAPE EXCERPTS 239

03:38:42:01   We may have to _____ not that she was so over _____ inside. The _____ are really _____. _____ let me help this, and make the effort. Anyway, [CLEARS THROAT] we didn't have to it, she didn't have to _____ chase it.
03:39:14:22   And so I said, well, _____ and ____. So I pulled it, _____ and _____ the bathroom floor. And it was filled _____ leg. And [CLEARS THROAT]
[IMPOSSIBLE TO HEAR]
[TAPE CLEARS UP FROM HERE]

DR. CORNELIA WILBUR

03:42:42:22   Very much of it.

FLORA SCHREIBER

Yeah.

DR. CORNELIA WILBUR

03:42:47:12   You know, that, the, the ten-year-old logic in this girl. You have confusion on the one hand.

FLORA SCHREIBER

Yeah.

DR. CORNELIA WILBUR

03:42:51:15   Angry and the confusion on the other hand, you have logic. [OVERLAP] not exactly matching.

FLORA SCHREIBER

No.

DR. CORNELIA WILBUR

03:43:04:05   Now, in terms of your psychiatric techniques. Oh yeah, she walks and knows how to take the dogs out. And _____ tight four years, and take some responsibility in your work. _____.

FLORA SCHREIBER

03:43:18:13   But well, you know, she was a good typist, and uh, and really, _____ of course. And you know, she could do something. And she could get back to _____. She went by on those other things, good jobs, and these other things like. She had already _____.

03:43:41:14 She _____ you know. But she would go back. She was maybe _____ she's ending the job. And then she just, _____ somebody else somewhere. So that uh [OVERLAP].

DR. CORNELIA WILBUR

03:43:52:20 Do you know she was a typist?

FLORA SCHREIBER

No, I, I Peggy said she was going to get through. And I hope she is. She's going to stay _____.
03:43:07:19 But you know, _____.

DR. CORNELIA WILBUR

Uh, now is _____ and Sylvia said you, got Christmas card signed Sylvia, and _____?

FLORA SCHREIBER

Yeah.

DR. CORNELIA WILBUR

03:44:26:09 And this kind of. You have a real conversation from the horror and blackout, and lost time, and _____. And on the other hand, she actually let you know that she was a lone personality.
3:44:46:17 Was that Sylvia's acceptance of the _____?

FLORA SCHREIBER

No. Not the _____.

DR. CORNELIA WILBUR

03:44:50:21 Not the kind of _____ uh, comments.

FLORA SCHREIBER

Right. Those are there too. The minute he did. The fact is, she did not come until she began to _____.
03:45:05:20 Now _____ had forgotten that by specific _____. There are only two techniques that I know of [OVERLAP] what?

DR. CORNELIA WILBUR

Mount?

FLORA SCHREIBER

03:45:14:02 Hmmm? No.

DR. CORNELIA WILBUR

Mount?

FLORA SCHREIBER

03:45:15:29 _____. Uh, the first time we got any memories back was, when, I gave her pentothal and then because what happened was this. Now I had given her the pentothol and I said, when you were on pentothol you said so and so, oh I hadn't thought about that in years. I've forgotten all about it.

03:45:48:22 And so she talked about it, and I also said, what you also talked about so and so and so and so, _____. So I decided that I lost too much . . . trying to tell her what she said so what I did was to tape what she said and then I played the tapes back.

03:46:10:09 So that she could hear herself say it. Now this was very interesting. She would remember this for a certain period of time. And then she would lose some of _____ it. Re-forget.

DR. CORNELIA WILBUR

Re-forget.

FLORA SCHREIBER

03:46:28:08 Yeah, less painful. So now one of the things that happened was that she liked it a great deal because it relieved her anxiety and the day after she had pentothol she felt perfectly well. Something she had never felt at any time in her life _____.

03:46:48:22 And as a consequence, she became quite involved. And on two or three occasions, very demanding about having pentothol.

DR. CORNELIA WILBUR

Now, that runs regret through the tapes. I've seen lots of references to that.

FLORA SCHREIBER

03:47:03:15 And it worried me because I had the feeling she was getting addicted. At least psychologically. And I didn't want to go, from a multiple personality to an addiction. You know, so, I've lost where she is. So I stopped it, And . . .

DR. CORNELIA WILBUR

03:47:18:04 By then, had you stopped the _____ and when did you stop it? What was the situation?

FLORA SCHREIBER

I did not look at my heart. Absolutely.

DR. CORNELIA WILBUR

03:47:25:22 You didn't check it one time?

FLORA SCHREIBER

No. All right. Uh, we stopped at _____. But _____.

DR. CORNELIA WILBUR

But had you at least _____ and her heart the magician _____.

FLORA SCHREIBER

03:47:46:11 The very first _____.

DR. CORNELIA WILBUR

Since all of us talked about _____.

FLORA SCHREIBER

The very first experience I did, I did _____. And uh, I did, some careful losses.

03:48:04:17 But I did more careful on the _____, and, and the work. And it's _____, because I would never have _____.

DR. CORNELIA WILBUR

Uh, what is this? An injection?

FLORA SCHREIBER

03:48:14:25 Yeah.

DR. CORNELIA WILBUR

And why?

FLORA SCHREIBER

Yeah, through there _____.

DR. CORNELIA WILBUR

03:48:21:03 Not painful, apparently, because she uh _____?

FLORA SCHREIBER

Well, uh, it's the drug is uh, in the concentrations used, can be irritating to seen if you give it too fast.

DR. CORNELIA WILBUR

03:48:32:24 Now, what is this? Sodium pentothol?

FLORA SCHREIBER

Sodium pentothol—yes.
Is that the so-called truth serum?

FLORA SCHREIBEN

03:48:39:09 Uh-huh, that's one of them.

DR. CORNELIA WILBUR

So that you will really be eliciting . . . pretty subtle stuff. The truth—so to speak.

FLORA SCHREIBER

03:48:47:26 Yeah, yeah . . . Anyway—

DR. CORNELIA WILBUR

Now, how does it work, it unleashes the unconscious?

FLORA SCHREIBER

03:48:55:02 Well, what, um what happened to her, was that, um, I would give her um, oh, 125 milligram. Which is, you know, a dose that may put you to sleep. Then she would go to sleep.

03:49:12:26 And I would clean up the equipment and and then I would try to wake her up and usually_____. But it was not—

DR. CORNELIA WILBUR

After how much time did you have to waken her?

FLORA SCHREIBER

03:49:24:13 Uh, it ran from 12 to 20 minutes and uh, but she wouldn't wake up into _____. She would wake up in an altered state of consciousness.

03:49:47:23 But if I talk to her, and said, here's the _____. In this way, she would to back to sleep and she would wake up no_____.

DR. CORNELIA WILBUR

Now, when you talk about the altered state of consciousness.

03:50:02:21 Does this happen to any one of you, _____ as well, or is it exclusively _____ person business. In the oldest day, you didn't have _____ some of that person.

FLORA SCHREIBER

Well, actually, we would get a _____ person. Who would _____ all of me.

DR. CORNELIA WILBUR

03:50:29:01 So it really kind of simulate it in relation?

FLORA SCHREIBER

Yeah. I thought maybe it was uh, actually the _____ thing. _____. She first being evicted. So I was _____.

DR. CORNELIA WILBUR

03:50:51:01 You mean Costeau and ____?

FLORA SCHREIBER

Oh no. _____ because I'm concerned at her _____. I say to her, that I'm_____ because she'll . . .

DR. CORNELIA WILBUR

03:51:14:17 But this is _____.

FLORA SCHREIBER

Uh-huh. And she said, no. And uh, _____ that she really needed _____. When she said, _____ new house. [LAUGHTER]

03:51:37:25 Look what I, I said, that _____. She laughed. She said yes. You know, what's your need? She said, break up _____ and throw it away.

DR. CORNELIA WILBUR

03:51:44:16   Well now, under hypnosis. You summon the various personalities.

FLORA SCHREIBER

Yes I could do this. As well . . . yeah [OVERLAP]

DR. CORNELIA WILBUR

03:51:51:22   You did it for me.

FLORA SCHREIBER

Yeah, yeah. I had . . .

FLORA SCHREIBER

03:51:54:23   Yeah.

DR. CORNELIA WILBUR

You introduced all the personalities. Uh, you did do that on the pentothol?

FLORA SCHREIBER

03:52:00:18   Well excepting sometimes um . . . Well, I did do it on pentothol too. I mean I would say to whoever was talking to me _____ you know, I'd say well, you know, who are you and well, I'm talking for you now, and name three or four. And I would say what does Peggy think of all this, what does Vicky think about this and they would know, I said, look, it's gotten me_____. I say I don't know and I would say, can I talk to Vicky. Yeah, well the same with effect I could summon them all like_____.

DR. CORNELIA WILBUR

03:52:27:28   Now, had they been operative in talking to each other before the analysis? My feeling is that Sylvia knew nothing about them but they knew about themselves. And about each other.
03:52:42:19   Now, was there any intercommunication?

FLORA SCHREIBER

Well, let me tell you something. The very . . . I ever asked Sylvia to explain this.

03:52:54:10   Now I said to Sylvia, isn't there some connection between you and these other personalities? And I lost Sylvia.

DR. CORNELIA WILBUR

Now when did you ask her this?

FLORA SCHREIBER

03:53:06:23   This was very early. This was right after I explained to her that she was a multiple personality. And I said, I am sure that there is a connection between you and these other states.

03:53:23:02   And you need to find that connection, then you need to build a bridge between you and the other states and you—

DR. CORNELIA WILBUR

You call them states rather than people?

FLORA SCHREIBER

03:53:34:17   Uh, I think so at that point. And I said uh, you know, I want to _____ why I lost Sylvia.

DR. CORNELIA WILBUR

I think it was Vicky and she said I can explain it to you. It's very hard. Were they under pentothol? Nothing. Just straight.

FLORA SCHREIBER

Um. I hadn't started using them. She said, I can explain it to you but it's very difficult. She said, have on this side is Sylvia. And have on this side is, me, and Peggy and I guess, some others.

03:54:06:16   See I knew almost Peggy and Vicky at this point but I didn't know much about the others at this point. That _____. And she said, that there isn't a connection between us at all. Except way underneath. She stuck her hand under her leg like this. Yeap. She said , except way underneath there isn't really a connection, there's just a possibility of a connection.

03:54:45:29   Well, [CLEARS THROAT] I thought about this many many times I found out this really and I think that what she was trying to say was that if you consider all the altered states of consciousness say in layers.

THREE TAPE EXCERPTS 247

03:55:10:16 The waking is the most usual cerebral layer, you know.

DR. CORNELIA WILBUR

The most conscious.

FLORA SCHREIBER

03:55:17:23 And then you can have the uh, the sort of dream state, at least a , the somnambulism, or whatever you want to call it, then you _____, and so can have sleep and so on. That, what she was trying to say was that [OVERLAP] here—

DR. CORNELIA WILBUR

Consciousness and so forth. There isn't a connection between Sylvia and us.

03:55:38:29 But way way down deep, there is a connection.

DR. CORNELIA WILBUR

Yet, they shared Sylvia's experiences and have a healthy impact of that experience, individually. So there is a connection.

FLORA SCHREIBER

03:55:56:29 Yeah, but they often times didn't feel the impact, if Sylvia got put up on by somebody they were just terribly annoyed, just had to know that Sylvia didn't do something about it.

DR. CORNELIA WILBUR

03:56:09:29 Yeah, in childhood, when mother, uh, stuck a, you know, ice water up Sylvia's bladder, the rest of them felt it.

FLORA SCHREIBER

Uh. Yeah, because it showed the body. But they didn't have the emotions.

DR. CORNELIA WILBUR

03:56:31:08 Now, Peggy, and Clara, and Ruthie report cruelties. Several of the personalities report cruelties. What I don't understand . . .

FLORA SCHREIBER

03:56:40:01 But you need to watch it. Are they reporting cruelties that they were experiencing?

DR. CORNELIA WILBUR

Or, are they the Greek chorus for Sylvia?

FLORA SCHREIBER

Yeah. Yeah.

DR. CORNELIA WILBUR

03:56:49:11 Yeah. That's very important, you know, there are . . .

FLORA SCHREIBER

Because David said, _____ are actually another person. So,

DR. CORNELIA WILBUR

03:57:14:18 It was. But Peggy also says, momma did this to me. As an inconsistency or sometimes when they, even Vicky talks of her aunt, mother.

FLORA SCHREIBER

03:57:26:26 Yeah.

DR. CORNELIA WILBUR

Of the mother, her mother.

FLORA SCHREIBER

Uh, the part was only acted on, of course on_____.

DR. CORNELIA WILBUR

03:57:33:01 And cause of the later state is, I think the most marvelous lines, is when Vicky says, Sylvia's mother dash, why does_____.

FLORA SCHREIBER

03:57:53:11 But that is after they've discussed it. As kid. As _____ but you know, it's actually, she wasn't Peggy's mother. And she wasn't Vicky's mother, and so forth. Was_____.

DR. CORNELIA WILBUR

And there is one thing you mustn't forget is Sylvia's fantastic letter to you that gave me goose pimples. In this motel last summer. [LAUGHTER] when I discussed it—

03:58:10:27 In which Sylvia said, and that's all hotel, uh it's all a hoax, that she never was a multiple personality, and her mother was very good to her, and everything. And it was a total denial.

FLORA SCHREIBER

03:58:24:13 Yeah.

DR. CORNELIA WILBUR

And somewhere that has to take place. Cause it is very powerful stuff.
03:58:30:15 Now, did the personalities_____?

FLORA SCHREIBER

Do you know if she did that?

DR. CORNELIA WILBUR

Why?

FLORA SCHREIBER

03:58:37:13 Because I was pushing her. And uh, she wanted to get out from under. She didn't want to, really analyze. And well, actually, this came in, we better talk it over with her but I'm very definitely of the opinion that this came when
03:58:54:17 I was pushing in terms of you don't your mother, your mother was wicked, bad, cruel, painful. And you, really hate it. If you don't hate her you ought to, there is something the matter with you if you don't hate her because a normal response to this kind of treatment would be bitter hatred.
03:59:31:25 And she couldn't figure _____ I hate her. Clever tape. And she came in to listen to the _____. So what she did was to write this letter. Say I wanted to get _____. And it was after she wrote this letter, and it was after she wrote this letter that she came through work, I hate her, I hate her, I hate her.

DR. CORNELIA WILBUR

Now, this is not directly related to this. But did the personalities carry memories that preceded their individual emergencies?

FLORA SCHREIBER

03:59:56:24 I don't understand the question.

DR. CORNELIA WILBUR

Uh, did Vicky remember what happened? Before she arrived at St. Mary's Hospital?

FLORA SCHREIBER

04:00:10:25 Uh, yes, I asked her about that. And uh, she said, well, before I came out, I was always there.

DR. CORNELIA WILBUR

04:00:25:19 Now you have said that the doctors who were treating white coat, that denial of rescue haven't triggered uh the first emergence of Peggy and Vicky. Some, uh, they else would have at that point, it was already inevitable and ____ that she would become a multiple personality you know. Now you do believe that this is environmentally induced there is no genetic basis whatsoever.

FLORA SCHREIBER

04:00:52:00 Absolutely.

DR. CORNELIA WILBUR

And that if her early childhood had been totally different, she had had the loving kind, sweet dear mother, that all of the rest of it and if there hadn't been a fanatical grandfather.

04:01:06:27 And there hadn't been a over naïve religion, etc., etc., she never would become a multiple personality homeless?

FLORA SCHREIBER

That's right. That's right. Now if want to carry genetics, to their ultimate limit, I would say that there are people who are more susceptible to stress, than other people.

04:01:28:10 And say but, you know, you look at this case and say, how much stress can any human being hold? Well, I'm sure that this girl was a very solid, or [COUGHS]. I mean, she didn't believe about the things that ____ if she hadn't been put through stress.

04:01:46:06	And it's just incredible. There isn't a doubt that she was a battered child. She had bruises, she had a fractured ____, she would hide in the apartment. She was almost killed on two or three occasions. She was scared out of nightmares.
04:02:01:18	Incidents which almost killed her. We've been, the gas stove?

FLORA SCHREIBER

Yes, the gas stove. And the, the fact that she was punished for the _____.

DR. CORNELIA WILBUR

04:02:20:21	And we discussed it? About the ____ about the ____? The mother's intent wasn't necessarily to kill.

FLORA SCHREIBER

No.

DR. CORNELIA WILBUR

04:02:30:11	Only to inflict, to be vengeful, to hurt . . . [PAUSE]

TAPE ENDS

Sybil: Tape 3

Note: This transcript is comprised of what I believe to be the most salient excerpts from the tape of the Sybil therapeutic session in my possession. Unfortunately, technical problems—not least the poor audio quality—make it impractical to reproduce the entirety of the session here. However, readers who are interested can listen to the entire recording, copies of which are on deposit at John Jay College in New York and at the University of Akron, Akron, Ohio.

DR. CORNELIA WILBUR

00:00:00:00	Let it go. Now either leave it alone . . .

SYBIL

00:00:00:00	Well . . . . .

DR. CORNELIA WILBUR

00:00:00:00	Yes there is sweetie . . . .

SYBIL

00:00:00:00   . . . . no end to it.

DR. CORNELIA WILBUR

00:00:00:00   Yes there is honey . . . There is an end right now. Yes, you don't need to go on any further.

SYBIL

00:00:00:00   Not . . . . . not . . .

DR. CORNELIA WILBUR

00:00:00:00   No sweetie. You can do something else now. You can do all the numbers, so now you can do something else . . . . Now you can do something else. It's all right . . . . It's all right.

SYBIL

00:00:00:00   Mine. Mine. Mine.

DR. CORNELIA WILBUR

00:00:00:00   There are many things that are yours sweetie. You have many things and they belong to you.

TAPE RECORDER TURNED OFF.

SYBIL

00:00:00:00   (BREATHING) uh . . . . .uh

DR. CORNELIA WILBUR

00:00:00:00   Sweetie? You are very good. You know that when you can count to a hundred by twos that all the rest of them are exactly the same and then you don't have to go on any more. You can stop . . . .
. . . .You have learned it and that is all that is necessary . . . .It doesn't have to go on and on. You yourself can . . .

SYBIL

00:00:00:00   The man . . . and the baby . . . .the man and the baby . . . .

DR. CORNELIA WILBUR

00:00:00:00   Is that you and your daddy?

THREE TAPE EXCERPTS

SYBIL

00:00:00:00   Daddy . . .

DR. CORNELIA WILBUR

00:00:00:00   Is that daddy?

SYBIL

00:00:00:00   The baby . . . .very young baby . . . . . .Oh . . . . why? . . . .why?
Uh . . . uh . . . uh . . . .

DR. CORNELIA WILBUR

00:00:00:00   It's all right sweetie.

SYBIL

00:00:00:00   The book . . . .the book.

DR. CORNELIA WILBUR

00:00:00:00   What about the book?

SYBIL

00:00:00:00   The book.

DR. CORNELIA WILBUR

00:00:00:00   What about the book? What about the book, sweetie? (CLEARS THROAT) What about the book?

SYBIL

00:00:00:00   Uh . . . . . . (BREATHING)

DR. CORNELIA WILBUR

00:00:00:00   Do you want some books?
00:00:00:00   Would you like some books to read? . . . . .What about them, sweetie? Can I help you with the books?
It is all right dear. It's all right . . . . . . Sweetie, it's all right.

TAPE RECORDER TURNED OFF.

DR. CORNELIA WILBUR

00:00:00:00   How do you feel?

SYBIL

00:00:00:00   Numb.

DR. CORNELIA WILBUR

00:00:00:00   (CLEARS THROAT)

SYBIL

00:00:00:00   My legs . . .

TAPE RECORDER TURNED OFF.

SYBIL

00:00:00:00   . . . (UNINTELLIGIBLE) and the paper kept twirling. . . . (UNINTELLIGIBLE) . . . see where they set and I didn't even care. And I (UNINTELLIGIBLE) . . . .and I don't care. And I was playing with it and I push over it with my fingers and I think . . . and now, with this hand this way and with this hand like that, at the same time . . . see like that.

See? Up and downward. You are now looking at my hand up and down with one . . . (UNINTELLIGIBLE) . . . and that . . . .This is ice and this are walls.

And then in the tree, I had a big tree. I put in trees in and (UNINTELLIGIBLE) . . . and that way . . . .and the trees are all alike. And that's how they're built. And, they are not . . . and if I were going . . . And then that was all. And when I got through, that was, that's how it felt . . . .

. . . .And. And. And. If I were going to make them a new picture, I would have to mark out my . . . (UNINTELLIGIBLE) . . . .and I would put flowers . . . (UNINTELLIGIBLE) . . . and things you know I can't stand make a picture.

And I would have at the end a little dash of red and brighten up them . . . and I would get, I drew all together different things and I couldn't (UNINTELLIGIBLE) . . . I could make that into a picture but I didn't want to make it into a picture.

I didn't have to. I painted with, my hands put into it (UNINTELLIGIBLE) . . . and this is the way I want it and I just went all over it like that . . . and I just . . . very bad colors. Very bad!

THREE TAPE EXCERPTS   255

                    .... You said if I want to. I don't want to! (UNIN-
                    TELLIGIBLE).

                              DR. CORNELIA WILBUR
00:00:00:00   (UNINTELLIGIBLE) ... (CLEARS THROAT) ....
                    (UNINTELLIGIBLE)

                                       SYBIL
00:00:00:00   (UNINTELLIGIBLE) ... want to leave.

(PHONE RINGS)

                              DR. CORNELIA WILBUR
00:00:00:00   (UNINTELLIGIBLE)

                                       SYBIL
00:00:00:00   (UNINTELLIGIBLE) ... my arms and legs are ... weak
                    and I am sick and I couldn't draw.

                              DR. CORNELIA WILBUR
00:00:00:00   Hummm!

TAPE RECORDER TURNED OFF

                                       SYBIL
00:00:00:00   I don't know it.

                              DR. CORNELIA WILBUR
00:00:00:00   Are you reliving a time when you were sick?

                                       SYBIL
00:00:00:00   I am sick now. I am too sick to talk.

                              DR. CORNELIA WILBUR
00:00:00:00   Does that mean you don't want to talk?

                                       SYBIL
00:00:00:00   Uh-huh .... I want to do, I just want you to talk to
                    me.

                              DR. CORNELIA WILBUR
00:00:00:00   You want me to tell you what I thought about the pic-
                    ture with the black on it sweetie?

SYBIL

00:00:00:00   All right.

DR. CORNELIA WILBUR

00:00:00:00   You know . . . .you have said so many times that sometimes you feel like you come up against a stone wall. Huh? And the way you drew the black makes me think . . . that . . . this might be the stone wall.

SYBIL

00:00:00:00   No, it's in the other picture.

DR. CORNELIA WILBUR

00:00:00:00   Yes dear. But . . . .I think we will get to that.
I think actually that the wall that you were up against was the wall . . . .you couldn't get anywhere after. No? And I think that you could paint it . . . because now there are holes in it.

SYBIL

00:00:00:00   Yep.

DR. CORNELIA WILBUR

00:00:00:00   No? . . . . . . No what? . . . .I'm wrong. Is that right? It doesn't feel right to you. OK. (CLEARS THROAT)

SYBIL

00:00:00:00   It's like anger in some religion. The stone wall is something else.

DR. CORNELIA WILBUR

00:00:00:00   What is the stone wall dear?

SYBIL

00:00:00:00   The stone wall is doing things. And what I want. It doesn't have anything to do with the religion. It is something else.

DR. CORNELIA WILBUR

00:00:00:00   You mean that the religion hasn't kept you from doing what you want?

SYBIL

00:00:00:00 It's not the stone wall. (UNINTELLIGIBLE) religion has ....but it's not the stone wall. It's the black ... and it was all black, all black and alone ... and now it isn't (UNINTELLIGIBLE) ...

DR. CORNELIA WILBUR

00:00:00:00 What's happened to it?

SYBIL

00:00:00:00 You fixed it up .... (UNINTELLIGIBLE) ... put a lot of holes in it.

DR. CORNELIA WILBUR

00:00:00:00 There is a lot of black on that picture and I think we still have some to fix up.

SYBIL

00:00:00:00 Yes.

DR. CORNELIA WILBUR

00:00:00:00 Would you like to look at Neamiah? So that you can feel better and you won't feel sick? ... ...
Sweetie? ... ... Would you?

SYBIL

00:00:00:00 (UNINTELLIGIBLE)

DR. CORNELIA WILBUR

00:00:00:00 I see.

SYBIL

00:00:00:00 (UNINTELLIGIBLE) .... cold.

DR. CORNELIA WILBUR

00:00:00:00 All right. When you were little you always wanted to paint with your fingers but you weren't allowed to, were you?

00:00:00:00 Now you are free enough ... now that you can paint with your fingers. If that's the way you feel like painting, you can.

You still feel sick sweetie? Oh, let's look at Neamiah. . . . Will get rid of this sick feeling.

SYBIL

00:00:00:00   I just want . . . (UNINTELLIGIBLE) to let (UNINTELLIGIBLE) . . . do it.

(PHONE RINGS)

DR. CORNELIA WILBUR

00:00:00:00   (PERSONAL PHONE CONVERSATION)
00:00:00:00   Sweetie. You want to bring the book over here? . . . . . . Sweetie. How can you see? You haven't got your glasses.

SYBIL

00:00:00:00   I can see in the big book. And I can look at it if I want to look at it. I won't hurt it any.

DR. CORNELIA WILBUR

00:00:00:00   I didn't say you couldn't look at it. I said . . . .

SYBIL

00:00:00:00   I want to look at the big book .

DR. CORNELIA WILBUR

00:00:00:00   All right. I didn't say you could put it down. I said bring it over here . . . . . . Maybe there is something in there I could explain to you . . . . . That would be something that hadn't happened to you before. Wouldn't it?

SYBIL

00:00:00:00   Babies.

DR. CORNELIA WILBUR

00:00:00:00   Uh-huh. What about babies?

SYBIL

00:00:00:00   You got them in here.

DR. CORNELIA WILBUR

00:00:00:00   Uh-huh.

SYBIL

00.00:00:00   And they're tied up.

DR. CORNELIA WILBUR

00:00:00:00   Uh . . . .Well I guess I'll have to come over there. No honey. That's just the baby is still attached to the placenta. That is not all tied up.

(PHONE RINGS)

SYBIL

00:00:00:00   If that is my daddy, I am not here.

DR. CORNELIA WILBUR

00:00:00:00   (PERSONAL PHONE CALL)

SYBIL

00:00:00:00   Why is the baby upside down?

DR. CORNELIA WILBUR

00:00:00:00   Well, that's the way they grow sweetie.

SYBIL

00:00:00:00   Never seen any baby upside down.

DR. CORNELIA WILBUR

00:00:00:00   Well, you don't see babies upside down. But that's the way they grow inside the mommy.

SYBIL

00:00:00:00   Inside?

DR. CORNELIA WILBUR

00:00:00:00   Uh-huh. Don't you know how babies . . . grow?

SYBIL

00:00:00:00   No.

DR. CORNELIA WILBUR

00:00:00:00   Well, they grow inside the mommy . . . in a . . . . very . . . .

SYBIL

00:00:00:00 How do they get in there?

DR. CORNELIA WILBUR

00:00:00:00 Well, your mommy has one kind of cell. Called an ovum. And daddy has one kind of cell. It's called a sperm. And daddy puts the cell . . .

SYBIL

00:00:00:00 What's a cell?

DR. CORNELIA WILBUR

00:00:00:00 Well, a cell is a little, tiny . . . . You know when you scratch yourself . . . a little tiny flake comes off your skin? You know if you . . . if you scratch yourself sometime, you can scratch a little tiny flake off your skin? . . . . . . Hmmmm? Hmmmm?

SYBIL

00:00:00:00 Yes.

DR. CORNELIA WILBUR

00:00:00:00 Well that tiny, tiny, tiny, tiny, tiny flake is made up of several cells . . . .

SYBIL

00:00:00:00 Why?

DR. CORNELIA WILBUR

00:00:00:00 . . . . and you can't see a cell unless you look through a microscope. So the baby starts from this one little cell, see. And it's a special kind of cell. It's not like a skin cell. Or like a toenail cell. Or like a fingernail cell. It's a special kind of cell.

Mommy has one and daddy has the other one. And daddy puts the cell in mommy in the vagina. That's a special opening that the cell is put in . . . and . . . it has a little tail on it. And the tail wiggles. And the cell climbs up and . . . goes up and gets together with the ovum.

It grows to the cell and the baby starts to grow. And it grows and grows and grows and grows big enough to live in the outside world . . . . (UNINTELLIGIBLE) . . . nose and eyes and everything. And then

THREE TAPE EXCERPTS

	gets born ... (UNINTELLIGIBLE) ... just like it got in.
	SYBIL
00:00:00:00	It stops being .... (UNINTELLIGIBLE).
	DR. CORNELIA WILBUR
00:00:00:00	Uh-huh. And it grows ...
	SYBIL
00:00:00:00	.... all by itself.
	DR. CORNELIA WILBUR
00:00:00:00	Uh-huh.
	SYBIL
00:00:00:00	(UNINTELLIGIBLE) it upside down.
	DR. CORNELIA WILBUR
00:00:00:00	No, they didn't put it upside down. That's the way little babies ... (UNINTELLIGIBLE) ... all curled up.
	SYBIL
00:00:00:00	They grow all curled up?
	DR. CORNELIA WILBUR
00:00:00:00	Uh-huh. They grow all curled up.
	SYBIL
00:00:00:00	And how do they get straight?
	DR. CORNELIA WILBUR
00:00:00:00	Well, when they get born, they stretch out and stretch ... (UNINTELLIGIBLE) ...
	SYBIL
00:00:00:00	They don't grow up ....I don't know how they grow straight when they're curled up.
	DR. CORNELIA WILBUR
00:00:00:00	Well, that's one of the miracles about babies growing sweetie is that ... they grow like that ....And they move some but when they stretch out straight ....when

they are born they stretch out straight just like you stretch when you wake up in the morning.

SYBIL

00:00:00:00 There it is. Now I see it. I wish I had a cute little baby like that. A little tiny baby . . . .

DR. CORNELIA WILBUR

00:00:00:00 Umm. That's a very little, tiny baby.

SYBIL

00:00:00:00 I wouldn't keep it upside down. I wouldn't hang it upside down.

DR. CORNELIA WILBUR

00:00:00:00 (UNINTELLIGIBLE) . . . no. You know . . . you know about opossum? You know they go to sleep hanging upside down on trees.

SYBIL

00:00:00:00 (UNINTELLIGIBLE)

DR. CORNELIA WILBUR

00:00:00:00 (UNINTELLIGIBLE) Yeah . . . . and so the babies . . . . after they are born . . . don't sleep upside down. But babies grow upside down.

SYBIL

00:00:00:00 (UNINTELLIGIBLE) . . . babies. Is that a baby?

DR. CORNELIA WILBUR

00:00:00:00 No. I don't think that is a baby . . . . . Let's see. That little red "x." But that isn't a baby.

SYBIL

00:00:00:00 None of them . . . . (UNINTELLIGIBLE) took a book over there . . . . just 'cause you said that. 'Cause I was just trying to take a picture and I (UNINTELLIGIBLE) . . . somebody marked up in the book.

DR. CORNELIA WILBUR

00:00:00:00 I did. It's my book.

THREE TAPE EXCERPTS

SYBIL
00:00:00:00 Why.

DR. CORNELIA WILBUR
00:00:00:00 Remember, I said it was mine. Didn't I?

SYBIL
00:00:00:00 You did?

DR. CORNELIA WILBUR
00:00:00:00 Uh-huh. Good. That's what books are for. (CLEARS THROAT) When you are studying you underline things you want to know and then when you want to go back and see whether it's for sure the things you want to know . . . why you read what's underlined. (UNINTELLIGIBLE)

SYBIL
00:00:00:00 Momma said no . . . (UNINTELLIGIBLE) . . . my crayons and I colored in the book and she said no . . . . nothing.

DR. CORNELIA WILBUR
00:00:00:00 (UNINTELLIGIBLE) . . . I can't tell from here.

SYBIL
00:00:00:00 What's that?

DR. CORNELIA WILBUR
00:00:00:00 Well that's the . . . that's a sort of little . . . not little either . . . but sort of . . . a kind of a fleshy pancake . . . (UNINTELLIGIBLE) it has little fingers and the fingers fit in like that with the fingers in the mother's circulation. And then the blood all runs in all through here and into the umbilical cord and up to the baby . . . so the baby can grow . . . . while it's inside the mother.

SYBIL
00:00:00:00 I see more babies.

DR. CORNELIA WILBUR
00:00:00:00 Well maybe if you look in the back you will find some babies.

SYBIL

00:00:00:00 In the back?

DR. CORNELIA WILBUR

00:00:00:00 Uh-huh. I think I have gone too far back. Maybe if we go to the syllabus.

SYBIL

00:00:00:00 Grown-up people.

DR. CORNELIA WILBUR

00:00:00:00 Uh-huh.

SYBIL

00:00:00:00 That's a big head upside down.

DR. CORNELIA WILBUR

00:00:00:00 Uh-huh.

SYBIL

00:00:00:00 That one is not upside down.

DR. CORNELIA WILBUR

00:00:00:00 No.

SYBIL

00:00:00:00 That's a funny looking . . . (UNINTELLIGIBLE)

DR. CORNELIA WILBUR

00:00:00:00 (UNINTELLIGIBLE)

SYBIL

00:00:00:00 More grown-up people.

DR. CORNELIA WILBUR

00:00:00:00 Those are pregnant women. Remember they are going to have babies.

SYBIL

00:00:00:00 How do you know?

DR. CORNELIA WILBUR

00:00:00:00 See. Because you see, they are fat here.

THREE TAPE EXCERPTS

SYBIL
00:00:00:00   Oh.

DR. CORNELIA WILBUR
00:00:00:00   That means there's a baby inside.

SYBIL
00:00:00:00   Inside here?

DR. CORNELIA WILBUR
00:00:00:00   Uh-huh.

SYBIL
00:00:00:00   Are you sure?

DR. CORNELIA WILBUR
00:00:00:00   Uh-huh.

SYBIL
00:00:00:00   I don't... (UNINTELLIGIBLE)

DR. CORNELIA WILBUR
00:00:00:00   Well that one... (UNINTELLIGIBLE)... if that had grown right. Sometimes babies don't grow right. If that had grown right, that would have been (UNINTELLIGIBLE)... but they didn't get separated from each other like they should.

SYBIL
00:00:00:00   I have never seen a baby look.... (UNINTELLIGIBLE)

DR. CORNELIA WILBUR
00:00:00:00   That is very, very rare. Very, very rare occurrence. Once in a while, twins will fail to get separated. Here are a pair of twins that didn't get separated right through here. They are almost separated... (UNINTELLIGIBLE)... 'cause they have all the arms and the legs and everything. (UNINTELLIGIBLE)

SYBIL
00:00:00:00   Hmmmm.

DR. CORNELIA WILBUR

00:00:00:00 (UNINTELLIGIBLE)

SYBIL

00:00:00:00 (UNINTELLIGIBLE)

DR. CORNELIA WILBUR

00:00:00:00 (UNINTELLIGIBLE)

SYBIL

00:00:00:00 Hmmm.

DR. CORNELIA WILBUR

00:00:00:00 (CLEARS THROAT) (UNINTELLIGIBLE) .... That shows how the babies ... that shows how they aren't separated.

SYBIL

00:00:00:00 Hmmmm.

DR. CORNELIA WILBUR

00:00:00:00 (UNINTELLIGIBLE) ... healthy babies ... (UNINTELLIGIBLE) ... it happens once in a great while.

SYBIL

00:00:00:00 Look at that baby. Boy it looks bad.

DR. CORNELIA WILBUR

00:00:00:00 Why .... it looks bad ...

SYBIL

00:00:00:00 Is the baby unhappy?

DR. CORNELIA WILBUR

00:00:00:00 No ....

SYBIL

00:00:00:00 ... then why don't (UNINTELLIGIBLE) like it?

DR. CORNELIA WILBUR

00:00:00:00 (UNINTELLIGIBLE) ...

THREE TAPE EXCERPTS

SYBIL

00:00:00:00   Oh . . . .

DR. CORNELIA WILBUR

00:00:00:00   That's another thing. Couples . . . .(UNINTELLIGIBLE) . . .

SYBIL

00:00:00:00   Oh . . . .

DR. CORNELIA WILBUR

00:00:00:00   (CLEARS THROAT) . . . .(UNINTELLIGIBLE). . . so uncommon you don't see it.

SYBIL

00:00:00:00   . . . (UNINTELLIGIBLE) . . . their not upside down. Not that one . . .

DR. CORNELIA WILBUR

00:00:00:00   Cause they are sideways.

SYBIL

00:00:00:00   Uh-huh.

DR. CORNELIA WILBUR

00:00:00:00   (UNINTELLIGIBLE)

SYBIL

00:00:00:00   (UNINTELLIGIBLE) . . . it was born in the other picture.

DR. CORNELIA WILBUR

00:00:00:00   (UNINTELLIGIBLE) . . . shows how the baby goes through. When it gets born, you see it gets born in between the two bones . . . and comes out through the vagina. And that shows how the baby slides through there. OK?

SYBIL

00:00:00:00   Hmmmm.

DR. CORNELIA WILBUR

00:00:00:00 Isn't that cute? . . . (UNINTELLIGIBLE) . . . by itself and shows how the baby comes through the bones. And that's how babies get born.

SYBIL

00:00:00:00 What if they got caught there?

DR. CORNELIA WILBUR

00:00:00:00 Well honey . . . (UNINTELLIGIBLE) . . . is all covered with muscles . . . and it is real smooth . . . so the baby can slide through. What they did was to take all the muscles off to show how it is in relation . . . but that isn't how it really is. Because inside is all these muscles and everything is real smooth and the baby slides right through.

SYBIL

00:00:00:00 How come you never share this book like this, to look at? This one isn't upside down. How come you never did?

DR. CORNELIA WILBUR

00:00:00:00 Well because, I mean . . . well there is nothing wrong with showing it while you're interested . . . (UNINTELLIGIBLE) . . .

SYBIL

00:00:00:00 (UNINTELLIGIBLE) . . . to talk about people and babies and children and people.

DR. CORNELIA WILBUR

00:00:00:00 (UNINTELLIGIBLE) at the beginning of the book . . . . at the beginning of the book . . . I thought you would be lost . . . (UNINTELLIGIBLE) . . .

SYBIL

00:00:00:00 (UNINTELLIGIBLE) . . . I know you gave me certain books to read them. I can't understand them . . . . . . You read them. What's the little letters for?

DR. CORNELIA WILBUR

00:00:00:00 You mean here?

SYBIL

00:00:00:00 Uh-huh.

DR. CORNELIA WILBUR

00:00:00:00 Why those are just the little help at the end of the chapter. You see that the chapters . . . . And the big headings tell about something and the other big headings tell about something.

These are just all notes about where they get their information. And that's where (UNINTELLIGIBLE) . . .

SYBIL

00:00:00:00 Any more babies? Are they too far back like you . . . (UNINTELLIGIBLE) . . . .What are they doing to it? They got grey. They got grey. (UNINTELLIGIBLE) . . . .

DR. CORNELIA WILBUR

00:00:00:00 (UNINTELLIGIBLE) . . . the baby didn't breathe very well . . . so the doctor (UNINTELLIGIBLE) . . . have the baby breathe oxygen so they don't . . . (UNINTELLIGIBLE) . . .

SYBIL

00:00:00:00 (UNINTELLIGIBLE)

DR. CORNELIA WILBUR

00:00:00:00 Yeah. Sometimes when babies are born they are not very strong. And they, they don't breathe very well and you have to have them breathe a special kind of air with all the good things in it. You see.

SYBIL

00:00:00:00 (UNINTELLIGIBLE)

DR. CORNELIA WILBUR

00:00:00:00 Well, the reason they have a pillow here . . .

SKIPPED LENGTHY EXPLANATION ABOUT BABIES' WINDPIPES . . . .TO WILBUR BEGINNING TO HYPNOTIZE SYBIL

SYBIL

00:00:00:00 I guess you want Shirley this time under the . . . . (UNINTELLIGIBLE) . . . .

DR. CORNELIA WILBUR

00:00:00:00   Well I think maybe . . . as Shirley and I do . . . That you will feel better 'cause you didn't feel very good a few minutes ago.

SYBIL

00:00:00:00   (UNINTELLIGIBLE) put this down here . . . you can talk to Shirley.

DR. CORNELIA WILBUR

00:00:00:00   All right. I want Shirley to look at me when I . . . (UNINTELLIGIBLE). OK sweetie?

SYBIL

00:00:00:00   My shirt tail . . . won't come out.

DR. CORNELIA WILBUR

00:00:00:00   (UNINTELLIGIBLE)

SYBIL

00:00:00:00   It's too short.

DR. CORNELIA WILBUR

00:00:00:00   Will you look at me . . . (UNINTELLIGIBLE) . . . Hmmm?

SYBIL

00:00:00:00   (UNINTELLIGIBLE)

DR. CORNELIA WILBUR

00:00:00:00   OK.

SYBIL

00:00:00:00   My glasses.

DR. CORNELIA WILBUR

00:00:00:00   I . . . You took them off sweetie. And I . . . put them over here because you put them right down here. (CLEARS THROAT)
Now you look at me and my eyes and you begin to get sleepy.

(CRASH)

SYBIL

00:00:00:00   Oh. I'm sorry. I'm sorry. I just . . .

DR. CORNELIA WILBUR

00:00:00:00   We need a little more room in here.

SYBIL

00:00:00:00   I'm sorry.

DR. CORNELIA WILBUR

00:00:00:00   Now you look at me in my eyes and you begin to get sleepy. One.
As I count to five you get sleepier and sleepier. Two.
You are beginning to get sleepy. And you begin to relax. Two. Three.
Now you are getting very sleepy. It is hard for you to keep your eyes open. Four.
And now you are getting very, very sleepy. And you may go to sleep. Five. You are going deeply, deeply asleep. More deeply asleep than you were day before yesterday. Now you can tell me. What happened this morning, if you were foggy?

SYBIL

00:00:00:00   An awful dream.

DR. CORNELIA WILBUR

00:00:00:00   Uh-huh. Why do you think you had that dream, dear?

SYBIL

00:00:00:00   I don't know. I hoped that it would . . . fear and not wish. I don't want it to be that I wished that. You know how it is that you say it when you dream that sometime it's wish . . . and I don't want it to be that I wish anything like that.

DR. CORNELIA WILBUR

00:00:00:00   Could that be, rather than a wish that daddy was dead . . . . an expression of anger at daddy?

SYBIL

00:00:00:00   I wasn't mad at him. I was afraid because he still liked to take . . . (UNINTELLIGIBLE) . . .

DR. CORNELIA WILBUR

00:00:00:00 But it was your dream honey. And why would you have him do that?
Would you have him do that if you were very angry at him?

SYBIL

00:00:00:00 No. I wouldn't do that to anybody. I screamed and didn't...

DR. CORNELIA WILBUR

00:00:00:00 It's all right dear. You screamed and he didn't pay any attention to you. Hmmmm?

SYBIL

00:00:00:00 But it wasn't quick enough. The car came too fast.

DR. CORNELIA WILBUR

00:00:00:00 But honey, there has been times when daddy didn't pay any attention to you. Remember?

SYBIL

00:00:00:00 I wasn't calling him for me. I was trying to get....

DR. CORNELIA WILBUR

00:00:00:00 But if he wouldn't pay attention to you for your sake he might not pay attention to you for his sake. Hmmmm?

SYBIL

00:00:00:00 (CRYING)

DR. CORNELIA WILBUR

00:00:00:00 Could that be?

SYBIL

00:00:00:00 (CRYING)

DR. CORNELIA WILBUR

00:00:00:00 Could that be, sweetie?

SYBIL

00:00:00:00 (CRYING)

THREE TAPE EXCERPTS

DR. CORNELIA WILBUR

00:00:00:00   Could that be?

SYBIL

00:00:00:00   You know, I don't.

DR. CORNELIA WILBUR

00:00:00:00   Well, could you be saying in the dream . . . Daddy should pay attention to me because if he doesn't pay attention to me when I say something to him . . . I might have to say something to him someday to save his life . . . and if he doesn't pay attention, his life won't get saved.

SYBIL

00:00:00:00   I don't know. Don't know.

DR. CORNELIA WILBUR

00:00:00:00   Sweetie?

SYBIL

00:00:00:00   I want him to leave me alone.

DR. CORNELIA WILBUR

00:00:00:00   Who?

SYBIL

00:00:00:00   (UNINTELLIGIBLE) . . . it was just like the idea with daddy.

DR. CORNELIA WILBUR

00:00:00:00   What was Forrest's idea?

SYBIL

00:00:00:00   That I wasn't going to go to school here. We would come home.

DR. CORNELIA WILBUR

00:00:00:00   When?

SYBIL

00:00:00:00   Cheaper to sponge off daddy . . . at home then here. Why keep up an expensive New York apartment when you can live at home and have a . . . .

DR. CORNELIA WILBUR

00:00:00:00   When did he say this?

SYBIL

00:00:00:00   ... (UNINTELLIGIBLE) ... she said I want to go to my daddy and he called me and he said if I wanted to come home ... it would be cheaper but I could do as I liked. To any ... I could have the room upstairs ...

DR. CORNELIA WILBUR

00:00:00:00   (OVERLAP) When did he say that?

SYBIL

00:00:00:00   ... the big room upstairs and my own bathroom there and everything ... And ... and I would have my own entrance there ... and ...

DR. CORNELIA WILBUR

00:00:00:00   (OVERLAP) When did this happen?

SYBIL

00:00:00:00   ....and then I could start over again and go to school at ... in East Lansing if I wanted to. Just like we what we talked about when I was home the last time and I said "no" ....

DR. CORNELIA WILBUR

00:00:00:00   (OVERLAP) When did this happen?

SYBIL

00:00:00:00   ....And I said you know I have to see Dr. Wilbur. You know she is helping me. And he said, "I know." He said "That's what, what I told (UNINTELLIGIBLE) ... He said, "That's why I had to tell her about it because she couldn't understand why it's safer and costs so much ... and ... and you weren't doing anything. And ... and ... and ...

DR. CORNELIA WILBUR

00:00:00:00   When did ...

SYBIL

00:00:00:00   ... and ... he asked if I can't sell some paintings. And I ... didn't know. And my ... and I ... used to tell him sometimes when I sold something. And ... you know, like the animal ones I did or something ...

DR. CORNELIA WILBUR

00:00:00:00   Uh-huh.

SYBIL

00:00:00:00   ... and he said ... you better now take them to a gallery. And I said, I just can't do it dad, I just can't face them ... and say here ... look at my work. Here it is. And I said, I just can't do it. And he said, I understand. I understand. I got excited .... That ...

DR. CORNELIA WILBUR

00:00:00:00   When did this happen dear?

SYBIL

00:00:00:00   It was a little while ago. And uh ... somedays ago and I wanted to tell you about it.

DR. CORNELIA WILBUR

00:00:00:00   Was that what upset you last weekend?

SYBIL

00:00:00:00   I don't know. I think it was ... uh ... before. I don't know what the time ... mixed ... I don't know the day.

DR. CORNELIA WILBUR

00:00:00:00   Uh-huh. It's all right. We can find out about the day. Now you are ...

SYBIL

00:00:00:00   It was ... um ... some time ago. I don't know when it was.

DR. CORNELIA WILBUR

00:00:00:00   Uh-huh. Was it more than two weeks ago?

SYBIL

00:00:00:00   I don't know.

DR. CORNELIA WILBUR

00:00:00:00   All right sweetie.

SYBIL

00:00:00:00   I don't know. I don't think so. I don't know.

DR. CORNELIA WILBUR

00:00:00:00 It's all right. Now let's go back. This is Monday. Now it's Sunday. Now it's Saturday. Now it's Friday. Now it's Thursday.

I am going to go on. And you stop me on the day that daddy called and said this. It's Wednesday.

SYBIL

00:00:00:00 He wants ... (UNINTELLIGIBLE) ... go to the institute.

DR. CORNELIA WILBUR

00:00:00:00 That day.

SYBIL

00:00:00:00 He wanted ... (UNINTELLIGIBLE) ... he said Wednesday.

DR. CORNELIA WILBUR

00:00:00:00 It's Tuesday. It's Monday. It's Sunday.

SYBIL

00:00:00:00 That's when Dr. Speigal asked me about going.

DR. CORNELIA WILBUR

00:00:00:00 It's Saturday.

SYBIL

00:00:00:00 It was the Saturday before that one.

DR. CORNELIA WILBUR

00:00:00:00 So it was just two weeks ago tomorrow.

SYBIL

00:00:00:00 I don't know.

DR. CORNELIA WILBUR

00:00:00:00 I do sweetie.
00:00:00:00 Now we will come back to now. It's Monday. Tuesday. Wednesday. Thusday. Now it's Friday, January 22nd. Now sweetie ...

SYBIL

00:00:00:00 He made me get awful worried about the money.

THREE TAPE EXCERPTS

DR. CORNELIA WILBUR
00:00:00:00 Uh-huh.

SYBIL
00:00:00:00 And . . . I am not going to worry about.

DR. CORNELIA WILBUR
00:00:00:00 All right. You don't worry about it sweetie. And if he says anything else . . .

SYBIL
00:00:00:00 I stopped worrying about it . . . everything . . .

DR. CORNELIA WILBUR
00:00:00:00 Uh-huh. All right. If you stopped worrying about it, that's fine. Now if anything else comes up, and daddy calls you.

SYBIL
00:00:00:00 I am going to let him talk to you.

DR. CORNELIA WILBUR
00:00:00:00 Good. That's fine.

SYBIL
00:00:00:00 Or else ask you to write him a letter.

DR. CORNELIA WILBUR
00:00:00:00 (OVERLAP) I would rather talk to him.

SYBIL
00:00:00:00 And if I . . . I I

DR. CORNELIA WILBUR
00:00:00:00 And if he would let me . . .

SYBIL
00:00:00:00 I pretended that you wrote him letter. And I pretended every sentence and word . . . what it would have said to him . . . and explained something . . . and . . . I don't think he really knew that . . .

DR. CORNELIA WILBUR
00:00:00:00 That's right.

SYBIL

00:00:00:00   And then . . . then I didn't worry any more.

DR. CORNELIA WILBUR

00:00:00:00   That's good. But if this comes up again honey, I would like to talk to him on the telephone. Because I think we can say a good deal more if we talk on the phone. And he may have questions . . . that my letter.

SYBIL

00:00:00:00   I don't want him to come here.

DR. CORNELIA WILBUR

00:00:00:00   That's all right.

SYBIL

00:00:00:00   I don't want them to come here because they don't know how to tell Nadia how it is.

DR. CORNELIA WILBUR

00:00:00:00   Well that's all right honey. You don't have to tell them how it is. I'll tell them.

SYBIL

00:00:00:00   There too busy to come anyway. And it costs quite a lot. And it's better if he stays there . . . but I got to stay here.

DR. CORNELIA WILBUR

00:00:00:00   That's right.

SYBIL

00:00:00:00   And I can't . . . work . . . very well . . . at a job.

DR. CORNELIA WILBUR

00:00:00:00   Yes, I know.

SYBIL

00:00:00:00   And I don't like it that way and I . . . I . . . I just can't seem to get around to it.

DR. CORNELIA WILBUR

00:00:00:00   Uh-huh. You will dear. When we get some of these things taken care of.

THREE TAPE EXCERPTS

Now ... I want you to slowly. Carefully. Go back to last night at about ten minutes after ten. Something happened last at ten minutes after ten. Now it is last night at ten minutes after ten. What happened.

SYBIL

00:00:00:00 She dialed RE 77177.

DR. CORNELIA WILBUR

00:00:00:00 Who is she?

SYBIL

00:00:00:00 That ... that other girl.

DR. CORNELIA WILBUR

00:00:00:00 What's her name? You know it.

SYBIL

00:00:00:00 I don't know her name.

DR. CORNELIA WILBUR

00:00:00:00 Yes dear, you do.

SYBIL

00:00:00:00 No doctor. Don't know her name. I don't see her very many times. This Saturday I saw her. And ...

DR. CORNELIA WILBUR

00:00:00:00 She has a name.

SYBIL

00:00:00:00 ....and there wasn't anybody answer it. And it just rang and rang and rang. So she hung up.

DR. CORNELIA WILBUR

00:00:00:00 Uh-huh.

SYBIL

00:00:00:00 And then when it was about another ten or fifteen minutes ... and you said hello to her.

DR. CORNELIA WILBUR

00:00:00:00 Uh-huh. And what did she say?

SYBIL

00:00:00:00   She talked to you.

DR. CORNELIA WILBUR

00:00:00:00   And what did she talk about?

SYBIL

00:00:00:00   (UNINTELLIGIBLE)

DR. CORNELIA WILBUR

00:00:00:00   It's all right sweetie. It's all right. What did she talk about?

SYBIL

00:00:00:00   My grandma.

DR. CORNELIA WILBUR

00:00:00:00   What's your name?

SYBIL

00:00:00:00   I'm Shirley.

DR. CORNELIA WILBUR

00:00:00:00   She said her name was Shirley.

SYBIL

00:00:00:00   She didn't say that last night.

DR. CORNELIA WILBUR

00:00:00:00   And she said it about my grandma and her . . .

SYBIL

00:00:00:00   I know it. She said it was her grandma and her mother.

DR. CORNELIA WILBUR

00:00:00:00   Uh-huh. Is this another part of you? Huh? Sweetie?

SYBIL

00:00:00:00   I'm thinking about it. It feels . . . like it sort of . . .

DR. CORNELIA WILBUR

00:00:00:00   Uh-huh.

THREE TAPE EXCERPTS 281

SYBIL
00:00:00:00 Where it . . . (UNINTELLIGIBLE) . . . over there.

DR. CORNELIA WILBUR
00:00:00:00 Yeah. If feels like it's sorta another part of you.

SYBIL
00:00:00:00 It wasn't me cause I don't bother you. I just call you when I'm bad or don't know what to take.

DR. CORNELIA WILBUR
00:00:00:00 Well, that was why she called me, dear. Because it was bad. And she wanted to tell me about it. And that is just exactly what you do. So this is another part of you. Now why do you have to divide yourself up in parts?

SYBIL
00:00:00:00 Safer.

DR. CORNELIA WILBUR
00:00:00:00 How is it safer sweetie?

SYBIL
00:00:00:00 It takes away some things.

DR. CORNELIA WILBUR
00:00:00:00 It takes away some things.

SYBIL
00:00:00:00 And it is not all of them at once.

DR. CORNELIA WILBUR
00:00:00:00 Uh-huh.

SYBIL
00:00:00:00 It's not so much.

DR. CORNELIA WILBUR
00:00:00:00 And that takes care of the too much feeling to divide yourself up into parts. Is that right?

SYBIL
00:00:00:00 It helps a little.

DR. CORNELIA WILBUR

00:00:00:00   I see.

SYBIL

00:00:00:00   Some take care of it.

DR. CORNELIA WILBUR

00:00:00:00   Uh-huh. (CLEARS THROAT) Now what did she say about your grandma and your mama.

SYBIL

00:00:00:00   I don't know.

DR. CORNELIA WILBUR

00:00:00:00   What do you think about that. Because you know too.

SYBIL

00:00:00:00   I don't want to think about it. I may even forget.

DR. CORNELIA WILBUR

00:00:00:00   Why would you forget it, dear?

SYBIL

00:00:00:00   I won't have to talk about it.

DR. CORNELIA WILBUR

00:00:00:00   Well sweetie. Didn't you learn something important from that?

SYBIL

00:00:00:00   From what?

DR. CORNELIA WILBUR

00:00:00:00   From what she said about grandma and about mama?

SYBIL

00:00:00:00   Uh-huh.

DR. CORNELIA WILBUR

00:00:00:00   You didn't learn that the grief and the tears were because she . . . because you all grieved when grandma died. And you didn't learn that . . . grandma loved you.

SYBIL

00:00:00:00 She cried . . . .with tears all over her face. And I always had more cause it was on my face too.

DR. CORNELIA WILBUR

00:00:00:00 Uh-huh. Because you and she are the same person.

SYBIL

00:00:00:00 Uh-huh. She was there.

DR. CORNELIA WILBUR

00:00:00:00 No dear. Because she couldn't cry . . . and use your eyes and your face to cry with if you and she were the same person.

2

Excerpt from the TV Movie *Sybil*

S: Dr. Wilbur, it's getting worse, do you know those pains. I don't tell you them, and who does those drawings? (agitated and talking fast)
W: You do. But you do them as other people.
S: uh hmmm
W: Do you understand?
S: uh hmmm
W: You do them as other parts of yourself.
S: NO, I DON'T. (stern)
W: Who are still children.
S: uh hmmm
W: It's true.
S: uh hmmm
W: You've got to understand it is true.
S: This is not possible.
W: It is possible.
S: uh hmmm
W: In fact through most of the analysis I've been talking to you through them. They all have names and they come here and they

protect you, they keep your appointments and there are the ones who pour out the information that you are afraid to face.
S: (crying)...
W: You've got to understand this.
S: (crying) NO, it's not true.
W: IT'S TRUE.
S: It's not, it's not, no.

Therapeutic Session Sybil & Wilbur

W: You are 11 years old Shirley... Shirley.
S: What? (sleepy)
W: You are 11 years old.
S: No I'm not. You know I'm not, you know I'm older than that. (slowed, slurred speech)
W: Alright, we're going to...
S: I'm 36.
W: Alright.
S: I'm almost 37.
W: Alright, now we're going to...
S: I don't want anybody to know that.
W: Now we are going to go back in time.
S: I don't want to.
W: Why?
S: 'Cause it's not better back there.
W: Seems to me that actually it's better up here than it was back there. Isn't that right?
S: Sometimes it is.
W: But the thing about it is sweetie, that there is a little 11-year-old that I want to help to grow up.
S: Alright, you can help her I will go home.
W: She is inside of you sweetie, if you go home I can't help her.
S: Nooo____(unintelligible)
W: uh hmmm
W: Do you remember what happened last night?
S: I lost the time.
W: uh hmmm...what happened last night?
S: I couldn't lay down.
W: Well you can dear.
S: No.

[LOUD NOISE]

EXCERPT FROM THE TV MOVIE *SYBIL*

W: Yes you can.
S: ____(unintelligible)
W: Sure.
S: (unintelligible)
W: Put your feet up now, that's the way.
S: (inaudible)
W: (inaudible)
S: Well that's nice.
W: What happened last night at 10:20?
S: Last night?
W: uh hmmm
S: ___(unintelligible)____ in my car.

3

Sybil's Letter of Denial to Dr. Cornelia Wilbur and Sybil's IQ Report

This letter, of which only a brief and heavily edited excerpt appeared in *Sybil*, was probably the most important of the scores written by Sybil (Shirley Mason) to her therapist Cornelia Wilbur. In it she denies that she had multiple personality disorder and goes on to assert that she was to a large extent inventing symptoms because she knew that this stratagem would keep Wilbur intrigued. The first page of the letter is missing; the following six pages are reproduced in their entirety.

several reasons....why I ask this....I've thought about it..etc;"
I felt very defensive and immediately (or simultaneously) pictured
you being against it. I did not, as probably implied,`, picture you
being cross or stern or flatly refusing because you are not like this.
But, I did feature you turning a little to one side and saying rather
casually (as you sometimes do when approaching something 'touchy')
"Well, Shirley, it would seem....." etc. and I at once felt you would
say it was better to wait until I felt stronger and could handle what
new material we already had from last time that we have not talked
over as yet......all very logical...but still NO.

My thoughts are going in all directions now....I have felt this
MANY times before.....I think up to what I want to say to you and then
I think of your saying no in a round-about manner, and I (pause... I
had a thought and then changed it to this: ...round about manner and I
then don't ask it.....but the first thought was right and I sat here
for awhile and then felt I could write it just the way I thought it, so
here it is) felt rejected. ....the tension has let up....I even
smiled just then because I had an amusing (to me, anyway) thought:
Dr. Wilbur has rejected me more times on issues she hadn't even heard
of yet......etc. Guess I don't give you much of a chance sometimes; do
I? If I wouldn't carry on these two-way conversations with you when
you aren't present I would save myself some trouble.

But why did I think you would convince me logically that I was
asking for something unwisely? (Dad could. I used to be even more
gulible than I am now with people and anyone could talk me into anything if they were logical enough---in tone, at least---but I learned
to do it too, and Dad no longer does that and neither does Jean.) My
first response to thinking of asking anything of anyone is that they
will refuse and then I feel rejected...so I don't ask. .....is that
why I never asked for things much when I was a kid? There is another
probable candidate for answer to the question above....because I think
it is unwise (most of my ideas are....or else they have repercusions
I don't enjoy.).

Now I've got this far, I want to tell you why I thought I did
want it this week.......first, last and always (cliche!) my thoughts
revolve around getting better as fast as I can, therefore, when I had
pentothal a few times and found that I felt better and talked easier
for a few days afterwards etc. I was all for the idea. Not doing
it....(oh dear, now I have changed my mind again and don't want to
say any of this....not sure I even want the pentothal)...but I'll try
to finish the explanation in spite of the heat I feel in my neck and
face......not having pentothal constitutes in my mind a delay of progress. Then I think it slows it and then I think it means I am not
getting well fast, then not going to get well at all and there I am
back on that merry-go-round. ....also, there is this: certain
times I feel better than others and we have better results....by my
measuring and also according to some of your remarks....well, this is
one of those times. The week of and the week after I have a period
more was accomplished than the week before it..generally speaking.
This week you made some suggestions that brought about some new feelings as you know...don't even know what I am feeling sometimes...but
it seems to me rather opportune to latch onto some of this before it
gets away again. I felt this at other times.....and lost it again....

.....I guess you are saying that it is not going to get lost forever and will appear later if not now and we can deal with it then. That is true, I am sure, yet it makes me feel rejection again. I want to do all I can WHEN I can and not has a remainder of it lurking just under the surface where it can become Peggy by my trying to combat depression or by being combined with some actual event such as "house is being sold!" What I am trying to say is, there are times when I feel something close to the surface and can't always get at it with words....last few days haven't know WHAT it is even, but the feeling I have learned to recognize as something to be said and I don't want to wait so long to find out what it is that bothers me that I dissociate or loose it. Now I have the distinct feeling that I have said all this for nothing...that it is not anything you do not already know....well, that may be for you know alot about me.....and you probably know a number of good reasons for not having pentothal these two weeks in a row. So I will try to understand.

There have been times when I dreaded the pentothal and from Friday until Monday the fear would grow, but still underneath that feeling was the reassuring one that it did help in the total picture. A few times it sort of knocked me for a loop afterwards, but when it has been like it was last week, it doesn't affect me much that I can notice and it is okay and nothing to dread. Oh, I don't know....this seems so trivial.....yet it ISN'T or it would not have bothered me so much......there is more to it, tho.....and everytime I think of the rest of it I want to quit writing and tear this up. At least I don't want to show it to you. Why? Same old struggle I've had for years and had at the hospital when I asked to come home......if you say, "No" it is rejection....if you say, "Yes", I feel guilty......feel then as if you did not want me to have or do whatever it is I ask but give in because I have asked...gets all mixed-up...can't win either way.

Sometimes I have blamed you for a dissociation when I very well know it was not your fault...but I could not, I think, face the fact it was in essence my own fault..........I am aware I have used the terms 'blame' and 'fault', but that is how it felt and I know better as to what it should be, but I do not know adequate words......so I say those. And, as long as I believed that I COULD avoid losing time if I tried hard enough, then it did feel as if I were at fault if I 'let' myself loose time...and then I blamed myself. Only now I (was going to say the word 'know', but I couldn't....my fingers got stiff and I got hot and the sentence stuck...and I felt the crying inside....so I have been just sitting here trying to breathe for...oh, maybe 5 or 6 minutes.. now I feel better and shall try again.....)..........it's just so HARD to have to feel and believe and admit that I do not have the conscious control over it......it is so much more threatening to have something 'out of hand' as it seems.... than to believe that at any moment I can stop (I started to say 'this foolishness'....mother's words, eh?) any time I need to. Sometimes that is why I have felt blame from you and guilt on my part when I thought or expected you would do or say certain things to help me and you did not react that way.....I felt you were implying that I could do it for myself and the fact that I didn't made me feel guilty.........if enough so, I'd dissociate...then I could not sometimes stand it to think I should have avoided it by holding on and trying harder...I thought I HAD tried and so there was (it seemed) only one recourse and that was to blame you for 'letting' me push myself too far. I never could have said this just this way...with this feeling, I mean, before.....I've said similar things, I know......but this is different because of the prompting...but that's some other train of thought I better not follow it here...

Almost all of what I said in that first paragraph has been off the subject of what I started to say....I did not have more than a few vague sentences when I began, but I did have a very definite feeling of an idea I meant to say.......and I WILL get it said. Right now. I only have to preface it with one 'reason'.....I can say this today because I am thinking of you and talking to you as doctor more than friend.....there is a difference sometimes....sometimes not...they blend at times. But this I can not talk about when I think we are friends because I cannot say to a friend who has done as much for me as you have, "Why didn't you do more?" I didn't even think I could type what it was I couldn't say! Guess maybe by your standards this would be termed 'better'......I HOPE SO. But to get back to the subject.........now I am so tired I can hardly lift my arms.....if I did not think it was resistance to saying it, I would have to lie down....but I am not going to if I can help it.....(ooops, lungs just collapsed too!......well, it won't do them any good, I feel I must say this whether it is important or not, and I keep telling myself that you said I was doing all right with it and that I should do it when I can .....and that encourages me.....I am not pressuring beyond endurance, I am writing and trying to be reasonable about when and how much, but I do think it is not pushing when I keep on over a rough spot that makes me tired just for a few minutes until it is said.......is that right?)

Now I can breathe more easily again, so will try once more.....if I can JUST BE DIRECT ABOUT IT AND SKIP THE FOOL DETAILS, then I'll get it over sooner..... ...it does not cost me quite as much as it used to when I skip details of some sorts..................all right, getting back to the matter of blaming you when I dissociate..........I know now that this was something other than the truth, but I still do not know WHAT it really was, but you will tell me.....this is how it seemed, felt and then happens at times: everything seemed to stack up and get to the place where it seemed to be too much to take.....sometimes I could call you and talk to you....or talk to you during the office hour.....and that would be sufficient, but the other times, NO..........and that is where this so-called blame I used to think I felt came in........I'd call you when I felt I could not manage any longer and we'd talk about the troubles and you would say much what you had on other occassions when it helped, but at these times it did not help enough and I'd keep saying I did not know what to do or how to hold on or that I was afraid,.....and inside I was hoping and half-way expecting you would say that you would come and help me........but you would not say this and then I would do one of two things (neither purposely) either dissociate from what seemed to be unbearable pressure, or I'd get terribly defiant feeling inside and think okay I will do it myself if you are not going to come help me I will just do it myself and show you I do not need you...I will never ask for help again (had not actually asked, but hoped only) however, this attitude does not hold for long....it works sometimes all right enough but only until you break it down by being so very sweet and kind and understanding the next time or so that I see you, or else you see through it and say you are coming to see if we can't find out what is bothering so much...then I relent and think, "She does care after all.....".......it is not hard for me to relent for that is what I really want is to feel comfortable toward you, but at times I have been awfully stubborn inside.....I fight you with determination. (I can say this I think for just one reason....you used the word the other day....you implied that you knew I did this at times...so that freed the way for me to admit it......yes, "freed" and "admit"...that is how it feels.....not the best words, but.........). Some times I hold out quite a while (not too often) or I take a kind of parallel way out ....example, the time I decided you were not going to come help me it was certainly okay with me, I knew all the time you did not really care and it was pretense (why, I did not ponder...that would have revealed it made no sense.....and this HAD to make sense on my own basis...) so if you were no help I would just show you I had other resouces and could get along without you.......I made up my mind I would show you how I could be very composed and cool and not need to ask you to listen to me nor to explain anything to me nor need any help.... deciding this gave me some relief, I thought.....then the next thing I knew, I had lost almost two days and had awakened on a Saturday morning to find I had written a day or two previously that all this about the multiple personalities was not really true at all but just put on......that would mean I did not need you, I suppose.....however, but the time I got to the end of it, I found that "she" had written that she was sick and wanted to get well so would you help "her" (well, at least it was not ME asking for help) to understand why she had pretended...etc.....you probably recall that paper and that day.   Again, I do not know the REAL beginning (the "WHY" of it) but I do know I was hoping for relief from the pressure by having pentothal on the following Saturday and I believed for reasons I can't recall that I needed it and you were not coming.

There is only one difference that I see off-hand about the times I call you (or talk a certain way in the office....neither can I help) and get the needed support and help from what you say and the times I call and do not get the needed support and encouragement to try (in the REAL sense of trying) that would give you any clue whatever to the fact that 'this' call is any different from my others.....(you have said to me that you did not always know what I was really asking for....of course not....I did not say.....I only implied and thought you could and DID see what I was asking in my round about way...which was the only way I could ask it seemed.. .).....but the difference was this: when I called I usually did so with the idea that you would help me with words of explanation or encouragement etc. and I expected no more....and often this worked (as you've pointed out to me as being the thing that confuses you) and I felt 100% better and could hold on and go ahead.....this was fine, of course.......but other times I found your words did not help and the tension or whatever was wrong did not get less...in fact it got worse as I became frustrated talking with you and feeling what you said SHOULD help but WASN'T helping.....then, in those conversations I could not and did not say I was feeling better and I could try again etc., but I kept saying I don't know what to do, or I don't know what is wrong, or isn't there anything that will ever make me better, or to each suggestion you made (such as take seconal, or write it out, or paint etc.) I would say what I really felt...that I had tried it or that I could not face it ....seems as if I have been too detailed again, so I am going to try to get this one simple thought into one simple sentence:

The difference in calls that help and those that throw me into something worse is that if it helps I say so and feel better and you often say "you sound better already"....if it does not help I realize it is not enough and I can't stop talking and I can't let go (hang-up!) and then I keep repeating and asking (so indirectly, I see, but in essence obvious to ME) you for more help than words 'from a distance'.......these latter situations are unbearable to me and I get into deeper trouble. Then I blame you.

I could say some of that because I no longer feel that way....I was able t "take it" yesterday and I DID believe you were not coming last night.... and I did not feel lost nor rejected nor isolated......however, if I am completely honest about it there were a couple of 'side-lights' on it that may be worthwhile saying..........I was not sure I could take it if you said no....I had not the week before............and secondly, I think I did take it mainly because of one particular word and expression with it that you said.............I asked you if it were not correct that you did not intend to come tonight and you said , "Yes" and I got it all right, but it did not feel too comfortable inside and I was afraid, so I added with a touch of my own bitterness in my feeling,(but I think not in my voice) and you had no intension of it, right?! and you quickly and emphatically, though softly, said, "Oh, no"..............that made it all right inside and in my fear you would 'spoil' it by adding something that I might interpret as a promise and then get hurt, I reassured you quickly I did not need it nor plan on it and then I switched the subject and kept on my way out the door. The rest of the afternoon and last night when ever I would think of it, the feeling inside was one that was comfortable and secure because I'd think of the way you said, "Oh, no" and to me that meant you HAD thought about it and you HAD NOT ruled out forever and ever the possibility (even though I knew then as I do now this morning I never want nor plan to have pentothal again....we will talk about this sometime but not now) and this gave me some peace because it meant you did care. I was able to accept caring without action where as sometimes caring meant only action.   That is back to the telephone calls now.....if you cared I knew it by your voice and your words and I got better.. .if, on other occassions when you 'cared' you also had to 'prove' it by coming...else I could not accept it that you cared.   It does not make sense to me, but THAT is nevertheless the way it was. I keep saying "was"...I believe it and feel it as past-tense, and I only hope to Heaven it is past tense.... for ever and a day"(with apologies to Longfellow). ....This may

sound as if it ought to be the end......or at least a good stopping
place.......but I am not ready to stop. I think I would rather try to
get it all said.....I feel sickish...but even so, there IS more to this
before we can judge....and I do mean judge, because that is somewhat,
but not altogether of course, how it feels.........in a way I feel almost
on trial for having felt and thought some things I have.......also, at
one point, I felt you accused me.......that is probably as mixed-up as
some other things I have felt and later understood to be different, so I
am, for that reason, willing to admit it.....in the hopes I can understand it was not that way...or whatever way it was, I can see and accept
and get it straight.

......

o

That brings me right back to where I was on the previous pages
when I was talking about the "Why".........see why I said that all
thoughts lead to Rome? I always end with the same things even though
it never looks as if it is going to when I think of this or that as I
paint or work around here.........but what I just thought was that it is
not the things you say or don't say, as such, in the situations I was
referring to, but what I expected(evidently determined by the amount of
pressure building up the tensions) by way of help....and then I rational-
ized (is that what it's called?) with memories of 'details' as I called
them yesterday.....I picked out I suppose what I was going to remember...
I was not aware of that....all I thought I was doing was remembering the
promises you had made previously......and applying them to the present
situation....when this did not work out, I blamed you and felt you did
not really care nor understand.

o

PATIENT: Mason, Shirley
BIRTHDATE: 1/25/23
DATE TESTED: 3/25/60
TEST: WAIS

26 WEST 9TH STREET
NEW YORK 11, N. Y.
GRAMERCY 3-1047

Miss Mason achieved a full-scale IQ of 116: verbal 118, performance 113. Her distribution of sub-test scores was as follows:

Verbal

Information   12
Comprehension   18
Arithmetic   11
Similarities   13
Digit-Span   11

Performance

Digit Symbol   11
Picture Completion   8
Block Design   11
Picture Arrangement   14
Object Assembly   12

On the basis of this test data, it may be inferred that Miss M's intellectual potential extends up to the level of an IQ of 124. In the light of the operation of disturbing emotional factors in her test functioning, it may be assumed that this 124 altitude may be minimal.

Miss M's consistently lowest scores were in those tasks involving little more than an absence of anxiety and a capacity to apply oneself consistently. An outstandingly low score was that on Picture Completion, suggesting difficulty in tasks involving simple perceptual alertness. Finally, on Picture Arrangement, Miss M performed correctly, apparently perceiving the motivational sequences involved but not knowing or understanding what it was she was doing correctly despite her success. This array of low scores and this pattern of performance is consistent with the usual performance of the hysterical personality.

4

Schreiber's PR Bio and Dr. Ralph Allison's letter

Bell-McClure Syndicate, 1501 Broadway, New York, N.Y. 10036

The Diggers, Analysts and Writers of

SYNDROME '70

FLORA RHETA SCHREIBER

Professor Schreiber is the award-winning author of more than 400 articles for major magazines, she is psychiatry editor of Science Digest, and professor at City University of New York's John Jay College of Criminal Justice, and a member of the New School for Social Research. She was given an award by the Family Service Association of America for an article, "The Tragedy of Emotional Divorce," published in Cosmopolitan magazine.

She holds bachelor's and master's degrees from Columbia University and a certificate from the University of London.

Flora Rheta Schreiber has been a friend of every President since Franklin D. Roosevelt and has been a friend of most of their families. She has been a guest at the home of Mrs. Hugh F. Auchincloss, the mother of Jacqueline Kennedy Onassis, and at the home of Hannah Milhouse Nixon, the President's mother. On the latter visit Mrs. Hannah Nixon put her up for the night in Richard Nixon's former bed. Her friendships and acquaintances include most members of the Nixon Cabinet.

Her magazine articles have included 24 on President Johnson, the first magazine interview with Lady Bird Johnson, and articles on Presidents Eisenhower and Kennedy and their families. She has lost count of the many times she has been an invited guest at the White House.

She is now planning a book on what may be one of the most unusual psychiatric cases in the world.

Ralph B. Allison, M.D.

2162 Mountain View Dr.
Los Osos, CA 93402-3312
805/528-7599
Fax: 805/528-7599

August 18, 1998

Robert Rieber, Ph.D.
John Jay College of Criminal Justice
899 Tenth Ave.
New York, NY 10019

Dear Dr. Rieber,

    You are quoted in a recent newspaper article as believing that Sybil created her personalities during therapy, not before. As a retired psychiatrist who has known principles in the cases of "Eve White," "Sybil," and Billy Milligan, I want you to know that I agree that Sybil did not have a bona fide case of MPD, by my definition. In reading all three of these "prototype MPD" stories again recently, I believe that most of the "alter-personalities" reported were really the results of "emotional imagination," not dissociation. They were what I call Internalized Imaginary Companions (IIC), inner versions of Imaginary Playmates.

    Two papers of mine which describe this, and which have been accepted for publication in professional journals, are at the top of the list of Unpublished Papers on my website at www.dissociation.com, if you would care to download and read them. In the top paper, I propose a complete overhaul of the DSM-IV criteria for diagnosing MPD/DID, since the present list of criteria are inadequate to differentiate alter-personalities from IIC. I also do not accept the current idea that MPD is no more and DID includes all dissociators who make alter-personalities, regardless of the circumstances. I use MPD for one group, those Grade V hypnotizable patients who dissociate before the age of seven because of a life threatening trauma. I use DID for those who first dissociate after the age of seven, because of a trauma which was too much for them to handle, such as rape or assault.

    In my present reading of The Three Faces of Eve, I find no evidence that she made any alter-personality, ever. All her "faces" were creations of emotional imagination, IIC, in a person who was Grade V hypnotizable with a fantasy prone personality. She never suffered enough trauma to actually have a need to create an alter-personality.

    In reading Sybil, she started out making IIC at an early age. Because of her odd behavior and the psychosis of her mother, she had major problems during her preteens, and she may have made one or two actual alter-personalities in those years after age seven. So she might have what I call DID plus IIC. The same is true of Billy Milligan, when you look at how he reports making all of his "personalities." He may have made one real alter-personality in his preteens, when his life was quite chaotic.

Two patients I have treated wrote their own stories in the books, The Five of Me (Henry Hawksworth) and Tell Me Who I Am Before I Die (Christine Peters). Henry clearly describes how he created two IIC before he dissociated at age 4 and then created two alter-personalities. Christine clearly describes how she created only alter-personalities after her father brutally raped her at the age of three. Christine is dead by now, but Henry is alive and well, and I visited him at home a few months ago. He is quite clear on how it all happened, and his autobiography detailed it as well as anyone could. I have awaiting publication the detailed story of a subsequent patient, "Marie McKenize," who made lots of alter-personalities prior to my successful treatment, but then made a batch of IIC to bedevil me to try to keep me from moving on to a new job. We have in the manuscript detailed stories of how to deal with both kinds of "creatures." Marie is my partner on the website.

You might have already heard that Dr. Herbert Spiegel has spoken up recently about his views on Sybil. I heard him talk last year in San Diego at an hypnosis meeting. From his information, it seems Sybil was a Grade V hypnotizable person who most likely had a fantasy prone personality, but insufficient early trauma to dissociate prior to age seven. I had one of those myself, "Carrie," in my own book, Minds In Many Pieces. So I am not holding myself up as a better diagnostician than Dr. Wilbur, whom I knew personally. I made the same mistake in those early years, but I am trying to correct such misinformation today. Maybe you can help do this necessary job of clearing up the confusion which those famous cases created in this already controversial field.

Sincerely,

Ralph B. Allison, M.D.

Name Index

Abercrombie, J.,15, 17
Ackerknecht, E. H., 35
Acocella, J., 119
Alexander, F., 123
Allison, R., 106
Atkinson, 116
Azam, E., 141

Baker, R., 14, 137
Baldwin, J. M., 37
Bean, N.P., 88-89
Beauchamp, C., 81, 87-88, 90, 94
Beauchamp, M., 144
Bernays, E., 23
Bernheim, H., 49, 51
Bernstein, M., 171
Bilden, L.W., 14
Binet, A, 27
Bleuler, E., 128
Bliss, E.L., 184
Boerhaave, H., 12
Bogen, J., p.16
Bourne, Ansel, 16-17, 140
Braid, J., 49
Breuer, J, 51, 54-55, 61
Browne, A. J., 16

Bruce, L., 27
Buranelli, V., 45-49

Calot, D., 32
Campbell, J., 67
Carlson, T., 14
Carpenter, W., 24
Charcot, M., 18, 20, 22, 23
Charcot, J., 49, 51, 54
Cheyne, G., 12
Cleckley, H., 86, 128, 172, 193
Combe, G., 17, 39
Connelly, S., 86
Costner, C., 172
Crabtree, A, 25
Cullen, W., 12, 38

Damasio, A., 35
Darwin, C., 38
Dell, P., 188
Deslon, 47
Disraeli, B., 128
Dorsett, Hattie., 68-77, 80, 82, 92-94, 96, 98, 102
Dorsett, Sybil., 64, 67-83, 86, 88, 90-104, 106-107, 109-110, 115-130. *See* Chapter 5 for. Multiple Personalities

Dorsett, Sybil (*Cont.*)
Dorsett, Clara, 72
Dorsett, Helen, 72
Dorsett, Marcia Lynn, 71, 102
Dorsett, Marjorie, 72
Dorsett, Mary Lucinda, 72, 74, 90
Dorsett, Mike, 72
Dorsett, Ruthie, 72, 81-82, 101
Dorsett, Vanessa Gail, 72, 90
Peggy, 96-101
Peggy Ann, 70-71, 78-79, 90
Peggy Lou., 70-71, 73, 75, 77-82, 90
Peggy Louisiana, 70
Vicky., 71, 75, 78-82, 100, 102
Dorsett, W., 69-71
Dufrense, A., 117

Ellenberger, H., 51, 61
Elliotson, J., 25, 39-41
Esdaile, J., 25
Exner, S., 19

301

Fancher, Mollie, 138
Faria, A., 48
Felida, 141
Ferrier, D., 19
Field, S., 88
Finger, S., 34
Fischer, D., 155
Flourens, P., 34-35
Flournoy, T., 150
Fodor, J., 35
Franz, S., 165
Freud, S., 22, 23, 25, 29, 51, 53-64, 190

Gall, F.-J., 31, 33-41
Galvani, D., 38
Gieson, I. van, 28
Goddard, H. H., 164
Goodhart, S., 29
Greatrakes, V., 45

Hall, G.S., 50, 54
Haller, A., 38
Hanna, T., 29, 151
Hartley, D., 12
Hawthorne, N., 128
Hebb, D., 28
Heidenhain, R., 50-51
Herbart, J. F., 32, 34
Herman, J., 63
Hilgard, E., 61-62, 185, 188
Hinshelwood, R.D., 183-187, 191-192
Hippocrates, 43-44
Hodgson, R., 17
Hollander, B., 35
Hull, C L., 63
Hume, D., 12

Ingenhousz, J., 46

Jackson, J. H., 17, 26
Johnson, R. J., 106
James, H., 128
James, W., 17, 19, 22, 24, 27, 29, 33
Janet, P., 13, 19-26, 31-33, 61-62, 143, 188, 192

Kallinger, J., 92-95
Kames, H., 12
Kidder, J., 17
Kihlstsrom, J. F., 15
Kleinberg, H., 127
Kluft, R., 106, 115-117
Koppel, T., 127
Kurzweil, R., 195

Laing, R., 85-86
Lashley, K., 36
Lavater, J., 35
Laycock, T., 24
LeBlanc, A., 89
Lewis, S., 68
Liébault, A.-A, 47-51
Locke, J., 12

MacNish, R., 15, 17
Marceline, 143
Marks, O., 87
Mason, S., 68, 90-91, 104
Maudsley, H., 24
Maxwell, J., 45
Mayo, Herbert, 16-17
Mesmer, J., 14, 37, 39
McHugh, P., 111-112
Merskey, H., 184-185
Mesmer, A., 14, 45-48, 113
Mitchell, S., 14
Morgani, G. B., 38
Muller, G. E., 19
Murphy, Bridey, 171
Myers, F. W., 13, 24

Norma, 164

Oppenheimer, L, 188-189
Osgood, C., 189

Paracelsus, 44
Piper, A., 184-185
Poe, E. A., 43
Poultney, J. C., 165
Prel, K. du., 24
Preyer, W., 24
Pribram, K., 36
Prince, M., 13, 15, 19, 22, 25-27, 33, 86-89, 144, 188
Prince, W., 155
Puysegur, Marquis de, 48

Regnery, H., 67
Reynolds, M., 14, 135
Ribot, T., 19
Rieber, R., 23, 30, 56

Salzinger, K., 56
Sauvage, S., 38
Schreiber, F., 67, 68, 71, 72, 74, 78, 81, 83, 86, 88, 90-98, 104, 105-110, 117, 120-131
Sechenov, I., 19
Shelley, M., 43
Sherrington, C., 18
Sidgwick, H., 24
Sidis, B., 13, 19, 22, 27-29, 33, 151
Simpson, M., 14
Sinason, V., 73, 92
Smith, H., 150
Spiegel, D., 63-34, 113, 116-117, 188
Spiegel, H., 46-47, 107, 112-117, 130
Spinoza, B.D, 35-37
Spurzheim, J. C., 37-40
Stevenson, R. L., 43
Sutcliffe, J. P., 186, 190-193
Swales, P., 85-86

Tellegen, C., 116, 172
Thigpen, C., 6, 193

Watkins, J., 106
Warren H. C., 36
Weissberg, M., 188
White, Eve., 81-172
White, W. A., 28
Wigan, L., 15-16
Wilbur, C., 71, 75-83, 88, 90-104, 106-107, 109-110, 114-115, 117, 120-130
Wilhelm, Kaiser, 50
Winslow, F., 16
Wilson, A., 185
Wolberg, L., 55-56
Woodward, J., 88
Wundt, W., 19

Subject Index

Abuse excuse, 125, 127
Amnesia, 13-14, 22, 26, 29, 48, 56, 73, 108, 115-116, 121, 123, 127, 142-143, 146, 148, 155, 160, 167-168
Animal magnetism, 14, 25, 43, 46, 51

Brain, 11, 13, 15-16, 24, 26, 27, 30, 43, 51, 115

Clever Hans Effect, 38
Confession, 101, 125, 127
Consciousness, 12-14, 15-17, 19-20, 22, 24-29, 55, 57, 60-61, 64, 83, 113, 118, 127, 140-144, 146, 155, 171, 175

Dissociative Identity Disorder, 11, 21, 28, 103, 113, 127, 137, 139
DSM-IV, 95, 105, 107-108, 114

Electric shock treatment, 80
Epileptic condition, 23, 180

False memory, 107, 120, 122
Free association, 56, 58-59, 62
Fugue, 11, 15-17, 21, 143, 180, 182-183

Gestalt, 38

Hospitalization, 76
Hypnosis, 14, 17-18, 20, 22-23, 26-29, 42, 53-56, 58, 62-64, 80, 81, 83, 87, 99, 100, 102, 107, 112-123, 126, 135, 137, 141, 143, 145-147, 151-153, 155, 161, 163-164, 167, 173, 177, 180, 182
Hysteria, 9, 11-12, 18, 20, 22-23, 26, 58, 61-62, 114, 121, 133, 140, 145

Identity, 11-12, 15-17, 20, 28, 43, 64, 68, 103, 113, 115, 127, 130-132, 137, 139-140, 143, 152, 157, 159, 171, 174, 180
Imagination, 11, 15, 30, 44, 47-48, 87-88, 98, 153
Inhibition-excitation, 18
IQ, 5, 16, 22-24, 28, 74, 109, 111, 117, *See also* Appendix 3

Journal of the Society of Psychical Research, 18, 24, 26, 141

Media, 97, 100, 102, 114, 120, 127-129, 133, 169, 170-171
Memory, 15, 20, 26, 55, 60-61, 83, 92, 94, 107, 114-115, 118, 120-123, 131, 136, 138, 140, 145-146, 155-156, 161, 165, 167-169, 172, 183

SUBJECT INDEX

Mind, 9, 11-16, 18, 21, 3-27, 30, 43, 49-50, 57-59, 64, 67, 70, 77, 80, 85, 90, 93-94, 100, 109, 111, 114, 119, 122, 126, 129, 135, 137-138, 142, 149, 153, 156-157, 172, 175-177

Multiple personality, 11, 14, 16, 21, 25, 29, 43, 67-68, 78, 81, 85-86, 89, 91-92, 95, 101, 109, 111, 113, 117, 119, 121-124, 126-127, 132-133, 137, 139, 142, 145-146, 153, 173-174

Myth, 47, 65, 67, 86, 91, 105, 107, 109, 111, 113-115, 117, 119-121, 125, 127, 129, 131, 133, 173

Neurophysiology, 18, 26, 28, 39

Overdetermination, 58-59

Perception, 12, 15, 27, 79
Phrenology, 33-41
Primal scene, 98-99, 116, 122

Reductionism, 19
Religion, 12, 90, 139, 146-149, 162, 180
Repression, 58-59, 60-62, 99, 153

Seduction theory, 60-63
Sexuality, 58, 60, 63, 98, 174, 180
Schizophrenia, 186
Sleep, 12, 14-15, 18, 21, 27, 47-49, 73, 112, 115, 124, 138-140, 142, 144, 146, 148, 151, 156, 158-160, 162-164, 166-167, 170, 175, 181

Social distress, 118, 120, *See also* Chapter 9
Stream of thought, 19
Suggestion, 27, 44, 46, 48-49, 54, 63, 81-82, 87-88, 107, 118-119, 128-129, 145, 163, 169, 172

Sybil, the book, 86-87, 90-104, 107-133, 140, 146, 167, 182. *See also* Citings, 119
Sybil, the case of, 64-65, 67-133, 140, 146, 167, 182
Sybil, the movie, 86, 95-104
Sybil, the tapes, 107, 121, *See also* Appendices 1 and 2

Unconscious, the, 12, 14, 20, 22, 24-25, 29, 56, 59-62, 72, 111, 113-114, 126, 140, 149, 153, 159, 161, 169, 175

Ward's Island, 28